BRIDGE CONVENTIONS, DEFENCES AND COUNTERMEASURES

Bridge Conventions, Defences and Countermeasures rapidly established itself as the leading expert guide to those conventions most likely to be encountered. This new paperback takes account of recent changes in the use and popularity of conventions and selects the best of the new ideas and developments.

This is a book no keen bridge player can afford to be without.

'Explains each convention, and goes on to show how it should be used, and covers the good and bad sides of its use. I felt the best part of the book (and the part which makes it stand out from any other book on conventions) was that, first, he shows how you might set out to make any conventional understanding difficult to use well, when employed against you. Then he discusses how best to counter these (and other) defensive measures used against you when you yourself have used the convention ... Highly recommended.' – *Bridge Magazine*

BRIDGE CONVENTIONS, DEFENCES AND COUNTERMEASURES

Ron Klinger

IN ASSOCIATION WITH
PETER CRAWLEY

First published in Great Britain 1993
in association with Peter Crawley
by Victor Gollancz Ltd

Second edition published 1999
2nd impression 2009
in association with Peter Crawley
by Cassell

Third edition published 2017
in association with Peter Crawley
by Weidenfeld & Nicolson
an imprint of the Orion Publishing Group Ltd
Carmelite House, 50 Victoria Embankment,
London EC4Y 0DZ

An Hachette UK Company

A CIP catalogue record for this book
is available from the British Library.

ISBN 9781474605632

Typeset in Australia by Modern Bridge Publications, Northbridge, Australia

Printed and bound in Great Britain by Clays Ltd, St Ives plc

www.orionbooks.co.uk

Contents

INTRODUCTION

2017: Time passes and bridge moves forward. Changes were noted in the 1999 edition in Chapter 11, 'And The Beat Goes On . . .' Much more has happened since then, including transfer responses at the one-level, transfers after a 1X : 1Y, 2NT rebid, the X-Y-Z approach, splinters after a 1NT opening and much more. These appear in Chapter 12, 'Modern Times'.

'Know thine enemy.' 'Forewarned is forearmed.' 'Be prepared!'

This sound advice for life in general is even more important in the world of tournament bridge. This book contains the most common conventions you are likely to encounter at the duplicate table. Each convention is explained, when it is used, how it is used and the extent of its effect. You may care to adopt some of the conventions. If not, it will still be important for you to be familiar with most of them. You need to know what you are up against and how to combat their methods. It is not possible to include all the conventions. However, some of the effective newer approaches are included in Chapters 9, 11 and 12.

After each convention, you are provided with one or more defensive measures against that convention. Sometimes you are given the standard defence plus a more extensive, more effective defence. It is up to you and partner which defence you decide to adopt. After each defence, there are recommended countermeasures against each part of the defensive methods.

A note about terminology. The term 'advancer' is freely used, meaning the partner of the first defender to bid. The first defensive action may be an overcall, a double or some other takeout bid. Regardless of the nature of this bid, the partner of that bidder is the 'advancer'.

'Pass or correct' appears frequently in many of the multi conventions. The action by the bidder has more than one possibility. When partner bids catering for one possibility, the original bidder is expected to pass if holding that option. If not, make the cheapest bid which is consistent with the other option(s). The bidder 'corrects' to the actual option held. For example:

WEST EAST   Suppose West has opened 2 ◊ showing a
2 ◊   2 ♡   weak two in one of the majors. East's 2 ♡ is a
'pass or correct' action. If West has the weak two in hearts, West will *pass*. With the weak two in spades, West *corrects* to 2♠.

'No' or 'No bid' means a Pass.

Bids within brackets refer to bids made by the opponents. (2♠) means an opponent has opened the bidding with a 2♠ bid.

LHO = left-hand opponent, RHO = right-hand opponent, HCP = high card points. / = or. For example, 3♡/3♠ = 3♡ or 3♠. + = 'or more'. 5+ suit = 5-card or longer suit. 10+ points = 10 or more points.

There are two important aspects to your strategy when the opponents intervene. Firstly, it pays to use similar methods against similar interference. There are dozens, perhaps hundreds of variations of certain competitive areas. You cannot afford to devise a different counter to each different wrinkle. For example, if they come in against your 1NT opening, your methods should be able to cope with anything they might throw at you. Having just one basic counter saves on memory fatigue and countless discussions on how to deal with the latest fad. Where their methods do require a different tack, this is mentioned in the text.

Secondly, your basic approach should be 'strong action against their weak bids, weak action against their strong bids'. If they hit you with some weak action whether it is a pre-empt or weak interference, there is little value in retaliating with weak action on your part. You do not pre-empt against a pre-empt. Your object should be to cater for as many of your strongish hands as you can. You try to regain the ground that their action has taken away. That itself may be quite a task but it is foolish to rob yourself of bidding space crucial to covering as many of your strong types as possible.

On the other hand, when they have advertised great strength, either via a powerful opening bid (1♣ Precision, perhaps, or a strong 2♣ opening) or via a strong artificial response (game force relays), you should stretch to enter the bidding on the slightest values, subject to vulnerability and some decent distribution. When they have revealed enough strength to make game for your side unlikely, your priorities change. With game or slam no longer an aim, strive to disrupt their communications, particularly where their opening bid or response or both are artificial. Bid as high as you dare as quickly as possible. Either make a pre-emptive jump yourself or describe your hand type to partner and hope that partner will be able to strike a pre-emptive blow. Rob them of as much bidding space as you can and they will misguess their par spot often enough to reward you.

The text assumes that certain areas of the game are part and parcel of your basic bridge knowledge:

The Suit Quality Test

This guide measures how strong a suit you hold. This often determines whether the suit is strong enough to bid at a given level. It is useful for pre-empts, weak twos, overcalls, deciding whether you can afford to insist on your suit as trumps, just about whenever suit quality is a relevant criterion.

Count the number of honours in the long suit.
Add the total number of cards in the long suit.

The answer is the SQ, the Suit Quality, of that suit. For example, Q-8-7-4-2 has 1 honour and 5 cards. 1 + 5 = SQ of 6. For an overcall, the SQ should equal or exceed the number of tricks for which you are bidding. With an SQ of 6, such a suit is not good enough for an overcall even at the one-level (seven tricks requires an SQ of 7). K-J-9-5-4 has an SQ of 7 (2 honours + 5 cards). That is good enough to overcall at the one-level (assuming you have enough extra strength) but not strong enough for a two-level overcall.

Count the J or 10 as an honour card for the SQ Test only if you also hold a higher honour in the long suit.

J-8-5-4-3-2 has an SQ of 6. Do not count the jack if you have no higher honour. K-J-8-4-3-2, however, has an SQ of 8. The jack is full value as an honour because the king is also present.

The Rule of 10 is a useful product of the Suit Quality Test. If you have a suit with an SQ of 10, you may insist on that suit as trumps. K-Q-J-10-x-x or better is strong enough, for example, even though partner might have no support for you. Even if partner has a void, you should be able to knock out the ace and mop up the missing trumps for only one loser most of the time.

Suppose the bidding has started 1♣ : 1♡, 2♣ : ? You would be worth 4♡ with ♠ A5 ♡ KQJ1076 ◇ K52 ♣ 96 since your heart SQ is 10, but if you held ♠ AQ ♡ KJ7652 ◇ K52 ♣ 96, you should content yourself with 3♡. This suit is not strong enough to play opposite a singleton or a void. If partner has no fit for hearts, you are almost certainly better off playing in 3NT.

The Losing Trick Count

Counting losers is a sound way of estimating the playing strength of a hand, particularly a hand which contains one or two very long suits. High card points are best to assess the value of a balanced hand, counting losers works better for the more distributional hands.

Counting ♠ A ♡ AKQJ9765 ◇ 76 ♣ 42 as 14 HCP is missing the true value of the hand which is nine playing tricks. If you bid this as a 14-point hand you will be making a gross underbid. The Loser Count comes into play usually only after you and your partner have established at least an 8-card trump fit (see *The Modern Losing Trick Count* for a comprehensive exposition of this approach). Nevertheless, it often pays you to count your losers anyway. It will give you an idea of the potential of your own cards and if you can gauge how many tricks partner is likely to provide, you can estimate the playing strength of the partnership.

Many systems describe various bids or sequences not just in terms or points but in terms of losers or in terms of points *and* losers. A jump raise by a passed hand (No : 1♠, 3♠) for example would be described as showing 10-12 points *and* 8 losers. The value is in giving partner a clearer idea of the hand opposite.

Counting Your Losers

Void : No losers.
Singleton suit : Count one loser, except for ace singleton (0).
Doubleton Suit : Count two losers except for A-K (0), A-x (1) or K-x (1). Count Q-x as two losers.
3-card or longer suit : Count three losers (never more) but deduct one for ace, king or queen. Deduct one loser for each of these top cards. Maximum number of losers in your hand = 12.

Examples

A8765 = 2 losers	KJ4 = 2 losers	94 = 2 losers
KQJ93 = 1 loser	KQ4 = 1 loser	K4 = 1 loser
J8765 = 3 losers	973 = 3 losers	976542 = 3 losers
AKQ65 = 0 losers	AK = 0 losers	A = 0 losers

In a 3-card or longer suit, count the queen as a winner as long as there is at least one other honour in the suit. If not, count the queen as only half a winner.

AQ765 = 1 loser	QJ764 = 2 losers	Q104 = 2 losers
KQ765 = 1 loser	Q8764 = 2½ losers	Q74 = 2½ losers

Your losers minus partner's winners is one way to estimate the combined strength (7 losers − 4 winners = 3 losers, i.e. 10 tricks). Alternatively, count your losers, add partner's losers, deduct the total from 24. The answer is the trick-taking potential. (Maximum losers in each hand = 12; two × 12 = 24 together.)

1. Two Openings

Your opening bids at the one-level will naturally depend on the system you play. This includes the range for your 1NT opening, whether you play 4-card or 5-card majors and whether your one-openings in a minor are natural or semi-artificial. One-level openings are not generally conventional and if they are, the requirements and limitations will be stipulated by your chosen system.

At the two-level and higher, you may generally choose methods independently of your system requirements for the one-level. Thus, almost regardless of the system you use, you may combine it with Strong Twos, Weak Twos, Benjamin Twos, Multi-Twos or others. Natural strong twos are not conventional but other popular methods at the two-level and higher will be examined.

WEAK TWOS

Weak twos are generally played only in the majors. When weak twos first bounced into popularity, a weak 2◇ opening was also used. However, as the 2◇ opening can be harnessed for far more useful purposes, almost no top pair uses a weak 2◇ opening today.

Requirements for opening 2♡/2♠ in first or second seat :
- A strong 6-card suit
- 6-10 HCP
- 7-8 losers
- No void and not two singletons
- No four cards in the other major

Any of these hands would be suitable :

♠ AQJ876	♠ 87	♠ 9	♣ QJ9863
♡ 6	♡ KQ9852	♡ AKQ863	♡ 64
◇ 432	◇ A72	◇ 952	◇ KJ
♣ 984	♣ 63	♣ 632	♣ K32

Minimum suit strength : 3 HCP and two honours is a sound minimum, but many players accept 2 HCP plus two honours in the suit; Q-10-x-x-x-x in a suit is the minimum acceptable.

Responding to a weak two

- Raises are pre-emptive.
- Change of suit is forcing and denies support for opener's major.
- Any bid of game is to play.
- 2NT is used as a strong enquiry.
- 4♣ or 4◇ can be used as a splinter slam try. This shows 3-card or better support for opener's suit and sets opener's suit as trumps. It also promises a singleton or void in the suit bid and five winners or better. If opener has wasted values (king or queen) in the short suit, opener should sign off in the trump suit. With no king or queen in the short suit, opener should cue bid or with no ace, bid 4NT.

The 2NT Strong Enquiry

This may be played in various ways. Some use it to ask for a singleton (opener bids the suit in which a singleton is held or bids 3-Major with a minimum and no singleton and 3NT with a maximum and no singleton). Others use 2NT to ask for an outside feature (ace or king or Q-J-x outside opener's major). Opener bids the suit in which a suitable feature is held. With no such feature, opener bids 3-Major if minimum and 3NT if maximum.

However, the most popular and most effective use of the 2NT response is the Ogust Convention. The 2NT reply asks opener to indicate whether the hand is maximum or minimum and how many top honours are held in the major suit. Opener rebids :

3♣ = Minimum + only one top honour
3◇ = Minimum + two top honours
3♡ = Maximum + only one top honour
3♠ = Maximum + two top honours
3NT = A-K-Q-x-x-x or better in the major

The memory guide for this convention is:

Majors are maximum, minors are minimum.

The honours are shown in sequence : 1-2, 1-2-3. Top honour = ace, king or queen. The jack does not count as a top honour.

Responder's strategy

Singleton or void in opener's suit

Pass below 16 HCP. With 16+ points, bid a strong suit (new suit forcing) or use 2NT if you need to know whether opener is minimum or maximum. For example with a 16-18 point 4-4-4-1, bid 2NT and sign off in opener's major opposite a minimum but try 3NT opposite a maximum.

With support for opener's major

A maximum weak two will usually make six tricks (AKQxxx for example) and a minimum weak two about five. With support for opener and no more than three winners, pass. With a very weak hand, you might raise pre-emptively or with superb support but a hopeless hand, you might make a psychic bid. For example, if partner opens 2♠ and you hold ♠ K8642 ♡ 53 ◇ 8 ♣ Q8532, you know that the opponents have enough for at least a game, perhaps a slam, and at least eight cards in each red suit. If RHO passes, you could hardly bid less than 4♠, but there is scope for deception. You might try 2NT, a subtle psyche, suggesting you have far more strength than you hold. Less subtle would be 4NT, asking for aces, and signing off in 5♠, of course, no matter what partner replies. If you can buy the hand in 5♠ doubled, you will probably still show a profit. Another attractive psyche would be 3♡, new suit forcing. Again you revert to spades over partner's next action.

With 3½-4 tricks in support of partner's suit, you are worth an invitation to game. Bid 2NT and sign off in 3-Major opposite a minimum or 4-Major opposite a maximum.

With 4½-5½ support tricks, bid game. You should use the sequence 2-Major : 4-Major both pre-emptively and also on good hands short of slam potential. If the opponents intervene, pass if the raise was pre-emptive and double with the strong hand.

With 6 support tricks, there is potential for slam if partner has a maximum. Bid 2NT if you need to know whether opener is maximum or minimum or use a 4♣ or 4◇ splinter bid if you want partner to discount the king and queen in that suit.

Counting your support tricks

In opener's major suit, count the ace, king or queen as one trick. In outside suits, count the tricks only in the first two cards in each suit (quick tricks) : A-K = 2, A-Q = 1½, A-x = 1, K-Q = 1, K-x = ½ but count A-K-Q as three tricks. With three-card or better support, count a singleton as one trick and a void as two tricks.

If you do respond 2NT, then after opener's reply :
• A bid of 3-Major is to play (even after a maximum reply).
• A bid of any game is to play. For example, suppose you hold ♠ Q-x-x ♡ A-x-x ◇ A-x-x ♣ A-x-x-x. Partner opens 2♠, you bid 2NT and partner replies 3◇ (minimum points, but two top honours in spades). You can count nine tricks, so bid 3NT.
• A new suit is a cue bid with opener's suit set as trumps.

DEFENCE AGAINST WEAK TWOS

Recommended is to adopt an approach similar to defending against their one-openings. There is no value in playing weak jump-overcalls or using an unusual NT bid to show a weak hand with both minors. Follow the principle 'Against weak actions, your actions are strong.' Thus–

- 2NT = 16-18 balanced with at least one stopper in their suit.
- 3NT = 21-22 balanced, at least one stopper in their suit.
- Double is for takeout. The hand must be short in their major with four cards in the other major if it is a minimum doubling hand. The greater the strength, the less important is the need to be short in their suit. With 19-20 balanced, start by doubling.
- 4NT = Unusual for the minors but a strong hand. At least 5–5 in the minors and no more than 4 losers. This would be enough :
♠ 76 ♡ 2 ◇ KQJ107 ♣ AKQJ3 or ♠ 7 ♡ 6 ◇ AQJ754 ♣ KQJ82.
- Overcalls are natural and show a strong suit. 2♠ over their 2♡ might be a hand with 7 losers but overcalls at the three-level should be no worse than a 6-loser hand.

2♠ over 2♡ : 6-7 losers.

3♠ over 2♡ : 5 losers. If better than this, double first.

3♣/3◇ : 5-6 losers. With 4 losers or better, double first.

3♡ over 2♠ : 6 losers. With 5 losers and a strong suit, bid 4♡. With 4 losers or better, double first.

Suit quality for a 3-level overcall should be 8 or better.* It would be nice to have a suit quality of 9, but you cannot afford to wait for that before coming into the auction.

- Bid their suit. Old style is to treat this as a game-force hand, either 24 HCP or more or 3 losers or fewer. However, one can cope with this powerhouse quite comfortably by starting with a double and bidding their suit next whatever advancer replies to the double. If advancer happens to give a strong reply to the double, you would be looking for slam with such values.

A preferable approach is to treat the bid of the enemy suit as a Michaels Cue Bid but with a strong hand (strong actions over their weak actions). Michaels shows five cards in the other major and five or more cards in one of the minors. For example, (2♡) : 3♡ shows five spades and 5+ diamonds or clubs. The hand should be five losers or better. A reply of 3NT to this is to play. A bid of 4♣ in reply would be corrected to 4◇ by partner if that is the minor suit held. A bid of 4NT in reply to the cue bid asks partner to bid the minor (it is not asking for aces).

*see page 9.

After partner's 2NT overcall of a weak two-bid

3♣ = Stayman
3◇ = Transfer to the other major
Their-suit = 4-4-4-1 with a singleton in their suit, game force.
3-other-major = at least 5-4 in the minors, game force.
4♣/4◇ = Natural game force, slam interest.

If this artificial approach does not appeal, use 3♣ Stayman, 3◇ as diamonds, 3-their suit as short in their suit with both minors and 3-other major as 5+ in that suit and forcing.

In reply to partner's takeout double

The standard approach is to bid at the cheapest level with a poor hand and give a jump response with about 10 points or more. This leaves a very wide range for a reply of 3♣ or 3◇ to a double, perhaps next to nothing, perhaps a fair 7-9 points. There is a better method which gives up on the natural use of 2NT.

2NT can be used as the Lebensohl Convention, forcing partner to bid 3♣. Bid this on all poor hands (except if you can bid 2♠ after partner doubles 2♡). When partner bids 3♣, pass if that is your suit, else bid your suit over 3♣. For example, after (2♠) : Double, if you hold ♠ 762 ♡ 87 ◇ Q98543 ♣ 43, bid 2NT. When partner bids the 3♣ 'puppet', you convert to 3◇, indicating that your suit is diamonds and you are in the 0-6 point range.

3-level-bids in reply to the double are encouraging, 7-10 points. For example after (2♠) : Double, you would bid 3◇ at once with ♠ 762 ♡ 87 ◇ KQ8543 ♣ K3, showing a respectable hand. Of course, the suit you bid need not be more than a 4-card suit.

(2♡) : Double : 3♠ shows 7-10 points with five spades.

(2♡) : Double : 2NT, 3♣ : 3♠ shows the same values but with only four spades. The NT bid shows the more no-trumpish hand.

Bidding their suit in reply to the double is forcing to game.

3NT in reply to the double indicates a double stopper in their suit. If you have the values for 3NT but only a single stopper, bid 2NT first and then rebid 3NT over the forced 3♣. This sequence expresses doubt about no-trumps and partner should remove it with a singleton in their suit unless a running suit is also held.

If the doubler is very strong (normally 19 HCP or better) or has about a 4-loser hand, the doubler may decline the 3♣ puppet.
(2♠) : Double : 2NT, 3♡ = too strong a hand to risk being left in 3♣. Partner should bid on to game with one trick or better.

With 19-20 balanced, double but if advancer uses 2NT, it is advisable to accept the 3♣ puppet. Over a stronger bid you would rebid 3NT.

COUNTERMEASURES BY THE WEAK-TWO SIDE

1. After 2♡ : (Double) or 2♠ : (Double)

All actions remain the same except for the following :

• 3♣ or 3♢ are natural but are to play, not forcing. This is more practical after a double when you are unlikely to be strong. If you are short in opener's suit, there is some risk that fourth player will pass the takeout double. As the weak-two opener should not have a void suit, it makes sense to rescue opener into 3♣ or 3♢ with a good 6+ suit. For example, after 2♠ : (Double), bid 3♣ with

♠ – ♡ J732 ♢ 92 ♣ KQ108754. Your hand will surely play better in clubs than spades. In clubs, you may escape a double.

• Likewise, 2♠ : (Double) : 3♡ is to play.

• Redouble is for penalties. You should have a singleton or void in partner's suit and 13 or more HCP. Double any suit bid by them with a strong 4-card or longer holding in their suit.

2. After 2♡ : (2♠)

Double = Penalties. 2NT = Ogust Convention. This 2NT does not imply or suggest a stopper in their suit. It is purely an enquiry bid.

Other actions are the same as though second player had passed except for 3♠ which asks partner to bid 3NT with a stopper in their suit. For this action you would need something like ♠ 762 ♡ 4 ♢ AK2 ♣ AKQJ32.

3. After 2♡ : (2NT) or 2♠ : (2NT)

Double = penalties. Later doubles are also penalties.

New suit = Natural and forcing.

Bid of opener's suit is invitational (as you have lost the 2NT invitational sequence).

4. After suit bids at the 3-level or higher

Double = penalties.

Bid of opener's suit at the 3-level is invitational (as their bid has taken away your 2NT invitational sequence).

Without interference, invite game via 2NT and use 3-Major or 4-Major in opener's suit pre-emptively. Once second player has bid, there is far less incentive to pre-empt and there is a genuine need for an invitational bid (3-opener's-major).

New suit = natural and forcing.

5. Interference over Ogust

After 2♡/2♠ : (No) : 2NT, if fourth player bids 3♣, pass with a 3♣ bid (or double with club values). Other bids have normal meanings. If fourth player bids 3♢, pass with a 3♣ bid, double with a 3♢ bid. Over 3♡/3♠, pass if minimum, double if maximum.

THE 2♣ GAME FORCE

This is part of the Acol system and common in Standard American and many other natural-based systems. The 2♣ opening indicates a hand of 23 HCP + or a hand with fewer high card values but with ten playing tricks or better. Each of these hands would be suitable for a 2♣ game force :

♠ AQJ2	♠ AQJ4	♠ AQ	♠ AKJ3
♡ KQJ	♡ 8	♡ AK872	♡ 2
◇ AJ9	◇ AQJ87	◇ A	◇ AKQ4
♣ AJ3	♣ AKQ	♣ AQJ53	♣ AKJ2
Open 2♣	Open 2♣	Open 2♣	Open 2♣
Rebid 2NT	Rebid 3◇	Rebid 2♡	Rebid 2♠

These rebids assume a negative 2◇ response from partner. The 2NT rebid, showing 23-24 points balanced, is not forcing. All other rebids commit the partnership to game. Opener's suit rebid is expected to be a 5-card suit. With a 4-4-4-1, bid your cheapest 4-card suit and hope things will work out for the best.

The 2◇ negative response shows 0-7 points. With 7 points, bid the negative if you do not have 1½ quick tricks, but if your 7 points are made up of an ace and a king or include an A-Q combination, you are worth a positive response.

Any response other than 2◇ is a positive indicating 8 HCP + (or 7 HCP with 1½ quick tricks). The function of the positive is to indicate slam prospects. If opener has 23 HCP or more and responder has 8 +, slam is likely. Similarly, if opener's 2♣ indicates ten playing tricks and responder has 1½ or more, slam is likely to be a good bet, especially if a trump fit is found.

The 2NT response is used for balanced hands and suit responses should be taken as a 5-card or longer suit. With a 4-4-4-1 and positive values, bid 2♡ or 2♠, the cheaper 4-card suit, and do not worry. Most of the time it will not be critical that partner expects you to have five cards there.

Other responding schemes exist (such as showing aces at once in response, showing the number of controls in response or using 2◇ positive, 2♡ negative and others as semi-positive) but none of these have a large following. The above structure is by far the most popular.

Jump responses show a 6-card suit with four honours and exactly one loser : K-Q-J-10-x-x, A-Q-J-10-x-x, or A-K-J-10-x-x. With a stronger holding, give a non-jump positive. Slam is almost a certainty.

DEFENCE AGAINST THE 2♣ GAME FORCE

Many players are cowed into submission by the mere fact that the 2♣ opening shows a powerhouse. However, subject to the vulnerability it is worth coming into the bidding if you have a shapely hand. The drawbacks of bidding are that you might be doubled for penalties and if they win the bidding, as they usually do, declarer will have some idea of your hand pattern which may be helpful in the play of the hand. On the positive side, bidding may locate a profitable sacrifice and it may assist partner in finding the best lead and also later in the defence. It may also rob the opponents of bidding space, causing them to misjudge whether they belong in game or in slam.

If you belong to the bidding camp, it is best to adopt a free-and-easy style to coming in on shapely hands. If you have a strict approach that the hand must be a 5-5 pattern at least, declarer gains too much knowledge. If the vulnerability is right, 5-4, 6-4 and even 4-4-4-1 patterns should be included.

It is safer to venture into the bidding with a two-suiter and so the following structure works well :

Over (2♣) : 2◇ = diamonds and hearts, 2♡ = hearts and spades, 2♠ = spades and clubs, 3♣ = clubs and diamonds, Double = clubs and hearts and 2NT = diamonds and spades. Suit bid above 3♣ = long, strong one-suiter. A suit quality of 9 is recommended.* The hand should conform to the Rule of 3 and 2. After (2♣) : No : (2◇) : 2♡ = hearts and spades, 2♠ = spades and clubs, 3♣ = clubs and diamonds, 3◇ = diamonds and hearts, Double = diamonds and spades and 2NT = clubs and hearts. Suit bid above 3◇ = long, strong one-suiter.

Non-jump suit bids show the suit bid and the next suit up. With 4-card or better support, partner should bid at once as high as vulnerability allows. Make them guess at the highest possible level. The non-touching suits are shown by Double, showing the suit bid and its non-touching mate, or 2NT, showing the other non-touching suits. Again, with strong support, bid as high as you dare. For example :

WEST	WEST	NORTH	EAST	SOUTH
♠ J10873		2♣	2NT	No
♡ 6	?			
◇ 7				
♣ QJ6532	Bid 4♠. Let them guess how high to go.			

*see page 9.

COUNTERMEASURES BY THE 2♣ SIDE

1. After 2♣ : (Double)

Common agreements here are that redouble shows strong clubs, a desire to play in 2♣ redoubled or to penalise a club bid by the opponents. Other bids have their normal meaning, 2◇ negative, others positive and natural. 2NT shows a stopper in any suit shown by the double. With a balanced hand, positive values but no stopper in a suit shown by the double, bid their suit to ask for a stopper. Pass = a weak hand with club tolerance, while 2◇ suggests weakness in clubs.

If your partnership can handle a slightly more sophisticated counter, the following works well whether the double shows clubs or whether it indicates a two-suiter including clubs.

2◇ = Negative, singleton or void in clubs.

Pass = Negative, two or more clubs.

Redouble = Positive, two or more clubs, any shape other than balanced.

Suit bid = Natural, but promises a singleton or void in clubs.

2NT = Natural, balanced positive with a stopper in clubs.

3♣ = Same as 2NT but no stopper in clubs.

If the double showed a suit other than clubs (e.g., a transfer to diamonds or hearts plus another suit), actions by your side refer to the suit shown by the double. For example, if the double showed diamonds, then 3◇ would be the 2NT bid with no stopper in diamonds.

The advantage of showing shortage in their suit comes later when you have to decide whether to bid over their bid, whether to double for penalties or whether to try for a slam.

2. They bid a suit

Common agreements are pass = negative and double = penalties. Bids are natural and positive. Another method :

Pass = negative

Double = any positive with two or more in their suit and not suitable for a bid of no-trumps.

Suit bid = Natural but promises a singleton or void in their suit.

Again this helps later decisions if the auction becomes heated.

2NT = balanced positive with at least one stopper in their suit.

3-their suit = 2NT bid without a stopper in their suit.

If they bid their suit at the three-level, bid 3NT with 8-9 balanced and no 4-card major. With other hands, double to show a positive with two or more cards in their suit.

BENJAMIN TWOS

This clever structure, devised by Albert Benjamin of Glasgow, incorporates weak twos, game-forcing twos and Acol twos (hands about one trick short of game).

> 2NT = 21-22 points balanced.
>
> 2♣ = 21-22 points unbalanced. 2♣ is artificial and forcing for one round. It also caters for hands of 19-20 HCP and a 6+ suit, or 17-18 HCP and a 7+ suit.
>
> 2♦ = Artificial game force, 23 HCP or ten playing tricks or better if below 23 HCP. The 2♦ opening is equivalent to the 2♣ game force (see page 17).
>
> 2♡ or 2♠ = weak two (see pages 11-16).

Responding to 2♡ or 2♠

Same as weak twos, page 12.

Responding to 2NT

See Chapter 3, *Responses to 1NT and 2NT*.

Responding to 2♦

The style of response is akin to responding to the game-force 2♣ opening (see page 17). The major difference is that 2♡ is the negative response so that with a positive hand and hearts as the main suit, you must respond 3♡, not 2♡. This is a disadvantage, to be sure, but those who play Benjamin Twos believe this is a small price to pay for the ability to cope sensibly with those hands in the 21-22 zone or just short of game in playing tricks.

The 2♣ Opening

It is not recommended to open 2♣ with a balanced hand. With 21-22 balanced, open 2NT. With more, open 2♦. With less, start at the 1-level. If partner passes and you have a balanced hand in the 12-20 point range, it is unlikely that you have missed a game. Open 2♣ when you have an unbalanced hand of 21-22 points *or* 19-20 points and a 6+ suit *or* 17-18 points and a 7+ suit.

The playing strength for 2♣ is given as 8-9½ tricks but most hands with just 8 playing tricks should start with a 1-opening. If you have only 8 tricks, you will need two tricks or so from partner to make a game. With two tricks or thereabouts, partner will be strong enough to respond to a 1-level opening.

Responses to 2♣

2♦ = Negative, 0-7 points. After opener's rebid, responder should bid again with one trick or better and pass only with less than one trick in support.

Others = Positive, game-force.

Opener's rebids

Opener is able to reveal the playing strength very accurately when rebidding in a major suit. Suit bids at the cheapest level are taken to be at least a 5-card suit. Jump rebids are strong 6-card or longer suits.

2♣ : 2♢, 2♡/2♠ = 8½ playing tricks
2♣ : 2♢, 3♡/3♠ = 9 playing tricks
2♣ : 2♢, 4♡/4♠ = 9½ playing tricks
2♣ : 2♢, 3♣/3♢ = 8½-9 playing tricks
2♣ : 2♢, 4♣/4♢ = 9½-10 playing tricks
2♣ : 2♢, 3NT = Solid minor suit, 9 playing tricks
2♣ : 2♢, 2NT = Solid minor suit, 8 playing tricks

Example hands :

WEST	EAST	WEST	EAST
♠ AQJ1073	♠ 54	♠ AQJ1073	♠ K4
♡ KQJ	♡ 654	♡ KQJ	♡ 654
♢ AK	♢ 8732	♢ AK	♢ 8732
♣ 98	♣ J652	♣ 98	♣ J652
2♣ : 2♢		2♣ : 2♢	
3♠ : No		3♠ : 4♠	

WEST	EAST	WEST	EAST
♠ AKQ	♠ 754	♠ 53	♠ 9842
♡ KQJ1087	♡ 64	♡ A	♡ J8632
♢ AQ3	♢ J75	♢ A74	♢ 96
♣ 4	♣ J9853	♣ AKQ8643	♣ 72
2♣ : 2♢		2♣ : 2♢	
4♡ : No		3NT : No	

WEST	EAST	WEST	EAST
♠ A72	♠ 6	♠ 63	♠ 9854
♡ AKQ632	♡ 854	♡ A6	♡ K84
♢ AK	♢ 96432	♢ AKQJ85	♢ 732
♣ 98	♣ J1065	♣ A42	♣ 987
2♣ : 2♢		2♣ : 2♢	
3♡ : 4♡		2NT : 3NT	
No		No	

Try to bid the above hands without the use of the Benjamin 2♣ which expresses the playing strength of such hands so well.

DEFENCE TO 2NT

Covered in Chapter 4, *Responses to 1NT and 2NT*.

DEFENCE TO BENJAMIN 2◇

It is sensible to play a two-suited defence here just as against the 2♣ game force (see page 18).

>   Double = diamonds and spades (non-touching suits).
>   2♡ = hearts and spades.
>   2♠ = spades and clubs.
>   3♣ = clubs and diamonds.
>   3◇ = diamonds and hearts.
>   2NT = hearts and clubs (non-touching suits).
>   3♡, 3♠, 4♣, 4◇ = one-suiter

After (2◇) : No : (2♡) :
Use the same style of interference : Double = hearts + clubs,
2♠ = spades + clubs, 2NT = spades + diamonds,
3♣ = clubs + diamonds, 3◇ = diamonds + hearts,
3♡ = hearts + spades, and higher suit bids are one-suiters.

COUNTERMEASURES BY THE 2◇ SIDE

Use the same approach as on page 19 when they interfere over the 2♣ opening. If the partnership can manage the memory strain, it is worth dividing the responding structure into actions which show shortage in their suit and those which confirm two or more cards in their suit.

After 2◇ : (Double) :
   2♡ = Negative, 0-1 diamonds; Pass = negative, 2+ diamonds;
   Redouble = Positive, 2+ diamonds; suit bids = 0-1 diamond.

After 2◇ : (Suit bid) :
   Pass = negative
   Double = Positive with 2+ cards in their suit
   Suit bids = Positive with 0-1 cards in their suit

DEFENCE AGAINST THE BENJAMIN 2♣ OPENING

Adopt the same defence as against the 2♣ game force (see page 18). It is sensible to play like methods against all powerful opening bids.

COUNTERMEASURES BY THE 2♣ SIDE

Similarly, the side that opens with an artificial powerhouse opening should adopt like methods of counteracting their interference almost regardless of the nature and meaning of the interference. One method fits all!

MULTI-2◇

This popular structure at duplicate usually combines a number of weak possibilities and often one or two strong options as well. Some play that it shows just a weak two in one of the majors. Others use it to show a weak two in the majors *or* a strong balanced hand (23-24 points) *or* an Acol Two in the minors. Another possibility is a weak two in hearts *or* a weak two-suiter in the black suits *or* a strong balanced hand. The possibilities are limited only by their creators' imaginations.

The responding structure has many points of similarity regardless of the possibilities that exist. With a weak hand, responder usually bids the cheapest option, 2♡. If opener has that suit, opener passes. If not, opener indicates the hand held. This method is known as 'Pass or Correct' : Pass if you hold the suit bid by responder, correct to the appropriate strain if you do not hold that suit.

2NT is used as a strong enquiry. Responder will have a hand worth an invitation to game or stronger opposite opener's weak options. Jump bids in response to 2◇ are usually played as pre-emptive, with opener applying the 'pass or correct' approach.

Here are some sample responding structures :

1. 2◇ = a weak two in one of the majors
Responses
2♡ = Pass if you have hearts, otherwise bid 2♠.
2♠ = Pass if you have spades; with hearts, bid 3♡ if minimum, 4♡ if maximum. 2♠ operates as a game invitation with support for hearts.
2NT = artificial, strong enquiry. One possible rebid scheme :

    3NT = A-K-Q-x-x-x in the major held.
    3♠ = Spades, minimum points, only one top honour.
    3♡ = Hearts, minimum points, only one top honour.
    3◇ = Spades, better than the 3♠ bid.
    3♣ = Hearts, better than the 3♡ bid.

Over 3♣ or 3◇, responder can enquire further by bidding the next step (3◇ over 3♣, 3♡ over 3◇). Opener's rebids :
1st step = minimum points but two top honours in the major.
2nd step = maximum points, two top honours in the major.
3rd step = maximum points but only one top honour in the major.

This gives responder as much information as can be obtained by the Ogust 2NT enquiry after a weak two. The multi-2◇ here effectively telescopes two opening bids (2♠ and 2♡) into one.

2. 2◇ = weak two in the majors *or* strong balanced hand *or* Acol Two in one of the minors

Responses

2♡ = Pass if you have the weak two in hearts, otherwise show which option you hold. 2♡ is a weak response. Opener passes with the weak two in hearts, bids 2♠ with the weak two in spades, 2NT with the strong balanced hand or 3♣/3◇ to show the Acol Two in the suit bid.

2♠ = Pass if you have the weak two in spades. If opener has one of the other options, opener bids 2NT with the balanced hand, 3♣/3◇ with the Acol Two, 3♡ with hearts and a minimum, 4♡ with hearts and a maximum. 2♠ is a weak reply but acts as an invitation to game opposite a weak two in hearts.

2NT = Strong enquiry. The 2NT response, looking for game opposite a weak two, will be equivalent to an opening hand or stronger. Facing the big balanced hand or the 8½-9½ trick hand in a minor, such values will usually lead to slam. Opener therefore rebids at the three-level with the weak two type (use the same responding scheme as on page 23) and bids 4♣/4◇ with the Acol Two and 4NT if big and balanced. The four-level replies will be very rare.

3. 2◇ = weak two in hearts *or* weak two-suiter in spades and clubs (at least 5-5) *or* big and balanced *or* a powerful 4-4-4-1, 17 HCP or bigger.

Responses

2♡ = Pass with the weak two in hearts. If opener has one of the other possibilities, opener bids 2♠ (weak black two-suiter), 2NT (big and balanced) or 3♣/3◇/3♡/3♠ (powerful 4-4-4-1, showing the singleton suit).

2♠ = Pass if you have the black two-suiter. This operates as at least an invitational hand opposite a weak two in hearts. Without the black two-suiter, opener bids 2NT (big and balanced), 3♡ (minimum weak two in hearts), 4♡ (maximum weak two in hearts) or 3♣/3◇/3♠/ 3NT (bidding the singleton suit with the big 4-4-4-1, with 3NT showing the singleton heart).

2NT = strong enquiry, opening hand or better. Opener bids 3♣ (black two-suiter, minimum), 3◇ (minimum weak two in hearts), 3♡ (maximum weak two in hearts), 3♠ (black two-suiter, maximum), 3NT (A-K-Q-x-x-x in hearts), 4♣/4◇/4♡/4♠ (the big 4-4-4-1, bidding the singleton suit) or 4NT (big and balanced).

DEFENCE AGAINST THE MULTI-2◇

The tough part about defending against multi-bids is that no suit is promised by the opening bid (i.e. there is no 'anchor' suit). Against a natural weak two, you might double and advancer can bid the enemy suit to show a strong hand. The possibilities for the multi-2◇ do not usually have such a base suit and advancer has no cue bid of the enemy suit available in reply to a double. Mostly the multi-2◇ is one of the weak options and actions over the multi should be based on strong hands. This works well :

Over the 2◇ opening :
Double = 16+ points, any shape except for the 2NT/3NT bids.
2NT = 19-21 balanced.   3NT = 22-24 balanced.
Suit bids = Natural, but below 16 HCP. At the two-level, a strong 5-card major and a good opening hand is adequate. At the three-level, a good 6-card suit and a 6-loser hand is enough.

In reply to the double :
Bids at the 2-level = weak, not forcing.
2NT = puppet to 3♣. Allows advancer to show a weak hand in clubs or diamonds. When partner bids 3♣, advancer passes with clubs or converts to 3◇, intended as a sign-off.
Suit bids at the 3-level = natural, forcing to game, normally 8 HCP or better. 3♡/3♠ in reply to the double promise a 5-card or longer suit.
With 8+ points and only a 4-card major, bid 2NT and after partner bids 3♣, rebid 3♡ or 3♠. These cannot be weak actions (you would have bid 2♡ or 2♠ in reply to the double). This enables you to distinguish 4-card suits from longer suits.
3NT = 4-3-3-3, 8-11 points.
2NT-then-3NT = 4-3-3-3, 12-14 points.

If third player bids over the double, pass = weakness, bids = 8+ points and force to game, double = takeout, promising 0-1 cards in the suit bid on your right.

After (2◇) : No : (Bid)
Treat the bid on your right as the opening bid. For example, after (2◇) : No : (2♡), adopt the same defence you would against a weak 2♡ opening. If you are strong in hearts and not worth 2NT, pass. Opener will reveal the hand if they do not have hearts and if they pass, showing hearts, partner may be able to bid.

After later bidding
Use doubles freely for takeout at the two-level or three-level. For example, after (2◇) : No : (2♡) : No, (2♠) treat the position as a weak 2♠ opening.

COUNTERMEASURES BY THE MULTI-2◇ SIDE

1. After 2◇ : (Double)

All responder's actions remain the same except for No Bid and Redouble.

2◇ : (No) : No is hardly feasible when there are very strong hands among opener's possibilities. Where the 2◇ opening has only weak options, passing 2◇ is feasible, either with diamonds or with such a poor hand that you do not want to give both opponents the chance to take action. You are prepared to fail in 2◇ undoubled if they elect to pass it out when you judge that they probably have a game their way. If the bidding goes 2◇ : (No) : No : (Double), either partner or you can start rescue operations.

2◇ : (Double) : No = 'Partner, save yourself if fourth player passes, but if fourth player bids, we are well out of the auction.' The pass does not suggest diamonds. It is used merely to force fourth player to commit to some action. If you take action at once, fourth player can pass and second player has a chance to make a descriptive rebid opposite a known weak hand.

Redouble = 'Partner, bid 2♡ and then pass my next bid. I have a long, strong suit of my own in which I wish to play.' Of course, if opener has a strong option, opener does not bid 2♡ but shows the hand type held.

2. After 2◇ : (Suit bid)

Play double for takeout at the 2-level or 3-level (penalties at the 4-level). With a long, strong holding in their suit, opener may of course pass the double out. The strength for the double should be game invitational or better facing one of the weak options. Bidding the enemy suit is forcing to game and asks opener to show the hand type held.

3. After 2◇ : (2NT)

Double = penalties. Suit bids are correctable. For example, 2◇ : (2NT) : 3♡ where 2◇ might be a weak two in one of the majors asks opener to pass with hearts and minimum, bid 4♡ with hearts and maximum or bid 3♠ with spades (minimum) or 4♠ (maximum).

Later bidding

Once opener has clarified the hand type, all doubles become penalty doubles. For example,

WEST	NORTH	EAST	SOUTH
2◇	Dble	2♡	No
No	3♣	Dble	

East's double of 3♣ is for penalties. The pass of 2♡ by West confirmed the weak two in hearts.

2. Pre-Emptive Opening Bids

Almost every system plays suit openings at the three-level the same way : weak hand (normally up to at most 10 HCP and then a poor ten only), long strong suit (usually a 7+ suit but a strong 6-card suit is acceptable for 3♣ or 3♦) and 6 playing tricks when not vulnerable or 7 playing tricks when vulnerable. The most popular defence against natural pre-empts is double for takeout, 3NT to play and suit bids as natural (six losers at the 3-level, five losers at the 4-level, playing partner to hold two tricks for you) and 4NT as a huge takeout for the minors, about a 4-loser hand.

However, from time to time you may come across methods which include artificial pre-empts at the 3-level or 4-level. The 3NT opening is rarely played as a natural, strong balanced hand these days.

TRANSFER PRE-EMPTS

In this method, the opening bids at the 3-level show a pre-empt in the next suit up. Thus,

3♣ = a 3♦ pre-empt.
3♦ = a 3♡ pre-empt.
3♡ = a 3♠ pre-empt.
3♠ = a solid minor with seven playing tricks and little else.
3NT = a 4♣ pre-empt.

The theory behind this approach is that it allows partner to play the hand and the lead coming up to partner's hand will usually be more valuable than the lead coming up to the pre-emptor's hand. In addition, having the unknown hand (partner's) concealed, may make the defence more difficult. The loss of a natural 3♣ opening is not considered too damaging. 3♣ is not a very tough pre-empt to overcome and it puts an end to those weak 6-card pre-empts, in clubs anyway, if not in diamonds.

Responses

Responder normally bids opener's suit, at cheapest level if weak or at game-level if strong or if pre-empting. New suit is natural and forcing, except for 4♣ over 3♣/3♦/3♡ which is best played as Roman Key Card Blackwood with opener's suit set.

Over 3♠, 3NT is to play, while 4♣/4♦/5♣/5♦ asks opener to pass with that minor or correct to the other minor.

DEFENCE AGAINST TRANSFER PRE-EMPTS

The idea behind transfer pre-empts in allowing partner to become declarer is highly attractive. The major drawback is that it allows the opponents tremendous scope for their defensive methods.

After 3♣/3♢/3♡

Bid the pre-emptor's suit = takeout bid with 0-1 cards in their suit. The normal takeout strength is expected (a 6-loser hand or better is the recommended minimum).

Double = Strong balanced hand, 2+ cards in their suit. Suggests doubling the pre-emptor for penalties. This is a major disadvantage to transfer pre-empts : they allow the opponents a cheap takeout bid and penalty doubles as well. Double + later double = penalties.

Suit bids = Natural, six losers at the 3-level, five losers at the 4-level. If stronger, start with a bid of their suit or a double.

3NT = Natural, to play.

Pass and later double if third hand simply bids the pre-emptor's suit = takeout, weaker than immediate action.

WEST	NORTH	EAST	SOUTH	
3♣	No	3♢	No	North's double is for takeout but shows a weaker hand than an immediate
No	Dble			3♢ bid or an immediate double.

After third hand bids the pre-emptor's suit

WEST	NORTH	EAST	SOUTH	
3♢	No	3♡	?	Treat East's action as the opening and defend as you would against a 3♡ opening.

After 3♠ (showing a solid minor and 7 playing tricks)

Double = Strong, looking for penalties

3NT = Brave but not foolhardy. A strong hand is required with both minors stopped, of course. Their minor was not as solid as they thought (and therefore you should consider doubling).

4♣ = Takeout for the majors with preference for hearts.

4♢ = Takeout for the majors with preference for spades.

4♡ or 4♠ = Natural, to play.

After 3NT (showing a 4♣ pre-empt)

4♣ = Takeout with 0-1 clubs

Double = Strong hand with 2+ clubs. Suggests playing for penalties after the likely run to 4♣.

After (3NT) : No : (4♣)

Treat the situation just as a 4♣ opening. Recommended is to double for takeout and suit bids are natural.

THE GAMBLING 3NT

This shows a solid minor, 7 playing tricks, and little else.

A typical hand looks like this : ♠ 6 ♡ 72 ◇ AKQ9865 ♣ 852. It is permissible to hold a queen outside the long suit but a king or ace would be too much. With that, start with a 1-bid.

Partner is expected to pass with stoppers in the outside suits and potential for two tricks or better. With a weaker hand or with no cover in one or more suits, bid 4♣. Opener will pass with clubs or correct to 4◇. 3NT : 4◇ asks opener to pass with diamonds or bid 5♣ if clubs is the suit held. Responder has good support for clubs but is not worth as much opposite diamonds. You will know which minor suit opener has when you hold a top honour in the other minor. (Some play 3NT : 4◇ to ask for a singleton. In reply, opener bids 4♡ or 4♠ with a singleton in the bid suit, 4NT if 7-2-2-2, 5♣ with a singleton diamond, 5◇ with a singleton club.) 3NT : 5♣/5◇/6♣ asks opener to pass or correct to the other minor. 3NT : 4♡/4♠ = to play.

DEFENCE AGAINST THE GAMBLING 3NT

Double = Strong hand. Suggests doubling for penalties if they run to 4-minor.
4♣ = Takeout for the majors with preference for hearts.
4◇ = Takeout for the majors with preference for spades.
4♡/4♠ = to play.

DEFENSIVE PLAY

If their 3NT is passed out, it is often good to start by leading an ace. This is usually not a sound move against no-trumps, but it works well against the gambling 3NT. As opener has little outside the long minor, the ace lead does not set up extra winners in declarer's hand. The ace lead allows you to see dummy and you can almost always then find the best continuation. Dummy's strengths and weaknesses will be revealed and declarer is known to have little outside the long minor.

COUNTERMEASURES BY THE GAMBLING 3NT SIDE

After 3NT : (Double)

All actions have the same meaning including No Bid. Redouble does not ask partner to run. It indicates great confidence that 3NT will succeed and a desire to penalise them if they run.

After 3NT : (Suit bid)

Doubles are for penalties. Minor suit bids = Pass or correct.

Pre-Empts at the Four-Level

Against natural pre-empts at the 4-level, many partnerships play double as simply a very strong hand. You do not need trump winners (indeed, you rarely have them). Partner is expected to pass unless holding a long strong suit. 4NT over 4♡ is used as a strong two-suiter in the minors, while 4NT over 4♠ is played as any strong two-suiter.

Other pairs prefer to use double for takeout, which partner may still pass for penalties, of course. Playing takeout doubles means that with length in the enemy suit, you pass unless you have a long, strong suit to call. You cannot afford to double unless you can stand any suit partner may bid. 4NT over 4♡ still shows a strong two-suiter in the minors, while over 4♠, double shows a three-suiter short in spades and 4NT is a strong two-suiter.

NAMYATS

Artificial strong pre-empts of 4♣ and 4♢

Many pairs prefer not to use 4♣ and 4♢ as natural pre-empts but as strong pre-empts of 4♡ and 4♠ respectively. 4♡/4♠ show normal pre-empts while 4♣ and 4♢ show a hand about one trick stronger, usually with one defensive trick outside the trump suit. With
♠ AQJ87652 ♡ 62 ♢ 8 ♣ 42, open 4♠ but if you hold
♠ AQJ87652 ♡ 62 ♢ 8 ♣ A2, choose the 4♢ opening.
When playing this approach :

3NT = a 4♣ or a 4♢ pre-empt. Any minor suit bid by responder asks opener to pass or correct if holding the other minor.

4♣ = strong pre-empt in hearts. Responder converts to 4♡ or with slam-interest, bids 4NT for key cards or a new suit asking for control in that suit.

4♢ = strong pre-empt in spades. Responder converts to 4♠ or makes a slam move as over 4♣.

4♡/4♠ = standard pre-empt. With slam prospects, responder may ask for key cards via 4NT or bid a new suit to ask for control in that suit.

Answers to control asks :

Step 1 = no control.

Step 2 = king in the bid suit.

Step 3 = singleton in the bid suit.

Step 4 = ace in the bid suit.

Step 5 = void in the bid suit.

DEFENCE AGAINST NAMYATS

Against 3NT showing a 4♣ or 4♦ pre-empt

Use the same defence as against the Gambling 3NT (page 29).

Against 4♣ showing a strong pre-empt in hearts

4♥ = Strong takeout with 0-1 cards in their suit.

4NT = Strong two-suiter in the minors.

Double = Takeout but not as strong as the 4♥ bid. Allows the partnership to play in 4♦ whereas 4♥ would commit the partnership to game. The double is also attractive in allowing either partner to double their run to 4♥ for penalties.

WEST	NORTH	EAST	SOUTH
4♣	Dble	4♥	No
No	Dble		

North's second double is for penalties and shows two or more cards in their suit. With enough strength to bid again despite South's pass, bid 4♥ initially if short in their suit.

WEST	NORTH	EAST	SOUTH
4♣	Dble	4♥	Dble

South's double is for penalties. As North has already made a takeout double, South can bid a suit or use 4NT to ask partner to choose a minor.

Against 4♦ showing a strong pre-empt in spades

Double = Takeout, but not as strong as the 4♠ bid. Double on most takeout hands since you wish to keep 4♥ available.

4♠ = Very strong takeout, suggesting slam since it commits partner to 5♥ if that is partner's suit.

4NT = Strong two-suiter in the minors.

COUNTERMEASURES BY THE OPENING SIDE

After 4♣ : (Double) or 4♦ : (Double)

Responder can indicate a desire to compete to the 5-level.

Pass = No interest in bidding beyond the 4-level.

Opener's suit = Desire to be declarer (K-x or A-Q in the suit doubled) and prepared to push to the 5-level.

Redouble = Prepared to push to the 5-level but no holding in the suit doubled which makes it attractive to be declarer.

Other actions = Usual asking bids for slam (see page 30).

After 4♣/4♦ : (Double) : No : (No)

Opener bids the major held but may redouble to ask partner to bid the major in case partner has a holding such as K-x or A-Q in the suit doubled. Opener can also bid the in-between suit to ask partner to lead that suit if the opponents buy the contract.

After 4♣/4♦ : (Double) : Redouble : (No)

Bid the major or bid the in-between suit to ask for that lead. If the opponents bid, make a lead-directing bid en route to 5♥/5♠.

3. RESPONSES TO 1NT & 2NT

STAYMAN OVER 1NT

The simple version of Stayman asks opener whether a 4-card major is held and opener has only three responses :

2◇ = No 4-card major.
2♡ = 4 hearts, may have 4 spades as well.
2♠ = 4 spades, denies 4 hearts. If opener is 4-4 in the majors, opener replies 2♡, bidding 4-card suits up-the-line.

After 1NT : 2♣, 2◇

2♡/2♠ = Natural, usually a 5-card suit, asking to be passed.
2NT = Invites 3NT. Same value as 1NT : 2NT but responder has at least one 4-card major.
3♣ = Sign-off. Responder has a weak hand with long clubs.
3◇ = Forcing. Responder could have passed 2◇.
3♡/3♠ = Forcing, promises a 5-card suit.

After 1NT : 2♣, 2♡

2♠ = Weak with four spades and a longer minor, for example :
♠ J1053 ♡ 6 ◇ Q98632 ♣ 87. Responder was hoping to pass a 2◇ reply. Opener may pass 2♠ or bid 2NT without support for spades. Over 2NT responder will bid the minor held.
2NT = Invites 3NT but includes four spades. Opener may pass or bid 3♠ with a minimum hand. Bid 3NT or 4♠ if maximum.
3NT = Enough for game but includes four spades. Opener bids 4♠ with four spades or passes 3NT otherwise.
3♣/3◇ = Sign off with a long minor.
3♡ = Invitational.
3♠ = Forcing with *four* spades. Responder has slam in mind and cannot bid 3NT to show four spades in case that is passed. With *five* spades and not four hearts, responder bids 1NT : 3♠.

After 1NT : 2♣, 2♠

2NT = Invites 3NT. Responder will have four hearts.
3NT = To play, with four hearts but opener has denied hearts.
3♣/3◇ = Sign off with a long minor.
3♡ = Invitational. Responder could have signed off in 2♡ over 1NT or forced at once with 1NT : 3♡ if not holding spades also.
3♠ = Invitational.

DEFENCE AGAINST 1NT : 2♣

Double = Lead-directing with strong clubs. The minimum club holding for this double is five cards including three or more honours. It is dangerous to double with weaker holdings as the opponents can elect to play in 2♣ doubled or even redoubled. If they make it, you have a very poor result. To double you should also hold at least one sure entry outside clubs if the suit is weaker than A-K-Q-x-x.

Suit bids = Natural. If you bid at the three-level, you should be within two tricks of your contract.

2NT = two-suiter in the minors.

Against a weak no-trump, many partnerships use the double of 2♣ to say 'I would have doubled 1NT for penalties.' In this case, the double does not necessarily include strong clubs. If the double is used to show all-round strength, then later doubles are for penalties. With a weaker hand you may pass 2♣ and double a later suit bid at the two-level for takeout. For example :

WEST	NORTH	EAST	SOUTH
1NT	No	2♣	No
2♡	No	No	Dble

South's double of 2♡ is for takeout. It indicates a hand short in hearts and includes four spades plus tolerance for each minor.

COUNTERMEASURES BY THE OPENING SIDE

After 1NT : (No) : 2♣ : (Double)

If the double is lead-directing, opener can indicate whether a stopper in clubs is held :

Pass = No stopper in clubs. When this is passed to responder, redouble asks opener to give the Stayman reply.

WEST	NORTH	EAST	SOUTH
1NT	No	2♣	Dble
No	No	Rdbl	

West has denied a stopper in clubs. East's redouble asks West to make the normal reply regarding the majors.

Bids = Same meaning as usual but promise a stopper in clubs as well.

Redouble = To play in 2♣ redoubled. Opener judges that fourth player has made a serious error in doubling. Clearly opener will have a strong club holding, usually with a 5-card suit.

If the double was a general penalty double and not simply lead-directing for clubs :

Playing a weak no-trump, responder often uses 2♣ as the start of a rescue manoeuvre. Opener should pass with four fair clubs or make the normal reply otherwise. If the pass reverts to responder, redouble is for takeout. See page 85 for more details.

TRANSFERS

1NT : 2♣ is used almost universally as Stayman but other bids at the two-level are commonly harnessed as transfer bids which allow many hands to be bid more accurately than using the simple weakness takeout. A secondary benefit is that the no-trump opener becomes declarer very often, a likely advantage when responder has a very weak hand.

The transfer promises five or more cards in the next suit up. No particular strength is indicated by the transfer. Responder will indicate the strength held after opener 'accepts the transfer' (bids the suit shown by responder).

1NT : 2◇ = Transfer to 2♡.

1NT : 2♡ = Transfer to 2♠.

1NT : 2♠ = Transfer to 3♣. Some partnerships use only the 2◇/2♡ transfers to the majors and use a 2♠ bid for other purposes. However, transfers to the minors as well as the majors (four suit transfers) are highly recommended.

1NT : 2NT = Transfer to diamonds. If you have a quantitative 2NT raise, bid 2♣ and rebid 2NT. In this case, 1NT : 2♣ does not guarantee responder has a major. Some pairs prefer to use 1NT : 3♣ as the transfer to diamonds and retain 1NT : 2NT as quantitative. It is true that using 1NT : 2♣ just to invite game with a 2NT rebid gives information about opener's shape to the opponents but 1NT : 2NT as a transfer does have a significant advantage (see later) and leaves 1NT : 3♣ as a natural, slam-going one-suiter.

After 1NT : 2◇ or 1NT : 2♡

Normally opener simply bids the major suit shown. With a maximum 1NT *and* good support for the major *and* a doubleton, opener may jump to the three-of-the-major ('super-accept'). After opener has bid the major, responder rebids as follows :

Pass = weakness takeout. The opener is now the declarer.

2NT = Inviting 3NT or 4-Major.

3NT = Gives opener the choice of 3NT or 4-Major.

3-Responder's-Major = Shows 6-card suit and invites 4-Major.

New suit = 4+ cards in the suit bid and creates a game-force.

After 1NT : 2♠ or 1NT : 2NT

Opener normally bids the minor suit shown. However, with a maximum 1NT and Q-x-x or better in the minor, opener makes the in-between bid (1NT : 2♠, 2NT or 1NT : 2NT, 3♣). This may help responder bid 3NT. With a weakness takeout, responder simply bids the minor despite opener's 'super-accept'.

DEFENCE AGAINST TRANSFERS

Double = Lead-directing, showing a strong holding in the suit doubled. As the transfer is artificial, it is convenient to double to tell partner what to lead. Just like doubling 1NT : 2♣ Stayman for the lead, your suit should be at least five cards long and include three or more honours.

Bid the suit shown by the transfer

WEST	NORTH	EAST	SOUTH
1NT	No	2♡	2♠

If 2♡ is a transfer, 2♠ by South is a strong takeout with 0-1 spades.

WEST	NORTH	EAST	SOUTH
1NT	No	2♡	No
2♠	No	No	Dble

With a weaker hand or with two or more cards in spades, wait for the transfer to be completed and then double for takeout.

2NT = Two-suiter in the minors.

COUNTERMEASURES BY THE OPENING SIDE

After a double

WEST	NORTH	EAST	SOUTH
1NT	No	2♡	Dble
?			

Opener uses the opportunity to indicate support for responder's suit and thus the desirability of competing at the three-level when responder has the weakness hand.

Bid-the-major-shown = Doubleton support only and no desire to compete at the three-level.

Pass = 3+ support and prepared to compete at the three-level.

WEST	NORTH	EAST	SOUTH
1NT	No	2♡	Dble
No	No	Rdbl	

If this is passed back to responder, a redouble asks opener to accept the transfer anyway.

Redouble = 4-card support and maximum values. Certainly wants to compete at the three-level and is a strong invitation to game.

Super-accept of responder's major

WEST	NORTH	EAST	SOUTH
1NT	No	2♡	Dble
3♠			

Opener's hand could not be better. The super-accept shows 4-card support, a maximum 1NT and a doubleton in the suit doubled (hearts in the example). Opener can make no stronger invitation to game than this.

After they bid responder's major

WEST	NORTH	EAST	SOUTH
1NT	No	2♡	2♠

Opener passes to indicate only weak support for responder and no desire to compete at the three-level. Double by opener shows 3+ support, a maximum 1NT and a desire to compete at the three-level.

SOUTH AFRICAN TEXAS TRANSFERS

Before transfers at the two-level became popular, the Texas Convention was used to enable the 1NT or 2NT opener to be declarer when responder had a 4♡ or 4♠ response. 1NT : 4◇ was a transfer to 4♡ and 1NT : 4♡ was a transfer to 4♠. The natural-sounding 1NT : 4♡ posed a memory problem. A forgetful opener would occasionally pass 4♡ with dire results. On other occasions responder forgot the convention and bid 4♡, intending to show long hearts. After opener accepted the transfer and bid 4♠ responder woke up but now had to bid 5♡, of course.

The South African Texas variation overcame this flaw :
1NT : 4♣ = Transfer to 4♡. 1NT : 4◇ = Transfer to 4♠.

As the suits were minors, opener's memory would be jogged. In addition, if responder forgot and did bid 1NT : 4♡, no great damage was done. The only significant loss is that of 1NT : 4♣ as Gerber, asking for aces. This is no serious loss as it is always possible to make some other bid first (Stayman or a natural suit bid) before launching into an ace ask.

South African Texas Transfers are useful even when playing four suit transfers if responder simply wishes to rest in 4♡ or 4♠. One advantage is that a two-level transfer allows the opponents in cheaply, while a four-level transfer will almost always keep them out. Another consideration is whether you are worried about a lead-directing double. For example, you can reach 4♡ via 1NT : 2◇, 2♡ : 4♡ or via 1NT : 4♣, 4♡. If you do not relish a lead-directing double of 2◇, choose the 4♣ route. If, however, a lead-directing double of 4♣ concerns you, travel via 2◇.

You are not obliged to use the 4♣ or 4◇ transfer. If the lead up to your hand is desirable, simply bid the major game yourself. With ♠ QJ97632 ♡ – ◇ K93 ♣ K32, bid 1NT : 4♠.

DEFENCE AGAINST 1NT : 4♣ OR 1NT : 4◇

Double = Lead-directing.

COUNTERMEASURES BY THE OPENING SIDE

Opener may simply accept the transfer and bid responder's major. With K-x or A-Q or similar holdings in the suit doubled, opener certainly should bid the major. With nothing of value in the suit doubled, opener passes and allows responder to bid the major game. Responder can redouble to ask opener to take the transfer anyway. With A-x or A-x-x, opener can redouble so that responder can bid the game with holdings like Q-x or K-J-x.

RESPONDING TO 2NT

2NT : 3♣ – Stayman or Baron

Two types of structure are popular :

   3♣ = Baron Convention, asking for 4-card suits up-the-line. Opener bids the cheapest 4-card suit held. If clubs is the only suit, opener bids 3NT.

   3◇/3♡ = Transfer to hearts/spades.

   3♠ = 5 spades and 4 hearts exactly, the major two-suiter that cannot be shown otherwise with Baron 3♣ or transfers.

The other structure uses 3♣ as Stayman asking only for majors, not for all 4-card suits.

   3♣ = Stayman Convention, asking for 4-card majors.

   3◇/3♡ = Transfer to hearts/spades.

   3♠ = Minor two-suiter with some slam interest.

   4♣/4◇ = Natural, 6+ suit and slam interest.

One advantage of using 3♣ Stayman is that it reduces memory problems, as the same approach is used over 2NT as over 1NT. A more important benefit is that Stayman enables the stronger hand to be declarer more often when a 4-4 major fit is found. For example :

WEST	EAST	Playing Baron		Playing Stayman	
♠ AQ73	♠ K862	WEST	EAST	WEST	EAST
♡ K2	♡ 985	2NT	3♣	2NT	3♣
◇ AKJ3	◇ 74	3◇	3♠	3♠	4♠
♣ KJ5	♣ A432	4♠	No	No	

Both methods reach 4♠, but it will often be better to have West declarer. This type of situation arises frequently enough to prefer the use of 3♣ as Stayman. If you need to locate a minor suit with opener, you can use 3♣ Stayman and follow up with 4♣ as a minor suit enquiry over any reply by opener.

   With 5 hearts-4 spades, bid 3◇ (transfer to hearts) and rebid 3♠ over 3♡, allowing opener to choose the contract. With 5 spades-4 hearts, bid 3♣ Stayman. If opener bids 3◇, no major, you rebid 3♠ to show your 5-card suit.

   Using transfers over 2NT is very valuable. It enables responder to sign off at the three-level with a hopelessly weak hand and also to show a two-suiter at a comfortable level. In addition, with the great disparity in strength between opener and responder, it is usually preferable to have the strong hand as declarer.

DEFENCE AGAINST 2NT : 3♣

Given opener's strength, it will be rare for the defenders to enter the auction. Any suit bid would be based on exceptional playing strength (within two tricks of the bid made).

Double = Lead-directing. At least five clubs with 3+ honours.

3NT = Minor two-suiter, normally at least 6-5.

COUNTERMEASURES BY THE OPENING SIDE

After 2NT : (No) : 3♣ : (Double)

Redouble = To play. Opener has a strong 4-card or better club holding and expects to make 3♣ doubled if responder can stand to pass.

Pass = No stopper in clubs. This is conceivable although rare for a 2NT opener. If this is passed back to responder, redouble asks opener to make the normal reply. If responder has a decent club holding, responder may elect to pass out 3♣ doubled in anticipation of making the contract.

Bids = Normal meaning but promise a stopper in clubs as well.

After 2NT : (No) : 3♣ : (Bid)

Double = Penalties.

Pass = No stopper in their suit.

Bids = Natural meaning but promise a stopper in their suit.

DEFENCE AGAINST 2NT : TRANSFER

Double = Lead-directing. At least five cards in the suit doubled with 3+ honours.

3NT = Freak two-suiter in the minors, normally at least 6-5 at this level.

Bid their suit = Freak two-suiter, normally at least 6-5, with one of the suits being the other major and the other being a minor.

WEST	NORTH	EAST	SOUTH
2NT	No	3◇	3♡

South figures to have 5+ spades and 5+ in one of the minors in a 6-5 pattern. If advancer has no support for spades, advancer can bid 4♣. Partner will convert to diamonds if that is the minor.

COUNTERMEASURES BY THE OPENING SIDE

After 2NT : (No) : Transfer : (Double)

Opener will usually accept the transfer and with good support, maximum values and a doubleton in the suit doubled, opener may super-accept by bidding 4-Major. Accepting the transfer also promises a stopper in the suit doubled.

Pass = No stopper in the suit doubled (a rare occurrence). When this comes back to responder, a redouble asks opener to accept the transfer anyway.

4. Conventional Actions After a Suit Opening of One

THE BARON 2NT RESPONSE

The 2NT response to a suit opening bid of one shows 16+ HCP in a balanced hand with no 5-card suit. In addition, after a minor suit opening, the 2NT reply denies a 4-card major. The advantage of the response is that hands in the 16+ range are otherwise hard to describe. To bid 3NT with such values makes further exploration risky. Using 2NT as 16+, the 3NT response can be used as 13-15 with a 4-3-3-3 pattern.

   Further bidding is natural. A rebid of the suit opened asks for 3-card support. Without such support, responder bids 3NT. With support, responder cue bids the cheapest ace. Another attractive approach is to show the key cards* held in support of opener's suit. For example :

WEST	EAST
1♡	2NT
3♡	?

With two hearts, bid 3NT. With 3-4 hearts, responder shows key cards :

   3♠ = 0 or 3 key cards.
   4♣ = 1 or 4 key cards.
   4◇ = 2 key cards but no queen of trumps.
   4♡ = 2 key cards plus the queen of trumps.

Where opener bids a second suit, responder can show weak or strong support for either of opener's suits. For example :

WEST	EAST	Responder can support spades by bidding 3♠ (strong
1♠	2NT	support) or 4♠ (weak support). With support for clubs,
3♣	?	cue bid the cheapest ace. Alternatively, with support for

clubs, responder shows key cards, excluding 3♠ or 3NT as steps. Thus:

   3◇ = support for clubs + 0 or 3 key cards.
   3♡ = support for clubs + 1 or 4 key cards.
   3♠ = strong support for spades.
   3NT = no support for either of opener's suits (2-4-4-3 pattern).
   4♣ = support for clubs + 2 key cards but no queen of trumps.
   4◇ = support for clubs + 2 key cards and the queen of trumps.

*For more about key cards, see page 59.

THE JACOBY 2NT RESPONSE

The Jacoby 2NT response to a major suit one-opening shows support for opener's suit and is forcing to game. It is unlimited and there is no suggestion that responder wishes to play in no-trumps. However, if the partnership is also using splinters (see later) the Jacoby 2NT denies a singleton or a void.

Opener is asked to describe the shape of the hand by bidding a singleton at the three-level. If opener has a void, this is shown by bidding the void suit at the four-level. With no singleton, bid :

4-Major = The weakest rebid, showing a bare minimum opening.
3NT = 14-15 points.
3-Major = Stronger than 3NT.

After opener's initial rebid, 3-Major asks partner for key cards. If 3-Major is not available, 3NT can be used for key-cards. For example :

WEST	EAST	WEST	EAST
♠ AJ854	♠ KQ63	1♠	2NT
♡ 8	♡ 765	3♡	3♠ – key card ask
◇ A97	◇ K8	4◇(1)	5♣ – ask in clubs*
♣ K1052	♣ AQ93	5♡(2)	6♠
	(1) 2 key cards, no ♣Q		(2) ♣K, no ♣A, no ♣Q*

WEST	EAST	WEST	EAST
♠ 9	♠ A753	1♡	2NT
♡ AQ732	♡ K9654	3♠	3NT – key card ask
◇ AJ5	◇ K3	4♠(1)	5♣ – ask in clubs
♣ K742	♣ A3	5♡	7♡
		(1) 2 key cards plus the ♡Q	

WEST	EAST	WEST	EAST
♠ 9	♠ Q6	1♡	2NT
♡ KQ863	♡ AJ54	3♠	3NT – key card ask
◇ KJ4	◇ A72	4◇(1)	4♡
♣ K632	♣ QJ107	(1) 1 or 4 key cards	

WEST	EAST	WEST	EAST
♠ AK7642	♠ Q985	1♠	2NT
♡ A87	♡ K5	4◇(1)	4NT – key card ask
◇ –	◇ Q763	5♣(2)	7♠
♣ J752	♣ AKQ	(1) Void in diamonds	
		(2) 0 or 3 key cards, obviously 3	

*See page 126

DEFENCE TO BARON 2NT OR JACOBY 2NT

Given the high card strength contained in these responses, you will rarely have enough to enter the bidding. Bidding a suit is natural and your playing strength should be within two tricks of your bid. You might enter the auction with a freak two-suiter short in their suit, typically at least a 6-5 pattern. With such a hand, you could adopt the following approach :

Double = 6 spades + 5-minor. Partner supports spades if possible. If not, partner may bid a minor. Pass if holding that minor, otherwise convert to the other minor.

3-their-major = 5 spades + 6-minor. Partner supports spades if possible or bids a minor on the 'pass or correct' principle.

4-their-major = 6 spades + 6-minor.

3NT = Both minors, 6-5 (or great courage and a 5-5 hand).

4NT = Both minors, 6-6 at least.

Opposite any of these actions, the high card strength is not so important (you are not likely to have much) but the degree of fit should determine how high you take the bidding. Do not become too excited with just an 8-card fit. With a 9-card fit, you can afford to sacrifice at the 4-level and with a 10-card fit at the 5-level.

Where opener shows a singleton in reply to Jacoby 2NT

WEST	NORTH	EAST	SOUTH
1♡	No	2NT	No
3♢	Dble		

As North will be on lead against a heart contract, there is no point in using double for lead-directing. Best is to double with a long suit suggesting a sacrifice against their eventual game or slam.

COUNTERMEASURES BY THE OPENING SIDE

After they double the 2NT response

With most hands it will be best to make your normal descriptive rebid. This gives partner the best chance to make a sensible decision if they now pre-empt beyond your game. However, with a minimum balanced hand, pass is sensible. As 2NT was forcing to game, all passes below game are forcing : partner must either bid or double for penalties. Redouble should show a strong holding in a suit promised by the double. The redouble suggests your best result may come from a penalty double.

If they bid 3-of-your-major or 4-of-your-major

Pass with the minimum balanced hand. Double suggests it may be best to try for penalties.

If they bid 3NT or 4NT for the minors

Pass if minimum and balanced. Double for penalties.

THE SWISS CONVENTION

The Swiss Convention uses the responses of 4♣ and 4♢ to a major suit opening to show a balanced game raise with 4-card or better support for opener. If the partnership is using the Jacoby 2NT response, Swiss would be inappropriate as the 2NT bid covers the same hand type as that shown by the Swiss responses. Partnerships using the Jacoby 2NT response commonly use 4♣ and 4♢ as splinter responses (see later).

4♣ or 4♢ as natural pre-emptive responses being of little value to a major suit opening, it makes sense to harness them to show support for opener's suit. There are two basic approaches to the Swiss Convention. In one version responder shows the controls held :

4♣ = Three aces *or* two aces + trump king (three key cards).
4♢ = Two aces *or* one ace + trump king (two key cards).

As key cards can be comfortably located these days and often at a cheaper level, this version of Swiss has outlived its usefulness. In the other version, the focus is on the quality of the trump support :

4♣ = Strong trump support, two top trump honours at least.
4♢ = Poor trump support, worse than Q-x-x-x.

In both cases four trumps are promised. 4♣ may have more than four trumps but 4♢ has exactly four trumps. This is designed to avoid reaching a slam with a combined trump holding of K-6-5-3-2 opposite J-9-7-4 or similar.

If responder has exactly one top trump (ace, king or queen), choose a different sequence.

DEFENCE AGAINST SWISS 4♣ AND 4♢

As these are artificial responses, double if you want partner to lead that minor.

COUNTERMEASURES BY THE OPENING SIDE

4-of-your-major = Minimum and no control in the suit doubled.
Pass = no control but interested in slam if partner has control. When this is passed to responder, sign off with no control either, redouble to show the king but no queen and bid on with ace or king-queen in the doubled suit.
Redouble = control in the suit doubled. May still be a minimum opening.
Bid of the suit doubled = Void in that suit. Asks partner to show key cards outside the suit doubled.

SPLINTERS

How do you treat each of these sequences :

WEST	EAST	WEST	EAST	WEST	EAST
1♠	4♦	1♡	4♣	1♡	3♠

The standard meaning for a double jump response in a new suit is a pre-empt. However, after partner has opened, it is not attractive to pre-empt to the four-level. You may miss the best spot of 3NT. In general, it is of limited use to pre-empt opposite an opening bid, since the opponents are unlikely to enter the bidding anyway. Instead of shutting them out, your pre-empt is robbing your own side of valuable bidding space.

Many partnerships prefer to use the double jump responses to show support for opener's suit and a shortage in the suit bid. They are called 'splinters' because the shortage, the thinnest part of the hand, is shown.

A splinter bid shows :
- 4-card or better support for partner's suit,
- enough high card values for at least game, and
- a singleton or a void in the suit bid.

In response to a major suit opening, the splinters are :

WEST	EAST	WEST	EAST	WEST	EAST
1♡	3♠	1♡	4♣	1♡	4♦
WEST	EAST	WEST	EAST	WEST	EAST
1♠	4♣	1♠	4♦	1♠	4♡

The 1♠ : 4♡ response can take a while to absorb as it is such a natural sounding response. Splinters are not compatible with 4♣ Gerber or with the Swiss Convention. They do, however, work very well in conjunction with the Jacoby 2NT response (page 40). They also work well even without any other conventional method of showing strong raises of partner's suit.

Suppose partner has opened 1♡. These hands are worth a splinter raise :

♠ AJ2	♠ 9	♠ AK3
♡ KJ92	♡ A9763	♡ QJ872
♦ 5	♦ KQ6	♦ A642
♣ K7632	♣ K432	♣ 5
Bid 4♦.	Bid 3♠.	Bid 4♣.

The playing strength is 7 losers or better. It is best not to splinter with a very powerful side suit. Show this hand by bidding the side suit first, supporting partner later.

Splinters over minors

Splinters over minor suit openings are not as popular but they also work well, particularly in deciding whether to tackle 3NT. The more high cards you have opposite a short suit, the more you should lean towards 3NT rather than 5-of-a-minor. The splinter responses to a minor are :

1♣ : 3◇, 3♡ or 3♠ and 1◇ : 3♡, 3♠ or 4♣.

They replace the normal pre-emptive responses. 1◇ : 4♣ is a slam move since the splinter is beyond 3NT.

Splinter rebids

Splinters can also be used later in the auction. The general agreement is that where a change of suit would be forcing, the jump rebid can be used as a splinter. The last bid in each of these sequences is a splinter, agreeing partner's last mentioned suit as trumps and showing a shortage in the suit bid.

WEST	EAST	WEST	EAST	WEST	EAST
1♠	2♡	1♠	2◇	1♣	1♡
4◇...		2♠	4♣	1♠	4◇

The best way to consider a splinter is as a short suit slam try. With no wasted values in the short suit, you may try for a slam even with minimum values. Opposite a singleton, the ace is fine but all other honours are wasted. Opposite a void, even the ace should be considered a wasted value.

WEST	EAST	WEST	EAST
♠ KQ643	♠ A9875	1♠	4♡ – splinter
♡ 8742	♡ 6	4NT	5♡
◇ AQJ	◇ K95	6♠	No
♣ 6	♣ AJ43		

Both hands are minimum in high cards but the slam is excellent.

When you hold wasted values opposite the short suit, you need more than a minimum hand to push on, at least a king (one trick) stronger than minimum.

WEST	EAST	WEST	EAST
♠ KQ643	♠ A9875	1♠	4♡ – splinter
♡ AQJ	♡ 6	4♠	No
◇ 8742	◇ K95		
♣ 6	♣ AJ43		

West has a minimum opening and the Q-J in hearts are wasted opposite the shortage. Therefore, West signs off in 4♠. Even the five-level would be in jeopardy. The slam is not impossible but it is a very poor bet.

WEST	EAST	WEST	EAST
♠ KQ	♠ A964	1♡	4♣ – splinter
♡ KQ6432	♡ A975	4NT	5♠
♢ 62	♢ A743	6♡	No
♣ KQ7	♣ 8		

West has significant wastage opposite East's 4♣ splinter but also has better than a minimum opening hand (5 losers rather than 7, 15 HCP rather than 11-12, extra length in trumps). That entitles West to try for a slam despite the wasted club strength.

WEST	EAST	WEST	EAST
♠ KQJ	♠ 6	1♣	3♠ – splinter
♡ J87	♡ A62	3NT	No
♢ 84	♢ KQ72		
♣ AJ642	♣ KQ1097		

3NT might be defeated but it is a far better chance than 5♣. Even on a heart lead, 3NT might make but on a heart lead, 5♣ is doomed. In 3NT, the opponents tend to lead dummy's known singleton suit, while in 5♣ there is little value in that lead.

WEST	EAST	WEST	EAST
♠ J87	♠ 6	1♣	3♠ – splinter
♡ KQJ	♡ A62	4♣ (1)	4NT (2)
♢ 84	♢ KQ72	5♣	No
♣ AJ642	♣ KQ1097	(1) Sets clubs, asks for key cards	
		(2) 2 key cards plus the queen of clubs	

With no stopper opposite the short suit, 3NT is a ridiculous spot. The minor suit key card asking bids for slam can be found on page 63.

Mini-splinters

Most pairs are happy enough to give up pre-emptive responses and use the double jumps as splinters. Some are also prepared to give up the jump shift response and use that as a splinter try for game. In this method :

1♡ : 3♣ = short in clubs, strong enough for a limit raise in hearts (about 8-10 HCP). Opener can sign off in 3♡, bid game or even try for slam. Responder can still bid on after a sign-off with a stronger hand. Pairs using mini-splinters frequently play :

Jump shift response = singleton in suit bid, limit raise or better.
Double jump response = void in the suit bid.

This has the benefit of clarifying whether the shortage is a void or a singleton. After a mini-splinter and a sign-off, responder can still bid for game or try for slam.

DEFENCE AGAINST SPLINTER BIDS

When the opponents produce a splinter bid, they will have the majority of points. By all means bid an excellent suit if you are prepared to take a sacrifice. You can also bid their suit or 4NT to show two-suiters, e.g.,

WEST	NORTH	EAST	SOUTH	
1♡	No	4♣	?	4NT by South = Both minors.
				4♡ = Spades and a minor, probably clubs.

Obviously since you are outgunned, you will need excellent playing strength to enter the auction.

How do you play the double of a splinter bid? There are two schools of thought. One view is that the double shows length and strength in the splinter suit, the other uses the double as a lead-directing action. You and partner need to choose which approach to adopt.

It is reasonable to double to show length in the suit and to suggest a sacrifice. However, the vulnerability may be wrong, you may have defensive chances and you are not yet sure how high they are going. You may be happy to sacrifice against their game but not against a slam.

Recommended is to use the double as lead-directing, not for the suit doubled (there is little value in asking for the lead of dummy's singleton or void) but for *the suit below the short suit*.

WEST	NORTH	EAST	SOUTH	
1♡	No	4◇	Dble	Using lead-directing doubles. South is asking for a club lead, the suit below diamonds.

Where the splinter bid is clubs, double asks for a spade lead.

Some pairs play artificial splinters. A double of an artificial splinter asks you to lead the suit doubled. For example :

WEST	NORTH	EAST	SOUTH	
1♠	No	4♣*	Dble	Here the 4♣ splinter does not relate to clubs at all but shows a shortage in hearts. The double asks for a club lead.

*Splinter, short in hearts

Against natural splinters, double to ask for the lead *under* the splinter suit. Suppose you are playing this approach and you pick up as West :

♠ Q107 ♡ Q102 ◇ 10843 ♣ 1074.

The bidding has been :

WEST	NORTH	EAST	SOUTH
		No	1♠
No	4◇	No	4♣
No	No	No	

4◇ = natural splinter, singleton or void in diamonds.

What would you lead?

Under normal circumstances, there would be no clue which suit to try. However, using lead-directing doubles, it is valid to reason that partner could have doubled 4◇ to ask for a club lead. The failure to double indicates partner has no burning desire for a club lead. Therefore partner is likely to be stronger in hearts than in clubs. This is no certainty, of course, but it is enough of a guide to try the two of hearts. This was the complete deal :

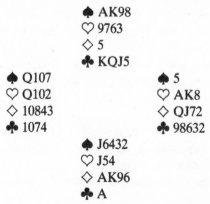

```
                    ♠ AK98
                    ♡ 9763
                    ◇ 5
                    ♣ KQJ5
        ♠ Q107                    ♠ 5
        ♡ Q102                    ♡ AK8
        ◇ 10843                   ◇ QJ72
        ♣ 1074                    ♣ 98632
                    ♠ J6432
                    ♡ J54
                    ◇ AK96
                    ♣ A
```

On a 'safe' minor suit lead, declarer wins and makes twelve tricks by discarding the heart losers on the clubs after two rounds of trumps. On a heart lead, the defence takes the first three tricks and declarer would need to be clairvoyant to pick up the trump suit for no loss.

COUNTERMEASURES BY THE SPLINTER SIDE

They bid 4NT for the minors : Double = Looking for penalties.

They bid opener's suit : Double = We are better off playing for penalties than bidding on.

They double showing the suit doubled : Bids have normal meanings, redouble = first round control in that suit and asks partner to cue bid, pass allows partner to redouble to show void in the splinter suit or to cue bid with singleton there.

They double to ask for the lead of some other suit : Sign off in your suit = no slam interest (normal meaning), pass = slam interest but no control in the key suit, cue bid or 4NT = second round control in the key suit, redouble = first round control of the key suit and asks partner to cue bid. After pass, partner signs off with no control, cue bids or uses 4NT with second round control and redoubles to show first round control.

LONG SUIT TRIALS

A trial bid is a change of suit after a major suit has been raised to the two-level. A long suit trial shows three or more cards in the suit bid with two or three losers in that suit. It is an invitation to game in the agreed major if partner has help in the trial suit.

♠ AQ876   After 1♠ : 2♠, you are worth a try for game. The typical
♡ A4   trial bid is in the 15-17 HCP range or a hand of six losers.
♢ J765   The best action is 3♢, asking for help in removing those
♣ KQ   diamond losers.

Partner might have ♠ KJ54 ♡ K82 ♢ 9843 ♣ 73 making 4♠ hopeless. Partner can also have ♠ KJ54 ♡ 982 ♢ A3 ♣ 7643 which makes 4♠ a good proposition.

After a trial bid :
- With three losers in the trial suit, sign off in 3-Major.
- With two losers in the trial suit, sign off in 3-Major with a minimum raise and bid 4-Major with a maximum raise.
- With one loser in the trial suit or no losers in the trial suit, bid 4-Major even with a minimum raise.

With the first hand above, responder would bid 3♠ and with the second 4♠ (only one loser in the trial suit).

DEFENCE AGAINST LONG SUIT TRIAL BIDS

If a long suit trial has been made and rejected via a sign-off at the three-level, it is often best to lead the trial suit. Declarer has shown weakness in that suit and dummy has indicated little help there. If a trial bid is accepted via a jump to 4-Major, there is less indication that you should lead the trial suit. If declarer has made a trial bid, received a rejection and bid on to game anyway, beware of leading the trial suit. Declarer may well have made a psychic trial bid with a holding like A-Q-x hoping to tempt you into leading that suit.

As a trial bid is made by the probable declarer, doubling the trial suit for the lead is not sensible in the normal sense. You can use the double to show a holding such as A-Q-x or longer, so that partner knows to return that suit when partner gains the lead. As you have not been in the bidding earlier, it is not likely to be of use to double a trial bid for a sacrifice when declarer is showing 3+ cards in the trial suit. In addition, it is not even certain that they will bid the game anyway.

COUNTERMEASURES BY THE OPENING SIDE

Bids have normal meanings. Redouble shows a strong holding such as K-J-10-x or Q-J-10-x inviting partner to pass or bid 3NT.

TRIAL BIDS IN COMPETITIVE AUCTIONS

Very often you will be involved in a competitive auction and will have lost one or more possible trial bids.

WEST	NORTH	EAST	SOUTH	
1♡	2◇	2♡	3◇	There are no trial bids available. Play
?				3♡ as merely competitive and use
				Double for any game invitation.

WEST	NORTH	EAST	SOUTH	
1♡	2♣	2♡	3♣	Play 3♡ as competitive. Double as a
?				general game invitation and 3◇ as a trial
				bid in diamonds.

WEST	NORTH	EAST	SOUTH	
1♡	1♠	2♡	2♠	Play 3♡ as competitive, Double as a
?				general game invitation. Use 3♣ and 3◇
				as trial bids.

It is important to be able to bid 3-Major simply to contest the partscore without reaching 4-Major every time partner happens to have a maximum raise. Otherwise you will have to let the opponents win the partscore battle too often.

The least necessary action in these sequences is the penalty double. When they bid and raise a suit immediately, it is highly unlikely that you will be able to do any significant damage to them at the two-level or three-level. It is better therefore to forego the penalty double and use Double simply to make a general invitation to game (like 1♡ : 2♡, 3♡ with no interference bidding).

DEFENCE AGAINST INVITATION DOUBLES IN COMPETITIVE AUCTIONS

If you feel you are worth a sacrifice, it is usually best to wait and see whether they do go to game. Often they will subside in 3-Major and it is silly to take an advance sacrifice against a game they would not have bid anyway.

WEST	NORTH	EAST	SOUTH	
1♠	2◇	2♠	3◇	Redouble in this auction has no value
Dble	?			in any natural sense. You could use it to
				tell partner you wish to defend against

their contract but that should not be necessary. South having bid 3◇ has said it all and should allow North to decide whether to defend or sacrifice later. A sensible agreement is to use Pass to ask partner to do nothing and Redouble to ask for partner's co-operation if they bid the game. Partner can then decide to defend on a flattish hand or to sacrifice with some distribution.

SHORT SUIT TRIALS

A short suit trial is a trial bid (new suit after a major suit raise to the two-level) which shows a singleton or a void in the suit bid (normally a singleton). It invites partner to bid game with little wastage in the trial suit. The best holding is three or more rags in the trial suit.

- With three losers in the trial suit, bid 4-Major.
- With ace and two losers in the trial suit, bid 4-Major.
- With no ace in the trial suit but two losers, bid 4-Major if maximum and 3-Major if minimum.
- With ace in the trial suit and one loser, bid 4-Major if maximum and 3-Major if minimum.
- With no ace and only one loser in the trial suit, bid 3-Major.
- With exceptional strength in the trial suit, bid 3NT if maximum.

WEST	EAST	WEST	EAST
♠ K8642	♠ A953	1♠	2♠
♡ AJ10	♡ Q72	3◇	4♠
◇ 9	◇ 8752	No	
♣ AJ62	♣ 84		3◇ = short suit trial bid

With no wasted high cards opposite the shortage, East should accept the invitation even with minimum values. 4♠ needs either a 2-2 spade break or the heart finesse, about a 70% chance in total.

WEST	EAST	WEST	EAST
♠ K8642	♠ A953	1♠	2♠
♡ AJ10	♡ 8752	3◇	3♠
◇ 9	◇ Q72	No	
♣ AJ62	♣ 84		3◇ = short suit trial bid

East's ◇Q is wasted and East is minimum. Therefore East should sign off. 4♠ may make but it needs spades 2-2 and no more than one loser in hearts. Total chance is only about 30%.

WEST	EAST	WEST	EAST
♠ K8642	♠ A953	1♠	2♠
♡ AJ10	♡ K752	3◇	4♠
◇ 9	◇ Q72	No	
♣ AJ62	♣ 84		3◇ = short suit trial bid ,

East's ◇Q is wasted but East has a maximum raise with 2+ losers in the trial suit. With ♠ Axxx ♡ Kxxx ◇ xxx ♣ xx East would have enough to accept the game invitation.

DEFENCE AGAINST SHORT SUIT TRIALS

Double = length in their short suit and suggests a sacrifice.

STOPPER SHOWING BIDS

Trial bids are used after a major suit has been raised to the two-level. Where a minor suit has been raised, the usual concern when a game is in the offing is whether to try for 3NT or whether to play 5-Minor. Common practice after a minor suit raise to the three-level is to use a new suit to show a stopper in the suit bid and suggest 3NT if partner has a stopper in the other suit(s).

WEST	EAST	
1♠	2♣	3♦ = I have diamonds covered. Am worried about the hearts.
3♣	?	3♥ = I have hearts covered. What about the diamonds?

WEST	EAST	
1♣	3♣	3♦ = I have diamonds covered. Am worried about at least one of the majors.
?		3♥ = Hearts stopped, but not diamonds.
		3♠ = Spades stopped. No stopper in hearts or diamonds.

Stopper showing can also be used after partner has rebid a minor at the three-level and thereby shows that no other suit is held. For example :

WEST	EAST	
1♣	1♥	West's 3♣ shows about 16-18 points and 6+ clubs with no second suit. It is safe for East to bid 3♦ or 3♠ as a
3♣	?	stopper-showing bid. West cannot have four cards to raise that suit.

After a minor suit raise to the two-level, change of suit is forcing but one can change suit at the two-level or jump to the three-level. At the two-level the bid is natural and shows strength in the suit bid. It may be a genuine suit or may be just a stopper. Jumps to the three-level (1♣ : 2♣, 3♠) can be used as a splinter, showing a singleton or void in that suit and aiming for 5-minor or 3NT if partner has at least a double stopper in the short suit.

Jumps to the four-level are natural and show a 6-5 pattern.

Bidding after a stopper showing bid

WEST	EAST	
1♥	2♣	Bid 3NT with the danger suit (spades) stopped. With no stopper, bid 3♥ with an excellent five-card suit including
3♣	3♦	at least three honours, *or* 4♣ with 2+ spades *or* 5♣ with a
?		singleton spade.

After a splinter bid

Bid 3NT with the short suit doubly stopped. Otherwise bid the minor at the 4-level if weak, particularly with wasted values in the short suit, or 5-minor if maximum.

STOPPER ASKING BIDS

Some pairs prefer to use stopper asks in situations where a stopper showing bid is commonly used (see previous page). After minor suit agreement, a new suit under this method says 'Do you have a stopper in the suit I have just bid?' With a stopper, bid no-trumps. Without a stopper, make some other descriptive bid. The stopper ask implies that the bidder holds stoppers in other unbid suits.

WEST	EAST	
1♡	2♣	Playing stopper asks, East's 3♠ bid says 'Bid 3NT if you have spades stopped.' It implies East has the diamonds
3♣	3♠	covered.

WEST	EAST	
1♣	1◇	Playing stopper asks East's 3♡ asks for a stopper in hearts. With a heart stopper, West bids 3NT. If West has a
3♣	3♡	heart stopper but is worried about the spades, West can

now bid 3♠ asking for a stopper there.

Stopper showing and stopper asking are reverse sides of the same coin. It matters little which approach is adopted as long as you and partner are both aware of the method you are using. It can lead to calamity if one of you is asking and the other thinks the bid is showing a stopper.

One reason pairs prefer to use stopper asks is that it produces some uniformity within your bidding system. Other stopper bids are commonly used as asking for a stopper. For example, bidding the enemy suit often includes an underlying question, 'Do you have their suit stopped?' Fourth-suit-forcing includes as part of its message, 'Do you have a stopper in the fourth suit?' Both of these *ask* for stoppers. Playing stopper asks in the minor suit auctions means that all stopper-related bids are asking for a stopper. You do not have some asking and others showing.

WEST	EAST	
1♣	2♣	After a minor suit raise to the two-level, it is still useful
2♡...		to use a new suit at the two-level as a natural bid showing a genuine suit. It may sometimes prove best to play in a

4-3 major fit. Jumps to the three-level. (e.g., 1◇ : 2◇, 3♠) can still be used as a splinter.

WEST	EAST	
1♣	2♣	Once the bidding has reached the three-level, it is back
2♠	3◇...	to stopper asking. In this sequence West has shown a strong holding in spades. East shows a maximum raise

(otherwise 3♣ would be bid) and is *asking* for a stopper in diamonds.

DEFENCE AGAINST STOPPER-SHOWING OR STOPPER-ASKING

As you probably are not in the auction and as the opponents are angling for 3NT, the only likely action is to double their stopper bid.

WEST	NORTH	EAST	SOUTH	
1◇	No	2♣	No	Whether 3♡ was asking or showing,
3♣	No	3♡	Dble	the double shows length and strength in
				hearts and asks partner to lead that suit.

WEST	NORTH	EAST	SOUTH	
1◇	No	2♣	No	If North has no obviously attractive
3♣	No	3♡	No	lead, or has an equal choice between
3NT	No	No	No	hearts and spades, there is a slight case

in favour of spades. Partner's failure to double 3♡ indicates partner has no burning desire for hearts.

WEST	NORTH	EAST	SOUTH	
1◇	No	2♣	No	The double of 3NT in an uncontested
3♣	No	3♡	No	auction normally asks for the lead of
3NT	No	No	Dble	dummy's first bid suit. This does not

make sense where the suit has been bid and raised. In this kind of auction partner is likely to choose a heart lead or a spade lead. You can demand a heart lead by doubling 3♡. It makes sense to use the double of 3NT in stopper auctions to demand the lead of the unbid stopper.

COUNTERMEASURES BY THE STOPPER SIDE

After a stopper bid has been doubled, you can still bid 3NT to show a stopper in the critical suit. However, if you are using stopper showing, bidding 3NT has the disadvantage that the opening lead will go through the stopper doubled.

WEST	NORTH	EAST	SOUTH	
1♣	No	2♣	No	One advantage of stopper asking is
3♣	No	3♡	Dble	that if the stopper ask is doubled and
?				you have a stopper, bidding 3NT will
				protect that stopper on opening lead.

If 3♡ shows a stopper, there is an obvious disadvantage for West to bid 3NT and allow North to lead through the stopper.

Using stopper showing : Redouble = 'I have the danger suit (the unbid suit) stopped. Please bid 3NT yourself to protect the stopper in the suit doubled.' In the above auction, West redoubles with the diamonds stopped if West wants East to be declarer. West can still choose 3NT instead of redoubling.

Using stopper asking : Bid 3NT if you have a stopper that needs protection on lead. Redouble with a sure stopper (A-x-x or A-K-x) allowing partner to bid 3NT in case partner has a useful secondary card in the suit such as Q-x or J-x-x.

THE CROWHURST 2♣ CONVENTION

Crowhurst is an artificial 2♣ rebid by responder after opener's 1NT
rebid. It applies whether the opening bid was 1♣ or not. The 2♣ rebid in
each of these sequences is Crowhurst.

WEST	EAST	WEST	EAST	WEST	EAST
1♣	1◇	1♣	1♡	1♣	1♠
1NT	2♣	1NT	2♣	1NT	2♣

WEST	EAST	WEST	EAST	WEST	EAST
1◇	1♡	1◇	1♠	1♡	1♠
1NT	2♣	1NT	2♣	1NT	2♣

The 2♣ rebid shows enough values to invite game. Using a 1NT rebid as
12-16, opener rebids 2◇, 2♡ or 2♠ with 12-13 points, showing relevant
features up-the-line. After 1♣ : 1♠, 1NT : 2♣, for example, opener's
2♠ would show 12-13 points, three spades but not four hearts. Opener's
2NT reply shows exactly 14 points, over which responder's 3♣ is a
further enquiry as to suit support features. Opener's reply to 2♣ at the
three-level promises 15-16 points, again bidding features up-the-line.

A feasible alternative scheme is to use a 2◇ reply with all 12-13 hands,
2♡/2♠/2NT with 14 and three-level replies with 15-16.

WEST	
♠ K72	After 1◇ : 1♡, 1NT (12-16), West is worth a try for game and rebids 2♣, Crowhurst. If opener rebids 2◇, 12-13, no 3
♡ AJ875	
◇ K76	hearts, or 2♡, 12-13 with 3 hearts, West can pass. Over 2NT,
♣ 54	14 points, West bids 3♣ to check on 3-card heart support, while West will choose the correct game over any three-level rebid.

♠ KJ765	After 1♣ : 1♠, 1NT responder can rebid 2♡ with this
♡ Q9862	without fear that opener might expect more. As 2♣ takes
◇ 6	care of the game invitations, other rebids at the two-level are
♣ 43	weak and distributional.

♠ KJ765	After 1♣ : 1♠, 1NT responder rebids 2♣ with this hand.
♡ KQ65	If opener rebids 2◇, 12-13, responder rebids 2♡, non-
◇ 98	forcing, describing the shape and strength. Over a rebid
♣ 73	showing 14 or more points, responder will know the right spot or explore for the best game.

With a weak hand with club support, rebid with a jump to 3♣ as a
sign-off (e.g., 1♣ : 1♠, 1NT : 3♣ = to play) and rebid 2NT (e.g.,
1♣ : 1♠, 1NT : 2NT) as a game force with club support.

Crowhurst also works well when using an 11-16 balancing 1NT.

THE DRURY CONVENTION

The Drury Convention is a 2♣ response to a major suit opening in third- or fourth-seat. It shows a maximum passed hand and normally will have support for opener's major. It enables the partnership to stop at a comfortable level if the opening bid was light. It also allows the partnership more room to explore the best spot, as a new suit response by a passed hand is not forcing.

Other bids by responder at the two-level (e.g., Pass : 1♠, 2◇) are natural, non-forcing and deny support for opener's major. Responder's jumps (e.g., Pass : 1♠, 3♣) show a maximum pass, a good five-card suit plus support for opener's major.

Opener's rebids after 2♣ Drury

2◇ = Sub-minimum opening or a minimum opening (11-13 HCP) with little interest in game opposite a passed hand.

All other bids by opener show a sound opening hand, 14 HCP or more and usually commit the partnership to game.

Responder's rebids

After 2◇, responder will usually revert to opener's major. A 3♣ rebid over 2◇, or any other reply, indicates a 6-card or longer club suit and denies support for opener's major. As a 3♣ reply at once shows support for opener and 2♣ is Drury, responder needs some means of showing a maximum pass with long clubs. The solution : bid 2♣ first, rebid 3♣. Opener's three-level jumps show 5-5 or 6-5 patterns.

WEST	EAST		WEST	EAST
♣ K932	♠ AQJ64		No	1♠
♡ KQJ3	♡ A742	Drury – 2♣	2♡
◇ 54	◇ A6		4♡	No
♣ J85	♣ 93			

Without Drury, the partnership is likely to end in 4♠. At matchpoints, 4♡ is clearly the better spot.

2♣ is still Drury if RHO doubles or bids over partner's opening.

DEFENCE AGAINST 2♣ DRURY

Your side has not entered the auction but you may still wish to overcall at the two-level. Most pairs would play a double of 2♣ as lead-directing, but there is a good case to play it as a takeout double of opener's major. You need to decide which to play.

COUNTERMEASURES BY THE DRURY SIDE

If there is a bid over 2♣, Pass = 2◇ reply, other actions are strong. If 2♣ is doubled to show clubs, Pass = minimum, 2◇ = maximum with diamonds and Redouble is to play in 2♣.

5. SLAM CONVENTIONS

BLACKWOOD 4NT

After a 1NT opening or a 2NT opening, most pairs play 4NT as a quantitative raise, inviting 6NT if opener is not minimum. With a minimum, opener passes. With one point extra, bid 5NT and with two extra bid 6NT. The same approach is often used after a 2NT response or a 2NT rebid showing a strong balanced hand.

After a suit bid, 4NT is generally played as asking for aces. The replies are :

    5♣ = 0 or 4 aces (all or none)
    5◇ = 1 ace
    5♡ = 2 aces
    5♠ = 3 aces

After the reply to 4NT, the asker may sign off at the 5-level or the 6-level. A rebid of 5NT after the reply to 4NT asks for kings.

    6♣ = 0 kings
    6◇ = 1 king
    6♡ = 2 kings
    6♠ = 3 kings
    6NT = 4 kings

The 5NT king ask is used only when there is some prospect for a grand slam (when all the aces are held). In some cases it is safe to use 5NT for kings even when an ace is missing if you hope to play 6NT rather than 6-in-your-suit (particularly at pairs).

If you wish to sign off in 5NT because you are missing two aces bid 5-in-an-unbid-suit. This asks partner to bid 5NT which you intend to pass. 5-in-a-new-suit cannot be a genuine attempt to play in that suit.

The 4NT asker's decision is normally final. A 5-level sign-off implies two aces are missing. A 6-level sign-off in a new suit is normally to play (e.g., 1♠ : 4NT, 5♡ : 6◇) if suit agreement has not been shown earlier. If a suit has been agreed, a new suit at the 6-level is a grand slam try, asking for help in the suit bid. It promises no aces are missing.

The most common mistake among average players is to use 4NT too early in the auction. First, make sure there is enough strength for a slam and you know which suit is to be trumps (or that you intend to play no-trumps).

DEFENCE AGAINST BLACKWOOD 4NT

If your side has been competing, a double of 4NT indicates a desire to defend against their contract and is designed to warn partner against sacrificing.

Bidding over 4NT may cause the opponents difficulty in deciding whether to push on to slam, compete at the 5-level or double for penalties.

You may also wish to double a reply to Blackwood to indicate a sound lead. You should hold at least A-K, A-Q or K-Q in the suit doubled.

COUNTERMEASURES BY THE BLACKWOOD SIDE

They double 4NT

Bids show aces as usual. A redouble suggests that 4NT may well be the best spot despite their double. Another approach is to redouble with 0 aces, pass with 1 (R=0, P=1 leads to the acronym ROPI), bid 5♣ with 2, 5◇ with 3 and 5♡ with 4.

They bid over 4NT

There are various ways to combat interference.

(a) *Double = Penalties*. In this method, if you feel that you could obtain more by doubling the opponents than by bidding on, you double for penalties. Other than that, No Bid = no aces (and partner may then choose to double them rather than bid on), the cheapest bid shows one ace, the next bid two aces and so on.

(b) *DOPI*. This stands for D=0, P=1, meaning Double = 0 aces, Pass = 1 ace. The next cheapest bid shows 2 aces, the next 3 and so on. When partner doubles to show no aces, you may well choose to leave the double in when slam is out of the question and the five-level may be in jeopardy. When partner passes to show one ace, you may again choose to double if slam is out of the question and the five-level is risky.

(c) *PODI*. This stands for P=0, D=1, meaning Pass = 0 aces and Double = 1 ace. There is no significant difference between this and *DOPI* and certainly no technical superiority. Most pairs prefer to use DOPI.

(d) *DEPO*. This is D = E, P = O, meaning Double = Even number of aces (0, 2 or 4) and Pass = Odd number of aces (1 or 3). This has the advantage of saving space but could lead to ambiguity. The theory is that partner should be able to tell from the earlier bidding and the cards held how many aces are shown. You and I know that in practice partner has every chance of getting it wrong. Some pairs use DOPI at the five-level and DEPO at the six-level where little bidding space is left.

They double a reply to 4NT

The double asks for the lead of the suit doubled. In addition to making sure you have enough aces, you also need to be confident that you can handle the lead of the suit requested.

WEST	EAST	WEST	EAST
♠ AQ8742	♠ K953		1♣
♡ A4	♡ KQ	1♠	4♠
♢ 75	♢ K4	4NT	5♢ (Double)
♣ Q73	♣ AKJ102	?	

Without the double, you would have bid 6♠. This makes all the tricks without a diamond lead and if a diamond is led, there is a 50-50 chance the ace is with North. After the double, however, the situation is serious. North is bound to find the right lead and the ace of diamonds is sure to be with South.

These are the actions for the 4NT bidder after partner's reply has been doubled :

Bid your agreed trump suit = 'We are missing two aces. Please pass.'
Pass = 'We are not missing two aces but I have no control in this suit. What about you?'

With no control in the suit doubled, partner will sign off in your agreed suit. With the K-Q in the suit doubled, partner may bid six in your agreed suit or 6NT if that is a reasonable choice. With K-x or longer in the suit doubled, partner should sign off in the agreed suit (the pass denies holding even the queen in the suit doubled – see redouble) or bid six in a contract in which partner is declarer so that the K-x is protected. Redouble = ace in the suit doubled. New suit = cue bid with first and second round control in the suit doubled. On the odd occasion when partner has a void in the suit doubled, partner bids six of the doubled suit.

On the hand above, West passes the Double and East should bid 6♣ (not 6NT as West is declarer in no-trumps).

Bid six in the agreed suit = 'There are no prospects for a grand slam but I have first or second round control of the suit doubled.'
Redouble = 'I hold the queen in the suit doubled and we are missing an ace.'

Partner should bid six in the agreed suit if holding the king or a singleton in the suit doubled. With the ace, partner can perhaps organise to be declarer and force the doubler to lead.

5NT = 'We have all the aces. Give me your kings, please.'

ROMAN KEY CARD BLACKWOOD

In this method, the answers to Blackwood include the king of trumps and possibly the queen of trumps as well. The trump suit is the suit specifically agreed. If there has been no agreement, the last mentioned suit is taken as trumps.

WEST	EAST
1♠	2♡
4NT	

Hearts are trumps.

WEST	EAST
1♠	2♡
2♠	4NT

Spades are trumps.

The answers to 4NT are :

> 5♣ = 0 or 3 key cards.
> 5♢ = 1 or 4 key cards.
> 5♡ = 2 key cards but no queen of trumps.
> 5♠ = 2 key cards plus the queen of trumps.
> 5NT = 5 key cards but no queen of trumps.
> 6♣ = 5 key cards plus the queen of trumps.

The key cards are the four aces and the trump king. If two key cards are missing, sign off at the five-level. If one key card is missing, bid six if you hold the trump queen. If not, check whether partner has it if you can do this without bypassing your trump suit at the five-level. If that is impossible, bid six if you hold the jack of trumps or you know there are nine or more trumps between you. Otherwise, sign off at the five-level.

The 5NT and 6♣ replies are naturally extremely rare. If partner is doing the asking and receives an answer showing all five key cards, there can hardly be anything else partner needs to know.

The 5♠ and 5♡ answers reveal the possession of the queen of trumps as well as holding two key cards. A 5NT rebid over any reply says, 'We hold all the key cards and the queen of trumps. Tell me your kings outside trumps.' The trump king has already been included in the answer to 4NT. The replies to 5NT asking for kings are the standard ones :

> 6♣ = 0
> 6♢ = 1
> 6♡ = 2
> 6♠ = 3

The 5♣ and 5♢ replies do not reveal the queen of trumps. The cheapest bid outside trumps now asks, 'Do you have the trump queen?' Next bid says 'No', second step says 'Yes' and any higher bid promises the queen and a near solid suit as well (at least K-Q-x-x-x or K-Q-J-x).

If partner asks for the queen of trumps and you know the partnership holds ten or more trumps, give the answer that shows the trump queen. Likewise with two key cards but no queen of trumps, answer 5♠ if you know the partnership has ten or more trumps. With A-x-x-x-x opposite K-x-x-x-x, the suit will break 2-1 almost 80% of the time.

The 5♣ and 5♦ replies are ambiguous. Most of the time you will be able to tell whether partner has the higher number of key cards or the lower number either from your own hand or from the earlier bidding. If you cannot tell, assume it is the lower number and sign off in your trump suit. Partner will pass if holding the lower number. However, the position is forcing if the higher number of key cards is held (it is not reasonable to ask for key cards if three or four key cards will not be enough).

With the higher number of key cards, partner bids next bid (Step 1) without the trump queen, Step 2 to show the trump queen and any other suit bid shows the queen of trumps and a strong suit as a source of tricks.

WEST	EAST	WEST	EAST
♠ AKQ	♠ J87	2♣	2♦
♡ 7	♡ K32	3♣	4♣
♦ AKQJ	♦ 96	4NT	5♣ – No key cards
♣ AQJ86	♣ 97532	No	

WEST	EAST	WEST	EAST
♠ AKQ	♠ J87	2♣	2♦
♡ 7	♡ 9643	3♣	4♣
♦ AKQJ	♦ 96	4NT	5♦ – 1 key card
♣ AQJ86	♣ K532	6♣	No

Note that in each case East's reply to simple Blackwood is 5♣.

WEST	EAST	WEST	EAST
♠ AKQ	♠ J8	2♣	2♡
♡ 7	♡ AK632	3♣	4♣
♦ AKQJ	♦ 96	4NT	5♦ – 1 key card
♣ AQJ86	♣ 9753	5NT	6♦
		6NT	No

WEST	EAST	WEST	EAST
♠ AKQ	♠ J8	2♣	2♡
♡ 7	♡ AJ632	3♣	4♣
♦ AKQJ	♦ 96	4NT	5♡ – 2 key cards, no ♣Q
♣ AQJ86	♣ K753	7NT	No

WEST	EAST	WEST	EAST
♠ KQJ	♠ 7	1◇	1♡
♡ QJ87	♡ A106532	3♡	4NT
◇ Q9842	◇ K5	5◇	5♡
♣ A	♣ KQJ4	No	

Uncertain whether West has 1 or 4 key cards, East signs off. With the lower number of key cards, West passes.

WEST	EAST	WEST	EAST
♠ A62	♠ 7	1◇	1♡
♡ K874	♡ A106532	3♡	4NT
◇ A9842	◇ K5	5◇	5♡
♣ A	♣ KQJ4	5♠	7NT
		No	

With the higher number of key cards, you *must* bid on over a sign-off. West's 5♠ says, 'I have the four key cards but no trump queen.' (With the trump queen as well, West would bid 5NT.)

3NT as Roman Key Card Blackwood

On the first hand above, 5♡ is at risk and it would clearly be better to stop in 4♡. A sensible agreement is to play 3NT after major suit agreement as Blackwood. In auctions which start 1♡ : 3♡ or 1◇ : 1♠, 3♠ or 1♠ : 2♡, 3♡ or 2♣ : 2◇, 2♠ : 3♠ it is almost never right to bid 3NT with the intention of playing there. Neither partner can be sure that every suit is well held and that 3NT offers better prospects than 4-Major. Since 3NT is virtually never used naturally, it makes sense to harness it as a cheap form of Blackwood. On the first hand above, East would bid 3NT after 1◇ : 1♡, 3♡ and sign off in 4♡ over West's 4◇.

Using 3NT as Blackwood not only keeps you lower when two key cards are missing, it also gives you more room to explore a grand slam when all the key cards are held.

3NT Blackwood is used only when a major suit has been bid and raised. It does not apply if there has been no suit agreement or when a minor suit is raised. 3NT after 1♡ : 2♣, 3♣ or 1◇ : 3◇ or 1♣ : 1◇, 3◇ or similar sequences is to play in 3NT.

DEFENCE AGAINST ROMAN KEY CARD BLACKWOOD

Exactly the same as defending against simple Blackwood.

COUNTERMEASURES BY THE RKCB SIDE

Exactly the same as the countermeasures used when they interfere over simple Blackwood (see pages 57-58).

GERBER 4♣

The Gerber 4♣ bid is an ask for aces. Its main benefit is keeping the bidding at a lower level than 4NT Blackwood. The answer to this contention is that your slam bidding should be accurate enough that you can afford to be at the five-level if two aces are missing. In addition, you can utilise 3NT as Blackwood after major suit agreement (see page 61) and this keeps the bidding lower still.

The answers to 4♣ Gerber are :

4◇ = 0 or 4 aces, 4♡ = 1 ace, 4♠ = 2 aces and 4NT = 3 aces.

After the reply to 4♣, 5♣ asks for kings and the answers are :

5◇ = 0 kings, 5♡ = 1, 5♠ = 2, 5NT = 3 and 6♣ = 4.

Some pairs use 4NT, if available, to ask for kings and others use the next available bid outside trumps as the king ask. However, 5♣ asking for kings is the most popular as it has least ambiguity and allows the partnership to play in 4NT when two aces are missing.

The main problem with 4♣ Gerber is the misunderstandings that pairs experience in regard to when is 4♣ Gerber and when is it natural. A sensible set of agreements would include :

● 4♣ is natural if clubs have previously been bid naturally.

● 4♣ is Gerber if a trump suit has been agreed (e.g., 1♠ : 3♠, 4♣). In this regard, 4♣ Gerber is incompatible with cue bidding.

● A jump to 4♣ is Gerber if a bid of 3♣ would be forcing (e.g., 1♠ : 2♡, 4♣). This use makes 4♣ Gerber incompatible with splinters.

● 4♣ is Gerber if it is a jump to 4♣ after a 1NT or 2NT opening.

● 4♣ is natural if it is not a jump and no suit agreement has yet been reached (e.g., 1♠ : 2♡, 3♠ : 4♣). This situation arises frequently when there has been opposition bidding pushing the bidding to the three-level.

Top players tend not to use Gerber, preferring to use 4♣ for cue bidding or splinters or other purposes.

It is possible (and sensible) to adapt the Roman Key Card Answers to 4♣ and play Roman Key Card Gerber. The structure is similar to the Roman Key Card Blackwood replies.

DEFENCE AGAINST 4♣ GERBER

Use the same as against simple Blackwood.

COUNTERMEASURES BY THE GERBER SIDE

Use the same as those when they interfere against simple Blackwood (see pages 57-58).

ROMAN KEY CARDS AFTER RAISING A MINOR SUIT TO THE FOUR-LEVEL

It is often awkward to check on aces after a minor suit has been raised to the four-level. Particularly with clubs you may receive a reply to 4NT Blackwood that carries the partnership beyond 5♣ when two (or more) key cards might be missing. It is usually better to cue bid in these situations but, of course, the hands may not lend themselves to cue bidding or the first cue bid may bypass two suits anyway.

One convenient solution is to treat the raise to the four-level as a key card ask itself. Partner can choose to answer by showing key cards or can ask for key cards. The cheapest bid says 'Tell me your key cards.' The other bids show key cards.

WEST	EAST	
1♡	2♣	Playing this method, 4◇ by East asks for Key Cards while 4♡/4♠/4NT/5♣ show 0 or 3/1 or 4/2 no trump Q/2
4♣	?	+ trump queen. In reply to the 4◇ ask, West's bids of 4♡/4♠/4NT/5♣ have the same meaning.

WEST	EAST	
1◇	1♠	Now, 4♡ by West asks for Key Cards and 4♠/4NT/5♣/5◇ show the Key Cards in the normal order.
3◇	4◇	In reply to the 4♡ ask, East bids 4♠/4NT/5♣/5◇ to show
?		Key Cards exactly the same way.

Notice that none of the replies takes you beyond five of your minor so that you will not bypass your safe game with two key cards missing.

In order to sign off after a raise to 4-minor, you will have to take control of the auction and use the Step 1 Key Card Ask. A direct bid of 5-minor over 4-minor would show two key cards plus the queen of trumps.

WEST	EAST		WEST	EAST	
♠ A8	♠ K752		1♡	2♣	
♡ AK963	♡ QJ		4♣	4◇ – Key Card Ask	
◇ J2	◇ A8		0 or 3 – 4♡	4♠ – Trump queen?	
♣ KQ92	♣ A8643		Yes – 5♣	5♡ – Heart holding?	
		King, no queen – 6♣		7NT	

In answering the 5♡ ask, the possession of ♡ A is known from the original answer to the 4◇ Key Card Ask (see page 127).

DEFENCE AND COUNTERMEASURES :

As against simple Blackwood (see pages 57–58).

5NT GRAND SLAM TRUMP ASK

With the popularity of Roman Key Card Blackwood which locates the trump honours as well as the aces, there is less call for a jump to 5NT asking for partner's trump holding. However, the 5NT Trump Ask may still be needed. You might have a void and be unable to tell which key cards partner has from the answer to RKCB. Perhaps your cue bidding sequence has taken you beyond 4NT.

Originally, 5NT Josephine (named after Josephine Culbertson) asked partner to bid seven with two of the top three trumps and otherwise to sign off in six. It is easy to have a more effective understanding than that. You will be better off even if you use a very simple approach, bidding 6♣/6♢/6♡/6♠ to show 0/1/2/3 top trumps. Only the ace, king or queen counts as a top trump.

Many regular partnerships have highly complex understandings. This structure works well :

Your suit	Reply	Meaning
Clubs	6♣	0 or 1 top trump
	6-other	2 top trumps
	7♣	3 top trumps
Diamonds	6♣	0 top trumps
	6♢	1 top trump
	6-other	2 top trumps
	7♣	3 top trumps
Hearts	6♣	0 top trumps
	6♢	1 top trump
	6♡	2 top trumps
	7♣	3 top trumps
Spades	6♣	0 top trumps
	6♢	1 top trump
	6♡	2 top trumps
	6♠	2 top trumps + an extra trump
	7♣	3 top trumps

Bidding beyond 6♣ and 6♢ with two top trumps when a minor suit is trumps assumes that two top trumps will be enough for a grand slam or if not, partner should have enough to play in 6NT. The 6-level bid chosen will be where you have extra strength. With no such suit, bid 6NT with two top trumps.

Bidding 7♣ whenever you hold the top three trumps enables partner to check the honours in one suit, but bid seven in another.

SLAM SACRIFICE DOUBLES

When your side has an excellent trump fit but the opponents bid a slam, the critical decision is whether to defend or whether it pays to sacrifice. It is silly to sacrifice if you can defeat them or might defeat them. On the other hand, if their slam is laydown, your sacrifice might be very cheap because of your good trump fit if the hands are also somewhat shapely.

How should East-West judge this decision :

Dealer West : North-South vulnerable

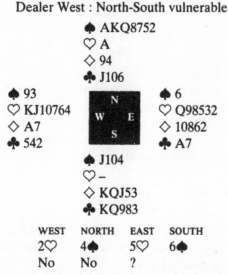

```
                 ♠ AKQ8752
                 ♡ A
                 ◇ 94
                 ♣ J106
   ♠ 93                          ♠ 6
   ♡ KJ10764       N             ♡ Q98532
   ◇ A7          W   E           ◇ 10862
   ♣ 542           S             ♣ A7
                 ♠ J104
                 ♡ -
                 ◇ KQJ53
                 ♣ KQ983
```

WEST	NORTH	EAST	SOUTH
2♡	4♠	5♡	6♠
No	No	?	

North-South have had a sensible auction but have reached a hopeless slam. West, the pre-emptor, is expected to pass and leave the decision to partner. The problem is that frequently partner will not be sure which way to go. To be sure, 7♡ will be a cheap sacrifice. That is clear to East. The flaw is that it is silly to sacrifice when North-South have two losers. Even though the North-South bidding is reasonable, the two losers are there.

It is a mistake to assume the opponents always know what they are doing or that they invariably make the right decision. This is particularly so when the auction has been pre-emptive and their decisions have been crowded.

If there were no better way, the recommended approach is to compete early and fiercely and then hope that they guess wrong. On that basis East should pass. However, the deal might be :

```
                        ♠ AK98752
                        ♡ A
                        ◇ A74
                        ♣ 105
        ♠ Q3                            ♠ 6
        ♡ KJ10764                       ♡ Q98532
        ◇ 9                             ◇ 10862
        ♣ J642                          ♣ A7
                        ♠ J104
                        ♡ –
                        ◇ KQJ53
                        ♣ KQ983
```

On this layout, 6♠ is laydown and 7♡ would be only four down. It is attractive to be on the right side of most of these decisions rather than just guess every time. Isn't it better to make a co-operative decision than play Russian Roulette?

When your side is clearly the sacrificing side and the opponents bid six or seven, slam sacrifice doubles work like this :

Against a small slam

The player in the direct seat :
>   Doubles with 2 defensive tricks. That ends the bidding.
>   Passes with 0 or 1 defensive trick. When this comes back to partner, the player in the pass-out seat :
>   Passes with 2 defensive tricks.
>   Sacrifices with 0 defensive tricks as partner has 0 or 1 trick.
>   Doubles with 1 defensive trick, after which partner passes with one trick also and sacrifices with no trick.

On each of the preceding deals, East doubles. On the first deal on page 65, West passes. On the deal above, West has no defensive trick against spades and sacrifices in 7♡.

Against a grand slam

Double in the direct seat with one trick. Partner must pass if you double. With no defence or merely potential for a trick, you pass. When this comes to partner in the pass out seat, partner should pass with one trick and double with potential for one trick.

If partner doubles, you should take the sacrifice with no trick at all. With potential for a trick, take your chances and pass. With both you and partner having potential for a trick, there is enough prospect in defending to reject the sacrifice.

The advantages of having a method are that you take fewer sacrifices when their slam is failing and that you do sacrifice when there is little potential for the defence. It takes a lot of the guesswork and gambling out of this area. Sometimes you score a bit extra by doubling their slam when you have one trick each.

Even though slam sacrifice doubles are recommended for regular partnerships, the situation is not always as rosy or as clearcut as on the preceding deals. One problem is that you may lose the opportunity for a Lightner Slam Double. For example :

WEST	NORTH	EAST	SOUTH
3♣	4♠	5♣	6♠
Dble			

The common approach is to treat the double by West as lead-directing. In this case, West is asking for an unusual lead and almost certainly has a void in one of the red suits.

Playing slam sacrifice doubles, West's double = two tricks and the lead-directing aspect of the double, is lost. This would definitely be the case if West had taken some other action consistent with strength. However, it does make sense to treat a pre-emptor's double as Lightner when the pre-emptor is not on lead. Still, this is something for the partnership to settle.

What constitutes a defensive trick? Do you count the ace in the partnership's long suit as a trick? The advice is to discount it but the opponents do not have to be void there. What about A-K in an outside suit? Looks like two tricks, right? Still, either opponent may have a singleton. What about deep tricks such as K-J-x or Q-J-x? They may turn out to be winners or they may be worth nothing in defence. A singleton in your hand could scuttle their slam if partner has that ace or the ace of trumps. Counting Q-x-x or J-x-x-x in trumps as a trick could enable declarer to pick up the trump suit without loss if declarer can detect you have counted that as a defensive trick.

Despite these drawbacks, the method has considerable value. Would you rather gamble the results in the slam area or try to estimate your side's defensive potential? Are you prepared to back your judgement as to how much defence you have? You do not have to be right every time to show a profit over those who take a sacrifice every time or those who always hope the opponents have guessed wrong. *If you have any doubts whether to defend or sacrifice,* it is better to let them play if the auction has been crowded and better to take the save if they have had plenty of room to explore.

6. BIDDING OVER THEIR ONE OPENINGS

THE UNUSUAL NT

(1♠) : 2NT and (1♡) : 2NT are commonly played as showing weak hands (usually in the 8-12 HCP zone) with at least 5-5 in the minors. The suits should have good texture, say five honours or better between the two suits. The high card strength and suit texture may be less if the shape is 6-5 or at favourable vulnerability. With a 6-6 pattern, any strength is acceptable.

Each of these hands is worth 2NT over their major opening :

♠ 5	♠ 8	♠ 9
♡ J3	♡ 7	♡ –
◇ KQ874	◇ J87642	◇ 1087542
♣ QJ1062	♣ KQJ54	♣ K109532

These hands are not suitable :

♠ A4	♠ 5	♠ J82
♡ 7	♡ K5	♡ 5
◇ K8532	◇ AJ987	◇ KQJ4
♣ Q7642	♣ AQ873	♣ QJ983
Suits too weak.	Hand too strong.	5-4 pattern is unsuitable.

After partner uses 2NT

With a weak hand, bid your longer minor. If the length is equal, bid the stronger. Do not pass unless you have 0-2 cards in each minor and double stoppers or better in the majors. With a great fit in one of the minors and little defence in the majors, pre-empt with an advance sacrifice in 5-minor.

With a strong hand, bid 4♣ or 4◇ to invite game, bid game, bid the other major (natural, forcing, at least a 6-card suit) or bid their major (looking for a stopper for 3NT). With an exceptionally strong playing hand, you might have enough to bid 4NT for aces. A bid of 4-in-their-major asks partner to choose the longer minor.

Suppose the auction has been (1♡) : 2NT : (No) and you have

♠ K76	♠ A7	♠ QJ109	♠ AK64
♡ KQ43	♡ A9842	♡ KQ105	♡ A53
◇ Q987	◇ K965	◇ K6	◇ 4
♣ 86	♣ 43	♣ AJ3	♣ KQ764
Bid 3◇	Bid 4◇	Bid 3NT	Bid 4NT

DEFENCE AGAINST THE UNUSUAL 2NT

A relatively uncomplicated defence is to double for penalties, bid 3-partner's-major as a sound raise, 3-other-major as natural and forcing and 3-minor as a stopper ask for 3NT.

For partnerships who wish to play more sophisticated methods :
Double = Looking for penalties. About 10 HCP or better, a strong 4+ holding in one of the minors and shortage in opener's suit are the key ingredients for a successful double of 3-minor.
3-opener's-major = Natural, weaker than a normal limit raise. A respectable 1-Major : 2-Major response.
4-opener's-major = To play, but essentially pre-emptive like 1-Major : 4-Major. The pre-emptive nature of the raise should help partner's decision if they sacrifice.
3-other-major = Long strong suit, about 6-9 HCP, no fit for opener's major, not forcing.
3♣ = Game invitation or better in hearts. If partner opened 1♠, the 3♣ response may also have spade support.
3♦ = Game invitation or better in spades. If partner opened 1♡, the 3♦ response denies heart support. With heart support and spades as well, start with a 3♣ response.

If opener signs off in 3-Major over 3♣ or 3♦, responder will still bid on, of course, with better than a limit raise. Responder may bid game, bid a minor as a cue bid or ask for aces.
3NT = To play. Responder judges game prospects are better than playing for penalties.
4♣ or 4♦ = Splinter raise of opener's major. See page 43.

COUNTERMEASURES BY THE 2NT SIDE

If they double 2NT

Make your normal reply unless you have a weak hand with equal length in the minors. With that, pass and let partner choose the minor. This enables the partnership to play in the longer minor (partner may be 6-5) and if your side is in deep trouble, it makes sure partner plays it, not you. Why suffer?

Redouble says, 'Please bid 3♣ and pass my next bid.' The redouble is used to allow you to play in 3-Major without partner running back to a minor.

Over other actions

With a weak hand, you would pass unless worth a pre-empt to 5♣ or 5♦. A bid of 4♣ or 4♦ is still invitational. If they bid a minor, double asks partner to lead that suit. This is better than doubling to suggest a sacrifice. If you are worth a sacrifice, bid it.

What if they open 1♣ or 1◇?

How does your partnership treat (1♣) : 2NT or (1◇) : 2NT? Some pairs play 2NT to show the two cheapest suits (hearts and the other minor). Given the prevalence of weak or phoney minor suit openings, it is also reasonable still to use 2NT for the minors. Your holding in their minor should be sound.

Other situations where the unusual NT shows both minors

The general rule is that if your no-trump can have a sensible natural sense, then it is a natural bid, not minors. Thus, 2NT over a weak two is played as natural (16-18). This is more important than showing the minors. Likewise, 1♠ : (2♡) : 2NT is natural, showing a heart stopper and 10-12 points. A balancing 2NT is natural : (1♡ or 1♠) : No : (No) : 2NT = 17-18 balanced.

The no-trump bid in these auctions, however, is generally used to show the minors :

WEST	NORTH	EAST	SOUTH	or	WEST	NORTH	EAST	SOUTH
No	1♡	No	1♠		No	No	No	1♡
1NT					1NT			

A natural no-trump overcall by a passed hand is suicidal.

WEST	NORTH	EAST	SOUTH	or	WEST	NORTH	EAST	SOUTH
No	1♡	No	2♡		1♣	No	2♣	No
2NT					No	2NT		

A natural 2NT overcall by a passed hand makes no sense. West's delayed 2NT in the second auction is for the minors but may be only 5-4 or 4-4 in the minors. With a normal 5-5 pattern and suitable strength, West would have bid 2NT at once over 1♠.

WEST	NORTH	EAST	SOUTH
1♠	No	2♠	2NT

Balanced or minors? This is arguable but it is a brave player who bids a natural 2NT in this sequence. Recommended is the minors.

WEST	NORTH	EAST	SOUTH
1♠	No	3♠	3NT

This is also arguable. South could hold a spade stopper and a running minor suit. Most pairs, however, would treat South's 3NT as both minors (but not strong enough or shapely enough for 4NT).

WEST	NORTH	EAST	SOUTH
1♡	1♠	No	2♠
No	No	2NT	

This should be for the minors. A natural no-trump bid was available on the previous round. The hand could look like this : ♠ 72 ♡ 4 ◇ K9742 ♣ J10754, too weak for a negative double over 1♠.

WEST	NORTH	EAST	SOUTH
1♠	2♣	2♠	No
No	2NT		

This is arguable but most pairs would treat 2NT here as both minors with clubs longer because of the 2♣ bid.

MICHAELS CUE BID

The original use of a cue bid of the suit opened, (1♡) : 2♡ for example, was to show a huge hand, one that would have been opened with a demand bid. It was like a takeout double except that it was forcing to game, whereas change of suit or a jump rebid after a takeout double would not be forcing at all after a weak suit reply to the double.

However, because of the rarity of such powerhouses, most tournament pairs adopt a different meaning for the bid of the enemy suit. The most popular is the Michaels Cue Bid which shows a 5+-5+ pattern in a weak hand, about the same strength as the unusual 2NT. After a major suit opening, Michaels shows 5+ in the other major and 5+ in one of the minors. Over a minor suit opening, Michaels shows at least 5-5 in the majors. Thus :

(1♡) : 2♡ = 5+ spades and 5+ in a minor.
(1♠) : 2♠ = 5+ hearts and 5+ in a minor.
(1◇) : 2◇ = at least 5-5 in the majors.
(1♣) : 2♣ = at least 5-5 in the majors.

After partner's Michaels Cue Bid over a major opening

With a weak hand, support partner's major if possible. Without support for the major, bid 3♣. Partner will pass with clubs or correct to 3◇ with diamonds.

With a strong hand, you may bid game, bid the enemy suit to ask for a stopper in that suit for 3NT or bid 2NT as a game try enquiry. The replies to the 2NT enquiry :

    3♣ = Minimum, second suit is clubs.
    3◇ = Minimum, second suit is diamonds.
    3♡ = Maximum, second suit is clubs.
    3♠ = Maximum, second suit is diamonds.
    3NT = 6-5 with 6-Major and 5 clubs.
    4♣ = 6-5 with 5-Major and 6 clubs.
    4◇ = 6-5 with 5-Major and 6 diamonds.
    4♡ = 6-5 with 6-Major and 5 diamonds.

After partner's Michaels Cue Bid over a minor opening

With a weak hand, support the major where you have more cards. With equal length, choose the stronger holding. Jumps to the three-level in a major are pre-emptive.

With a strong hand, bid game or bid the other minor (natural and forcing), bid their suit to ask for a stopper or bid 2NT to which opener replies 3♣ (minimum), 3◇ (maximum), 3♡ (six hearts) or 3♠ (six spades).

DEFENCE AGAINST THEIR MICHAELS OVERCALL AFTER A MAJOR OPENING

Suppose the bidding has started 1♡ : (2♡) : ?

3♡ = Equivalent to a sound raise to the two-level.

3♣/3♢ = New suit is natural and forcing.

2NT = Natural, stopper in their major, 10-12 points, not forcing.

Double = Looking for penalties, the same sort of hand that would redouble after 1♡ : (Double). Ideal is short in opener's suit, a strong trump holding in their suit(s) and 10 HCP or more.

2♠ = Limit raise or stronger. Guarantees support for opener and indicates an 8-loser or better hand. Opener may bid game, bid a new suit as a trial bid or sign off in 3-Major. Responder may bid on after a sign off. A new suit beyond 3-Major is a cue bid with slam potential.

3♠, 4♣ or 4♢ = Splinter just like 1♡ : 3♠/4♣/4♢.

COUNTERMEASURES BY THE MICHAELS SIDE

If they bid : Pass with a weak hand unless you have a strong fit for partner and wish to sacrifice. With a good hand, you may support partner's major, double for penalties, bid game or bid 4NT to ask for partner's minor.

If they double : Bids retain their usual meanings. Redouble = 'Make the cheapest bid and then pass my next bid.' This allows you to rescue the partnership into your own long suit.

Pass = No strong support for the major. This allows partner to describe the hand so that you can land in your best trump suit.

WEST	NORTH	EAST	SOUTH	
1♡	2♡	Dble	No	2♠ = Spades longer or better.
No	?			3♣/3♢ = Minor suit is longer.

2NT = Equal length suits, but if partner could not bid 2♠, the spades are too weak facing 0-2 support.

Redouble = 5-5-3-0 pattern with void in their suit. It may be best to have the 3-card fragment as trumps.

WEST	NORTH	EAST	SOUTH	
1♠	2♠	Dble	No	2NT = Hearts longer or much better.
No	?			3♣/3♢ = Prefer the minor to hearts.

Redouble = 5-5-3-0, void in spades.

After the redouble, 3♣ or 3♢ is to play and 2NT asks for the five-card minor.

WEST	EAST		WEST	NORTH	EAST	SOUTH
♠ –	♠ QJ872					1♠
♡ QJ874	♡ 5		2♠	Dble	No	No
♢ J84	♢ A10762		Rdble	No	3♢...	
♣ K10964	♣ A3					

West has chosen an unfortunate moment for Michaels but redouble locates the best spot for E-W.

DEFENCE AGAINST THEIR MICHAELS OVERCALL AFTER A MINOR OPENING

Suppose the bidding has started 1♢ : (2♢) : ? where the 2♢ bid shows both majors

3♢ = Equivalent to a sound raise to the two-level.

4♢ or 5♢ = Pre-emptive.

3♣ = 6-9 points, long clubs, not forcing.

2♡ = Game try or stronger with clubs. May have diamond support as well.

2♠ = Game try or better in diamonds, 10+ points.

3♡ or 3♠ or 4♣ = Splinter just like 1♢ : 3♡/3♠/4♣.

4♡ or 4♠ = Void splinter, slam try.

Double = Looking for penalties, the same sort of hand that would redouble after 1♢ : (Double). Ideal is short in opener's suit, a strong trump holding in their suit(s) and 10 HCP or more.

2NT = Natural and limited. Stoppers in both majors.

3NT = Natural with stoppers in both majors.

Wishing to explore 3NT, make a game try bid first (2♡ or 2♠), follow up by bidding 3-Major, asking for a stopper in the suit bid. Lacking good support or 5+ in the other minor, start with Double and bid 3-Major on the next round to ask for a stopper if a penalty double is less attractive than 3NT.

Where the bidding started 1♣ : (2♣), the structure is similar.

3♣ = A sound raise to the two-level, 6-9 points.

4♣ or 5♣ = Pre-emptive.

2♢ = Natural, long diamonds, 6-9 points, not forcing.

2♡/2♠ = Game try or better with clubs (2♡) or diamonds (2♠).

3♢ or 3♡ or 3♠ = Splinter just like 1♣ : 3♢/3♡/3♠.

Other actions are as above after 1♢ : (2♢).

COUNTERMEASURES BY THE MICHAELS SIDE

If they bid : Pass with a weak hand unless you have a strong fit for partner and wish to sacrifice. With a good hand, you may support either major, double for penalties, bid game or bid 2NT to ask for partner's range and major suit lengths. If 2NT is not available, 3♡ or 3♠ is used as a game invitation, not a pre-empt.

If they double : Bids retain their usual meanings. In addition :

Redouble = 'Make the cheapest bid and pass my next bid.' This allows you to rescue the partnership into your own long suit.

Pass = No preference for either major. This allows partner to escape into the longer or stronger major. In addition partner can redouble to show the 5-5-3-0 hand.

MICHAELS OVER MAJORS
NATURAL OVER MINORS

Using this approach, the Michaels Cue Bid is played only after a major
suit opening. Bidding the enemy's minor shows a genuine suit. Thus :

(1♣) : 2♣ = Natural overcall, same as (1◇) : 2♣
(1◇) : 2◇ = Natural overcall, same as (1♠) : 2◇

When the opponents open with a major suit, it would be extremely rare
for you to want to play in that major. Given the proliferation of artificial
and prepared club systems as well as fake diamonds, it is not
unreasonable to use the bid of their minor as a natural overcall.

WEST   If South opens 1♣, what is West supposed to do if unable
♠ K7   to bid clubs genuinely? Pass and hope that a cheap
♡ 98   opportunity will present itself on the next round? By then
◇ 652   the bidding may well be up to the three-level and if you are
♣ AKJ954 unable to show your clubs, you can imagine that partner's
             lead may not be best.

Hands with both majors are less pressing since you can bid one major
at once and bid the other one, or perhaps double, on the next round. If
strong enough with both majors, you can of course double at once.

There is a case for Michaels over minors since it is an advantage to
show two suits with one bid. In addition, if you bid one major first, a pre-
emptive raise of opener's minor by LHO may cause you to miss a fit in
the other major. On the other hand, one does want to be able to bid the
hands with a strong holding in their minor suit. Even when their minor
suit promises four or more cards, they could have 8-6-3-2 and you are
holding A-K-J-10-9-5.

A reasonable compromise between the competing objectives is to play
the simple cue bid as Michaels and the jump cue as an intermediate jump
overcall. Thus :

(1♣) : 2♣ or (1◇) : 2◇ = Michaels, weakish with both majors
(1♣) : 3♣ or (1◇) : 3◇ = Natural, 11-15 HCP and a strong 6-card
holding in the minor suit bid. This is sensible since you need virtually that
strength to overcall their suit anyway. Of course, if they double and catch
you, the cost is one extra undertrick.

(1♡) : 3♡ or (1♠) : 3♠ = Request to partner to bid 3NT with a stopper
in their suit. You will have a solid minor and 8-9 tricks.

Bidding your powerhouse hands if you play Michaels

Although it is rare to pick up a rockcrusher after an opponent has opened the bidding, it can occur from time to time, mostly after a light or psychic third hand opening. If you play Michaels, how can you show the rockcrusher?

The solution is to double first and bid the enemy suit on the next round. Hands which are too strong for a simple overcall are shown by doubling first and bidding again after partner's reply. This is a popular structure :

WEST	NORTH	EAST	SOUTH
1◇	Dble	No	1♠
No	2♡		

North's sequence shows a hand with about 16-18 points, five losers and a good 5+ heart suit. North will not have support for spades.

WEST	NORTH	EAST	SOUTH
1◇	Dble	No	1♠
No	3♡		

This time North is showing a hand of about 19-21 points, four losers and a good 5+ heart suit. Again North will not have support for spades. The jump is not forcing but partner is expected to bid again with one trick.

WEST	NORTH	EAST	SOUTH
1◇	Dble	No	1♠
No	2◇		

This shows North has 22+ HCP or a hand of three losers or better. North may have support for spades but need not. The situation is forcing but if South rebids 2♠, North may pass. In this situation, the repeat of the original suit is played, not as promising a 5+ suit but to show a worthless hand. With any values that make game likely, South bids anything other than a repeat of the original suit.

WEST	EAST	WEST	NORTH	EAST	SOUTH
♠ AJ5	♠ 9742				1◇
♡ AKJ4	♡ 63	Dble	No	1♠	No
◇ 87	◇ 6532	2◇	No	2♠	No
♣ AKQJ	♣ 964	No	No		

It would be silly for East-West to be any higher than this.

WEST	EAST	WEST	NORTH	EAST	SOUTH
♠ 5	♠ 872				1♠
♡ AKJ976	♡ –	Dble	No	2◇	No
◇ 6	◇ A8732	2♠	No	3♣	No
♣ AKQ97	♣ J10854	3♡	No	4♣	No
		4NT	No	5◇	No
		6♣	No	No	No

East's 3♣ confirms respectable values for game. West tries for hearts but when there is no fit there, the 6♣ slam is bid after making sure East has an ace.

COMPETING OVER 1NT

There are many conventions which deal with entering the auction after the opponents have opened 1NT. Almost all include Double for penalties, especially against the weak 1NT. The problem is to combine reasonable safety with describing two-suited and one-suited hands. It is safer to enter with a two-suiter, since if partner is short in one of your suits, partner is likely to have support or at least tolerance for the other.

To double a weak 1NT (12-14 or 13-15 HCP), a hand of 15+ points is recommended. You may have less with an obviously good lead such as ♠ KQJ1076 ♡ AK ◇ 94 ♣ 983.

A hand of about six losers is enough to bid a suit or show a two-suiter at the two-level. Seven losers is acceptable with good texture in your long suit(s). These hands are all worth a bid :

♠ KQ872	♠ KJ10742	♠ 8	♠ AK32
♡ AJ632	♡ 6	♡ AQ65	♡ KQ97
◇ 54	◇ AK4	◇ A108742	◇ 6
♣ 2	♣ 985	♣ 76	♣ J1052

The main problem is how many two-suiters you wish to cover and which one-suiters can be shown at the two-level.

Landy 2♣

The 2♣ overcall shows both majors. Other actions at the two-level are one-suiters. This is the simplest structure.

Ripstra

2♣ and 2◇ show two- or three-suiters, others are one-suiters. 2♣ = Both majors with clubs longer than diamonds. 2◇ = Both majors with diamonds longer than clubs. With no fit for either major, partner may be able to pass the minor. Ripstra does well on 5-4-3-1s and 4-4-4-1s with both majors.

Becker

2♣ = Both minors. 2◇ = Both majors. Others are one-suiters.

Astro

2♣ and 2◇ show two-suiters, others are one-suiters. 2♣ = Hearts and a minor. 2◇ = Spades and a second suit. This method can show all two-suiters (using 2NT for the minors). The suit shown is called the 'anchor suit'. If partner can support the anchor suit partner bids 2-Major if weak, 3-Major to invite game or 4-Major. Without support for the anchor, make the cheapest bid (the in-between step). Partner passes if holding that suit or bids on with some other second suit. With a strong hand, use 2NT to ask for the second suit.

There are variations of Astro which show the suit combinations more precisely. In Pinpoint Astro :

    2♣ = hearts and clubs.
    2◇ = hearts and diamonds.
    2♡ = hearts and spades.
    2♠ = spades and a minor.
    2NT = both minors.

This clears up the two-suiters involving hearts at the expense of showing a one-suiter in the majors. The Roth-Stone version of Astro :

    2♣ = clubs and spades.
    2◇ = diamonds and spades.
    3♣ = clubs and hearts.
    3◇ = diamonds and hearts.

Double = both majors over strong NT, penalties over weak NT.

This method covers the major-minor two-suiters although you have to reach the three-level with the hearts-minor combinations.

Using the double for takeout is also part of –

Brozel

where Double shows any one-suited hand worth a bid at the two-level. Partner is allowed to pass with scattered values and about a 10-count or better. Otherwise bid 2♣ to discover which is the long suit (pass = long suit is clubs). With a strong hand you may bid 2NT to find the long suit. Over 2♣, show a strong one-suiter by bidding it at the three-level.

Two-suiters in Brozel are shown exactly the same as in Pinpoint Astro (see top of page). Brozel shows one-suiters and two-suiters very effectively at the expense of the penalty double on strong balanced hands. However, it may gain penalties where partner can pass the double and other methods would have bid the one-suiter or passed 1NT.

There are two other attractive features playing Brozel. Jumps to the three-level show strong three-suiters, 4-4-4-1 or 5-4-4-0, the suit bid being the short suit. The Brozel double also applies after a 2-level takeout, e.g.,

WEST NORTH EAST SOUTH   South's double shows a one-suiter.
1NT   No   2♠   Dble   Partner may pass only with very strong spades. Otherwise bid 2NT if strong, 3♣ if weak. If the long suit is clubs, 3♣ will be passed. If not, the long suit is shown next. Bids over their takeout show two-suiters : 3♣ = clubs and diamonds, 3◇ = diamonds and hearts, 3♡ = hearts and clubs. 2NT is a three-suiter while 3♠ is a bigger three-suiter.

Brozel is recommended, especially against the strong 1NT but even against the weak 1NT it has much to offer, far more than the preceding conventions. One significant benefit is the ability to show a one-suiter in a minor and be able to play at the two-level.

With a powerful balanced hand, you have to pass 1NT but you may still collect penalties. Partner may double in fourth seat to show a one-suiter (fourth seat action is the same as second seat action) or third hand may run from 1NT.

WEST	NORTH	EAST	SOUTH
1NT	No	2♡	No
No	Dble		

North's belated double shows a powerful balanced hand. With a one-suiter or with a two-suiter, North would have taken action earlier.

WEST	NORTH	EAST	SOUTH
1NT	No	2◇*	No
2♡	Dble		

*Transfer to hearts

North's double here also shows the powerful balanced hand. There would be no reason to pass 1NT and double 2♡ before being sure of East's intentions.

A useful variation of Brozel would combine it with the RCO takeout structure (see Chapter 9, page 117) so that :

2♣ = two suits of the same rank.
2◇ = two suits of the same colour.
2♡ = hearts + clubs.
2♠ = spades + diamonds.

A takeout approach which retains the penalty double is :

Transfers over 1NT

This enables you to show one-suiters and two-suiters, although some reach the three-level.

2♣ = Puppet to 2◇. Shows either long diamonds (one-suiter or two-suiter) OR both majors. With a weak hand opposite, bid 2◇.

WEST	NORTH	EAST	SOUTH
1NT	2♣	No	2◇
No	?		

Pass = diamond one-suiter.
2♡ = both majors but not too strong. There are other routes to show a strong major two-suiter (see later).

2♠ = spades + diamonds two-suiter. The 2♣ was a transfer.
2NT = hearts + diamonds two-suiter. The 2♣ was a transfer.
3♣ + clubs and diamonds, either 5-5 or diamonds are longer.
3◇ = strong one-suiter in diamonds. Could have passed 2◇.

Over 2♣ if you have a strong fit for diamonds, bid 2♡ or 2♠. Partner bids 3◇ with the diamond hand. With a strong hand, bid 2NT. Partner bids 3◇ with diamonds only, 3♣ with both minors, 3♡ with hearts (may have spades also) or 3♠ with spades (denies hearts and therefore is a diamond-spade two-suiter).

2♦ over 1NT = Transfer to hearts. With a weak hand, bid 2♥ which will be passed if partner has a one-suiter or a two-suiter not worth pursuing opposite a weak hand. With a strong hand, bid 2NT. Partner rebids hearts or bids the second suit.

WEST	NORTH	EAST	SOUTH
1NT	2♦	No	2♥
No	?		

2♠ = spades is the second suit in a strong hand (else the 2♣ transfer would have been used – see previous page).

Also the spades are longer than the hearts. Otherwise, use 2♣ and rebid 3♥ if the hearts are longer than the spades.

    3♣/3♦ = second suit and the minor is longer than the hearts.

    3♥ = strong one-suiter in hearts.

    3♠ = strong 6-5 in the majors with six hearts.

    2NT = strong hand with hearts plus a minor. The pattern will be 5-5 or the hearts are longer.

2♥ over 1NT = Transfer to spades. With a weak hand, bid 2♠ which will be passed if partner has a one-suiter or a two-suiter not worth pursuing opposite a weak hand. With a strong hand, bid 2NT. Partner rebids spades or bids the second suit.

WEST	NORTH	EAST	SOUTH
1NT	2♥	No	2♠
No	?		

3♣/3♦ = second suit and the minor is longer than the spades. Strong hand.

    3♠ = strong one-suiter in spades.

    3♥ = strong 5-5 in the majors or 6-5 with six spades.

    2NT = strong hand with spades plus a minor. The pattern will be 5-5 or the spades are longer.

2♠ over 1NT = Transfer to clubs. With a weak hand, bid 3♣. With a strong hand, bid 2NT. Partner will rebid 3♣ if weak, bid a second suit (at least a 6-4 shape) or rebid 3NT with a strong one-suiter.

2NT over 1NT = Both minors but with the clubs longer. Not strong enough to transfer to 3♣ and then bid 3♦. With 5-5 in the minors or diamonds longer, bid 2♣ over 1NT and rebid 3♣ over partner's reply.

    If your original transfer is to a 4-card suit, your hand should be strong enough to show the longer suit on the next round. Partner may be forced to accept the transfer with a doubleton or worse.

    Transfers enable you to show all strong two-suited hands and also a moderate two-suiter in the majors. You may not be able to show other weak two-suiters if it entails reaching the three-level.

    The jumps to the 3-level may be used as purely pre-emptive (or if you prefer as strong three-suiters à la Brozel – see page 77).

COUNTERMEASURES BY THE 1NT SIDE

1. The opponents bid a genuine suit

WEST	NORTH	EAST	SOUTH
1NT	2♡	?	

There are different ways to approach this kind of position.
Standard approach
Double = Penalties. Some do play takeout doubles here but the popular approach is still penalties.
New suit (2♠/3♣/3♢) = Natural and not forcing.
2NT = Natural and invitational.
Jump bids (3♠/4♣/4♢) = Natural and forcing.
Their suit (3♡) = Stayman.
3NT = To play. Need not have a stopper in their suit but may have one. As the opponents would not overcall with a solid suit (pass and defend is the best strategy with a solid suit), you can expect (hope for, pray for) a stopper or two in opener's hand.

Lebensohl

The Lebensohl convention does away with the natural use of 2NT. It enables you to make forcing bids at a cheaper level and also to indicate to opener whether you do hold a stopper in the enemy suit. The 2NT reply is a 'puppet'. It requires opener to bid 3♣ and responder then clarifies the hand type. Auctions at the three-level which do not use 2NT either are forcing or promise a stopper in their suit. For example :

WEST	NORTH	EAST	SOUTH	2♠ = Natural but not forcing. Bids at
1NT	2♡	?		two-level are not strong.

3♣ = Natural and forcing.
3♢ = Natural and forcing.
3♡ = Enemy suit, Stayman *plus* a stopper in their suit.
3♠ = Natural and forcing.
3NT = Enough for 3NT *with* a stopper in their suit (denies four cards in any unbid major – would use their suit as Stayman).
2NT = Forces opener to bid 3♣.

WEST	NORTH	EAST	SOUTH	Pass = Weak with long clubs.
1NT	2♡	2NT	No	3♢ = Weak with long diamonds.
3♣	No	?		3♡ = Enemy suit, Stayman but *with no* stopper in their suit.

3♠ = Natural and forcing but no stopper in their suit. As 2♠ was available for a weak hand with long spades, 3♠ at once shows spades plus a stopper, 3♠ via 2NT = spades + no stopper.
3NT = Enough for 3NT but *denies* a stopper in their suit.

Pairs using Lebensohl often use takeout doubles over natural interference. The takeout double promises the values to bid 2NT but not enough for game. There are plenty of other actions available when you have game values. In reply to the takeout double, opener can bid a suit or 2NT if minimum or bid 3NT with a maximum. The takeout double does not guarantee the other major. If opener has a maximum and has a major suit, opener can bid the enemy suit as Stayman.

WEST	NORTH	EAST	SOUTH	
1NT	2♥	Dble	No	Pass = Penalties, very good hearts
?				2♠ = Minimum with spades. Without
				spades, responder converts to 2NT.

2NT = Minimum, no 4 spades.

3♣ or 3♦ = Minimum, strong 5-card suit.

3♥ = Their suit, Stayman with a maximum hand.

3♠ = Maximum with four spades if the partnership never opens 1NT with five spades. If five spades is possible with opener, 3♠ shows a maximum with five spades and 3♥ is used to locate the 4-4 fit. Over 3♥, responder can still ensure opener is declarer in spades by bidding 4♥ over 3♥.

3NT = Maximum but denies any unbid major (here spades).

Pairs using takeout doubles allow (and encourage) the 1NT opener to re-open the bidding with a takeout double if short in the suit doubled. This way you may still score some penalties.

Transfer Lebensohl

In standard methods, interference over 1NT causes you the loss of Stayman 2♣ and you also lose your transfer structure. 2♣ Stayman can be recaptured by bidding the enemy suit (with or without Lebensohl 2NT). Transfer Lebensohl enables you to recoup both Stayman and many of your transfer advantages.

Responder's bids at the two-level are natural and weak. Double is penalties or takeout according to partnership taste. 2NT and bids at the three-level are Lebensohl or Transfers as follows :

WEST	NORTH	EAST	SOUTH	
1NT	2♥	?		2♠ = natural, not forcing.
				2NT = opener must reply 3♣.

3♣ = Transfer to diamonds.

3♦ = Transfer to the other major (here spades).

3♥ = Their suit = Stayman plus a stopper in their suit.

3♠ = The other major = Slam try with both minors.

3NT = To play plus a stopper in their suit.

After 1NT : (2♦), then 3♣ = transfer to hearts, 3♦ = Stayman, no stopper, 3♥ = transfer to spades, 3♠ = five spades-four hearts.

Transfer Lebensohl : Further Developments

WEST	NORTH	EAST	SOUTH	
1NT	2♥	2NT	No	Pass = Weak with long clubs.
3♣	No	?		3◇ = Clubs + diamonds. The 2NT bid operated as a transfer.

3♥ = Their suit = Lebensohl = Stayman but no stopper. With a stopper bid 3♥ at once over 2♥ without using 2NT.

3♠ = 4 spades and 5+ clubs. 2NT operated as a transfer.

3NT = Enough for 3NT but no stopper in their suit. With a stopper, bid 3NT at once over 2♥ (see page 81).

WEST	NORTH	EAST	SOUTH	
1NT	2♥	3♣	No	Pass = Weak with long diamonds.
3◇	No	?		3♥ = Game force with long diamonds but no stopper in hearts. Some interest in slam.

3♠ = 4 spades and 5+ diamonds. Normal transfer sequence.

3NT = Long diamonds + stopper in their suit. Mild slam interest.

4♣ = 5-5 in the minors, very strong slam interest.

4◇ = 6+ diamonds, forcing, slam interest. Asks opener to start cue bidding.

WEST	NORTH	EAST	SOUTH	
1NT	2♥	3◇	No	3◇ is a transfer to the other major
?				(spades here but a transfer to hearts if they had overcalled 2♠). Normally

opener would simply bid the major and leave further action to responder. Here opener could bid 3♥ to show a maximum hand with spade support and the ace of hearts. In this sequence, the transfer to spades cannot be weak as 2♠ was available. Had the bidding started 1NT : (2♠) : 3◇, opener should bid 3♥. Responder may have quite a weak hand.

WEST	NORTH	EAST	SOUTH	
1NT	2♥	3♥	No	Responder has four spades and a
?				stopper in hearts. Bid 3♠ with four spades and a maximum (allowing

responder to start cue bidding), or 3NT without spades. A jump to 4♠ would show spade support but a minimum 1NT, discouraging slam ambitions.

WEST	NORTH	EAST	SOUTH	or	WEST	NORTH	EAST	SOUTH
1NT	2♥	3♠	No		1NT	2♠	3♥	No
?					?			

As responder can always transfer to the other major, bidding the other major can be used as a slam try with both minors. With no fit or no slam interest, opener can bid 3NT. With support and slam interest opener bids the minor suit chosen.

COUNTERMEASURES BY THE 1NT SIDE (*continued*)

2. The opponents make a conventional bid

When they intervene artificially, their bid normally promises one suit definitely. That suit is known as the 'anchor' suit and your actions will revolve around that suit.

WEST	NORTH	EAST	SOUTH
1NT	2♣	?	

If 2♣ is Landy (both majors), treat hearts as the anchor suit. If 2♣ is Astro (hearts and a minor), hearts is the anchor. If 2♣ is a transfer, diamonds will be the anchor.

WEST	NORTH	EAST	SOUTH
1NT	2◇	?	

If 2◇ is a transfer, hearts is the anchor. If 2◇ is Astro, showing spades and another suit, spades is the anchor.

WEST	NORTH	EAST	SOUTH
1NT	2♡	?	

If 2♡ shows hearts and another suit, hearts is the anchor. If 2♡ is a transfer, spades is the anchor.

After any of these bids, actions by the responder will generally be the same as after a natural overcall. This is so whether the partnership uses standard methods, Lebensohl or Transfer Lebensohl. Where stoppers are concerned, the suit referred to is the anchor suit. The only change comes in bidding the enemy suit. Most of the time you will have the option of bidding their anchor suit at the two-level or at the three-level.

WEST	NORTH	EAST	SOUTH
1NT	2◇	?	

Suppose that 2◇ shows spades and another suit so that spades is the anchor suit. Using standard methods:

2♠ = Stayman.

3♠ = Game force, short in spades, three hearts and at least 5-4 in the minors. For example :

    ♠ 6 ♡ KJ3 ◇ AJ763 ♣ A872

Using Lebensohl or Transfer Lebensohl :

2♠ = Stayman, plus a stopper in their suit.

2NT followed by 3♠ = Stayman but no stopper in their suit.

3♠ = Game force, short in spades, three hearts and at least 5-4 in the minors (as above). The main benefit of this 'splinter' is to ensure that opener has their suit well stopped for 3NT. Holding three cards in the other major allows opener to choose a 4-3 major contract.

Responder might also use the jump to 3♠ with shortage in their suit and a long minor. If opener can rebid 3NT, fine. If not, responder can convert any action by opener to 5-minor.

COUNTERMEASURES BY THE 1NT SIDE (continued)

3. The opponents make a conventional bid with no anchor

Occasionally you will come across pairs who intervene over 1NT with bids like 2♣ = majors or minors, 2◇ = red suits or black suits, and the like. It is not necessarily safe to pass if you have a good hand as fourth player may also pass, either with extreme weakness (highly likely if you have a good hand) or because fourth hand can deduce the suits actually held. Against such bids :

Standard methods

Double = Penalties.

2NT = Natural, invitational.

Non-jump suit bids = Natural, not forcing.

Jump bids below game = Natural and forcing.

Lebensohl

As there is no anchor suit, there is no scope for bidding their suit as Stayman or bidding 3NT immediately to show a stopper and via 2NT to deny a stopper. You either play standard methods as above or adopt a transfer structure akin to this :

2-level suit bids : Natural and not forcing.

2NT = Transfer to clubs. After opener accepts the transfer, a new suit is natural and forcing.

3♣ = Transfer to diamonds.

3◇ = Transfer to hearts.

3♡ = Transfer to spades.

3♠ = 5+ spades and 4+ hearts. This shape is difficult to show below 3NT when using transfers over interference.

Double = Good hand, at least invitational strength, but short in the suit doubled. This operates as a kind of takeout double but opener may of course leave the double in with strength in that suit. As responder is short in the suit, it is likely that the suit is one of the suits held by second hand.

If you have length in the suit bid, it is much more likely that you will have another chance as fourth player figures to be short in that suit and thus is likely to bid.

Double-and-later-double = Penalties.

Pass-and-later-double = Takeout.

COUNTERMEASURES BY THE 1NT *(continued)*

4. After a penalty double of 1NT – The Great Escape

Playing a strong 1NT opening, you are unlikely to have to scamper from a penalty double. Playing a weak no-trump, however, the need for an escape mechanism is far greater. The first important point is that if the bidding starts 1NT (weak) : (No) and you have a hopeless hand, you should start running before the doubling starts. Most pairs play a double of 1NT as penalties in both positions but most also play the double of a suit bid as a takeout double. You are therefore likely to escape if you bid at once rather than wait for the doubling to start.

With ♠ 764 ♡ J87 ◇ 9873 ♣ 763, bid 2♣ and pass any reply from opener. You may not survive but it is worth taking the chance. Your result is not likely to be any worse than playing in 1NT doubled and may well be much better.

After 1NT : (Double) : ?

There are several possible ways to try to minimise the loss. Most of these use the redouble as a transfer or puppet to 2♣. This is a simple enough scheme :

Redouble = Puppet to 2♣. Responder has a 1-suited hand and will pass 2♣ if that is the long suit, else bid the long suit over 2♣.

2♣ = 4+ clubs and a second suit.

2◇ = 4+ diamonds and a major.

2♡ = both majors.

Opener passes with 3+ support or bids a higher suit in which 3+ cards are held. The method ensures that you reach at least a 4-3 fit but of course you may miss a better fit in the process.

Transfers over the double

This method allows opener to be the declarer and forces the strong doubling hand to lead into opener's strength.

Redouble = Transfer to clubs.

2♣ = Transfer to diamonds.

2◇ = Transfer to hearts.

2♡ = Transfer to spades.

Pass = Forces opener to redouble if fourth hand also passes. This enables you to play 1NT redoubled if responder happens to have a strong hand and if not, responder then runs to show a 2-suiter as above.

WEST	NORTH	EAST	SOUTH	
1NT	Dble	No	No	2♣ = Clubs and another suit.
Rdbl	No	?		2◇ = Diamonds and a major.
				2♡ = Both majors.

Two-Way Transfers over the double :

This method has all the benefits of transfers and allows responder to show some 3-suiters and particular 2-suiters.

Redouble = Transfer to clubs *or* a 3-suiter short in clubs *or* both majors with the hearts longer. After opener bids 2♣, responder's removal to 2◇ shows the 3-suiter short in clubs while 2♡ shows both majors with hearts longer.

2♣ = Transfer to diamonds *or* both majors with spades longer. After opener bids 2◇, responder's removal to 2♡ shows the majors with longer spades.

2◇ = Transfer to hearts.

2♡ = Transfer to spades.

Pass = Forces opener to redouble.

WEST	NORTH	EAST	SOUTH	
1NT	Dble	No	No	2♣ = Clubs and another suit.
Rdbl	No	?		2◇ = Diamonds and a major.
				2♡ = Both majors, equal length.

With a major suit fit, this method enables you to play in your longer combined major.

Swine

This was devised by Bob Sebesfi and Alan Woods. *Swine* stands for 'Sebesfi-Woods-1-Notrump-Escape'. Aside from its benefits, it is attractive just to be able to say 'We play Swine!'

Pass requires opener to Redouble. Responder may then pass for penalties, while any suit bid shows that suit and the next-higher-suit.

WEST	NORTH	EAST	SOUTH	
1NT	Dble	No	No	Pass = To play.
Rdbl	No	?		2♣ = Clubs and diamonds.
				2◇ = Diamonds and hearts.
				2♡ = Hearts and spades.

Redouble immediately over the double requires opener to bid 2♣ and shows a 1-suiter. With clubs, responder will pass, otherwise bid the long suit.

WEST	NORTH	EAST	SOUTH	
1NT	Dble	?		2♣ = Clubs and a major. The aim is to avoid reaching the three-level when they

are doubling for penalties. That is why you do not use 2♠ to show spades and clubs, for example.

2◇ = Diamonds and spades.

2♡ = Genuine hearts and respectable values. A mild game invite.

2♠ = Genuine spades, mild game invitation. Opener needs a maximum 1NT and a strong fit to accept the invitation.

2NT = Strong and unbalanced, at least a 5-5 pattern.

7. BIDDING OVER THEIR STRONG OPENINGS

AGAINST STRONG 1♣ SYSTEMS

The most common strong 1♣ system you are likely to encounter is the Precision 1♣ (16+ points) but there are many others and many versions of Precision. As values in the world in general are eroded over time, so the strong 1♣ on 15+ points is not uncommon these days.

These systems share a common approach : all very strong hands are opened 1♣. One major advantage enjoyed by these systems is when the opening is not 1♣. Limiting opener's hand to 11-15 or 10-14 allows responder to judge accurately the offensive potential of the two hands. The Achilles heel, however, is the strong 1♣ opening itself. Opener has shown 15/16 points or more but has not yet shown any shape. If the defenders can intervene and in particular push the bidding to the three-level quickly, the opening side may have a tough time unravelling their combined potential.

Following the basic philosophy of 'bid with weak hands over their strong actions and with strong hands over their weak actions', second player should pass 1♣ with all hands of 13+ points. This is safe since the 1♣ opening is forcing. You will have a chance on the next round. It follows from this that :

Pass over 1♣ and later action = 13+ points

This is so whether your later action is a bid or a takeout double.

If third player bids 1◇, artificial negative, you can choose your action over opener's rebid. If their bidding starts, (1♣) : (1◇), (1NT), you bid over the 1NT rebid as you would have bid over a 1NT opening. The only difference is that your bid now promises 13+ points.

If third player gives a positive response, usually forcing to game in their methods, you are invariably well out of the auction with your 13+ points. They are unlikely to reach a slam and your points, sitting over the opener, give you a decent chance to defeat their game. You may still bid, of course, after a positive if you have a long, strong suit.

Even if you do not adopt any special methods, you should be quick to bid over 1♣ even on the slightest values. Overcall often at the 1-level on any decent suit. K-Q-x-x-x is enough even with no additional values if you are not vulnerable. It is rare for you to suffer a significant penalty at the one-level. With one extra playing trick (K-Q-x-x-x-x) you should bid vulnerable. Play your jumps to the two-level as weak with a 6+ suit. Use the Rule of 2 and 3 to judge whether you can afford the two-level or only the one-level. Jump to the three-level with a seven-card suit, again depending on vulnerability and the Rule of 2 and 3.

However, regular partnerships will have a more systemic approach. These methods will give you even better results.

1. Double = Majors, 1NT = Minors

Suit bids are weak, jumps are weak with 6+ suits. (1♣) : Double is a weak takeout with both majors and (1♣) : 1NT is a weak takeout with both minors.

This is simple and works well enough on the hands it covers. The main drawback is that there are four combinations of two-suiters not covered.

2. Exclusion bids

In this approach a suit bid up to 2♣ is equivalent to a weak takeout double of the suit bid. For example, (1♣) : 1♠ = short in spades, support or tolerance for the other suits. The hand type is a 3-suiter including 4-4-3-2 and 5-4-3-1 patterns. Partner bids as though responding to a takeout double of the suit bid but with the understanding that the bid shows under 13 points.

The method is fine for the hands it covers but again there are many two-suited patterns (5-4-2-2, 5-5-2-1) which are not covered. One could play jumps to the two-level are two-suiters but then one-suited hands cannot bid below the three-level.

3. Wonder bids

In this method, a suit bid up to 2♣ shows *either* a one-suiter in the suit bid *or* a three-suiter short in the suit bid. The bid is natural or an exclusion. 'Wonder' bids are so called because everyone wonders which one it is. Each of these hands is worth a 'wonder' bid of 1♠ over (1♣).

♠ AJ1076	♠ 6	♠ 5	♠ KQ10862
♡ 97	♡ K764	♡ J984	♡ 763
◇ 83	◇ QJ85	◇ QJ7	◇ 432
♣ J1063	♣ K962	♣ Q9832	♣ 5

After a Wonder Bid, partner is expected to act taking both possibilities into account. With strong support for the 1-suiter possibility, bid the best of your other suits as high as you dare, below the level to which you would be prepared to support the one-suiter.

WEST	NORTH	EAST	SOUTH	
1♣	1♠	No	3♦	$3\diamond$ = 'Pass if you have the 3-suiter, bid 3♠ if you have the 1-suiter.'

With strong support for the 1-suiter option but no good suit outside, bid your longest outside suit at the cheapest level. With equal length, choose the strongest holding. For example, suppose the bidding has started (1♣) : 1♠ : (No) : ? and you hold ♠ 97632 ♡ A5 ♢ KQ7 ♣ 983, bid 2♢. Partner will remove to spades with the 1-suiter and if partner has the 3-suiter, you have indicated a good lead to partner.

If you are short in the 1-suiter, it is best to pass with a weak hand and bid 1NT with a strong hand. Partner should pass 1NT with the 1-suiter unless it is playable opposite a singleton. With the 3-suiter, partner will bid a long suit at the two-level or, if maximum, at the three-level. If the wonder bid is passed and opener doubles, Pass = the 1-suiter, Bid = the 3-suiter. With equal length in the three suits, Redouble.

With an exceptionally powerful hand opposite a wonder bid, bid 2NT. Partner bids a new suit with the 3-suiter or rebids the long suit with the 1-suiter (at the three-level if playable opposite a doubleton, at the four-level if a major playable opposite a singleton). The 3NT rebid shows the 1-suiter type but only a five-card suit needing better than doubleton support.

Playing wonder bids, you can show two-suited hands quite comfortably at the two-level using also 1NT and Double. Suit bids show the suit bid and the next suit up. The structure is :

(1♣) : 2♢ = diamonds + hearts
(1♣) : 2♡ = hearts + spades
(1♣) : 2♠ = spades + clubs
(1♣) : 2NT = both minors

The non-touching two suiters are shown via :

(1♣) : Double = clubs + hearts
(1♣) : 1NT = diamonds + spades

Wonder Bids provide a strong offensive weapon allowing you to enter the bidding on most patterns with weak hands. The drawback is that if partner makes a wonder bid and you are on lead, you may not be sure of the best start if the opponents' bidding has made it impossible for you to clarify partner's hand.

4. Truscott Defence

This method, devised by Alan Truscott, bridge editor of the *New York Times*, shows two-suiters at the one-level. Bids up to 2♣ all show two-suiters, higher suit bids show one-suiters. Suit bids up to 2♣ show the suit bid and the next higher suit :

(1♣) : 1◇ = diamonds + hearts
(1♣) : 1♡ = hearts + spades
(1♣) : 1♠ = spades + clubs
(1♣) : 2♣ = clubs and diamonds

The non-touching suits are shown by double and 1NT. You may by now have realised that NT stands for 'Non-Touching'!

(1♣) : Double = clubs + hearts
(1♣) : 1NT = diamonds + spades

The suit lengths promised depend on the vulnerability, the bidding level and your personal courage. Naturally the playing strength should be better when vulnerable and when your bid commits your side to the two-level (the 1NT and 2♣ overcalls). Aside from that, 4-4 in the suits is acceptable. Opposite a passed partner when you know the opponents can make game or slam, you might try a semi-psychic on 5-3 or even 4-3 patterns. It is best not to be too conservative with your patterns. If the opponents buy the contract, as they often will, you do not want declarer to be sure you are 5-4 or 5-5 in your suits, as that gives declarer too good a reading on the hand. Play the two-suiters as free-and-easy and declarer will obtain less benefit in the play.

(1♣) : 2◇/2♡/2♠/3♣ = one-suiters. Higher suit bids are one-suiters but with at least a 7-card suit.

(1♣) : 2NT = An extreme two-suiter, at least 6-5, any two suits.

When partner makes a two-suited overcall, bid as high as you dare with a weak hand and good support for one of the two suits. Especially against pairs using relay methods, you need to take up as much bidding space as possible to eliminate their relays. 4+ support and 8 losers is enough to jump to the three-level. Such jump bids put maximum pressure on to the opponents.

With a weak hand but only 3-card support, choose the suit you wish to support at the cheapest level. Naturally you would pass if your preference is for partner's bid suit. The 1NT response is natural and indicates no desire to play in partner's suits.

With a strong hand, bid 2NT asking partner to clarify suit length or whether a third suit is held. A new suit over 2NT shows four cards in the suit bid and hence a three-suiter.

Where their bidding has started (1♣) : No : (1♢), fourth player may use the same defensive methods as directly over 1♣. However, there is also a strong case for playing a more natural approach. Firstly, it is not absolutely safe to pass with a very strong hand. Although the 1♣ opener usually bids over 1♢, there is no compulsion and opener is permitted to pass 1♢. Secondly, in view of the weak 1♢ response, there is less incentive to interfere with a weak hand. It is unlikely the opponents will have a sophisticated relay action. Recommended over 1♢ is to double for takeout, promising both majors and other low-level bids are natural with sound values. Jumps can be played as natural, weak one-suiters.

* * *

These defensive methods can be adapted over other strong opening bids. The Truscott Defence works well over strong 2♣ or 2♢ openings (see page 18 and page 22). On the odd occasion you may meet a pair playing a strong artificial 1♢ opening. Over this you can play Wonder Bids. If you choose the Truscott Defence, your actions over 1♢ would be :
1♡/1♠/2♣/2♢ = the suit bid + the next suit up. Higher suit bids are one-suiters.
Double = diamonds + spades.
1NT = hearts + clubs.

The rule is that Double = non-touching suits, showing the suit doubled and its non-touching mate, while 1NT shows the other pair of non-touching suits.

If you play a lot of duplicate, you may come across Forcing Pass systems, although these are banned from many lower-grade tournaments. If you should meet a Forcing Pass pair, their Pass shows a strongish hand (perhaps only 13+ points). The pass is the most vulnerable part of their system as it shows strength but is not descriptive in any other way. Interfere against that as you would against a strong 1♣ and you will cause them to regret their methods. Over their Pass :
1♣/1♢/1♡/1♠ = the suit bid and the next suit up.
1NT = non-touching suits, diamonds + spades.
2♣ = non-touching suits, clubs + hearts.
Higher suit bids = one-suiters.

As their Pass is forcing, you can afford to pass on hands with 13+ points and take action if you wish on the next round. Pass + later action promises 13+ points as over strong 1♣ methods.

Against Relay Methods

If you play in reasonably strong duplicates, you will strike pairs who use relay methods after any opening bid. Such pairs often make natural openings but use the next suit up as an artificial force to game. Their bidding approach is not a dialogue as in natural methods but rather a question-and-answer interrogation where one partner finds out all there is to know about the other partner's hand (shape, strength, controls, key cards), or all that is needed, and then decides on the contract.

Relay methods are highly effective especially for slam bidding. You should therefore adapt your style to interfere after a relay bid as often as possible. As the relay is either forcing to game or shows enough to invite game, the opponents will always hold the majority of the points.

In order to operate, relays need bidding space. Rob them of their space and you rob them of their relays. Bids usually need to be three or four bids above the relay in order to remove enough space to destroy them. A two-suited overcall structure works well here. If partner has a good fit for one of your suits, partner may be able to bid high enough to knock out the relays.

If you are used to the Truscott Defence to a strong 1♣ opening, it is easy to adapt this to bidding over their relay responses.

Suppose the bidding has started (1♡) : No : (1♠) where the 1♠ bid is a relay. Since they have opened a natural 1♡, there is little point in showing 2-suiters including hearts. Try this method :

> Double = spades + clubs.
> 2♣ = clubs + diamonds.
> 2♢ = diamonds + spades.
> 1NT = weak takeout, three-suiter short in hearts.

Bids beyond 2♢ are weak one-suiters.

The general rule is that suit bids show the suit bid and the next suit along (excluding their suit), double shows the suit doubled and the next suit up, while bidding NT or their suit, whichever is cheaper, is the three-suiter short in the suit they have shown.

Suppose the bidding has been (1♠) : No : (2♢) where the 2♢ reply is an artificial game force relay. Again there is no value in showing spades, their suit, among your two-suiters. Try these :

> Double = diamonds + hearts.
> 2♡ = hearts + clubs.
> 3♣ = clubs + diamonds.
> 2♠ = three-suiter short in spades.

COUNTERMEASURES BY THE STRONG 1♣ OPENING SIDE

Where the interference is a natural bid your system will already provide you with methods to deal with their intervention. What about when they use multi-bids, either Truscott or Wonder Bids?

There are three important points to consider :

1. You rarely get rich planning penalties at the low levels. It is better to use Double in some constructive sense for your side than to reserve double for penalties.

2. If their bid shows a two-suiter or a three-suiter, you may yet wish to play in a major suit even though one opponent may hold four cards in that suit. However, it is less likely you will want to play in a minor suit where they have length. Therefore, you should play that bidding a major they have shown is natural, bidding a minor they have shown is artificial.

3. Do not overdo artificial countermeasures. Often their bid will not have robbed you of any significant bidding space. In that case, treat bids by your side as having their usual meanings and make use of Pass and Double (or Redouble) to clarify hands which you would otherwise be unable to clarify.

After 1♣ : (Double) : ? (where double = some two-suiter)

They have robbed you of nothing. Your bids of 1♡ and higher have normal meanings. You can play :

Pass = 0-4 points, any shape.

Redouble = the other two suits and the upper range of your negative response (5-7 or 6-8 points). This is useful information which you would otherwise have been unable to show without their double.

1♢ = the upper end of the negative reply but not holding the suits required by the redouble.

After 1♣ : (1♢) : ? (where 1♢ shows some two-suiter)

Again you have lost no bidding space. Bids of 1♡ and higher have your usual meanings.

Double = upper end of your negative + the other two suits.

Pass = all other negative hands.

After 1♣ : (1♡) : ? (where 1♡ shows some two-suiter)

They have still not robbed you of any significant space (yet).

Double = upper end of your negative + the other two suits.

Pass = all other negatives.

Bids = the usual positives. If 1♡ showed the majors, play 1♠ as natural, 5+ spades and a positive, and 2♡ as natural, 5+ hearts and a positive.

After 1♣ : (1♠) : ? (where 1♠ shows some 2-suiter)

Double = upper end of your negative + the other two suits.

Bids = in general, the usual positives. If 1♠ showed spades + clubs, play 2♠ as natural, 5+ spades and a positive. Use 2♣, a bid of their minor, as competitive values in the other major : here 2♣ would show 5-8 points with hearts.

Pass = all other negatives.

After 1♣ : (1NT) : ? (where 1NT = some two-suiter, perhaps the minors, perhaps diamonds + spades, the non-touching suits).

Double = the upper end of your negative + the other two suits (both majors if 1NT = the minors; hearts + clubs if 1NT showed spades + diamonds).

Note that your approach is virtually the same regardless of the meaning of their interference. This is important since it reduces the memory strain and allows you to play the same approach no matter which suits are shown by their bids.

2♣ = competitive values in hearts if 1NT = the minors.

2◇ = competitive values in spades if 1NT = the minors.

2◇ = competitive values in hearts if 1NT = spades + diamonds.

Other bids are generally natural and Pass = negative outside the scope provided by the competitive bids above.

Jump bids in their suits or bidding one of their suits at the three-level should be taken as a no-trump probe, asking for a stopper in the suit bid.

Over Wonder Bids

Use Double to show competitive values with support for any unbid major. Over, for example, 1♣ : (1♠), use double to show the upper end of your negative range and 4+ hearts. With other negatives, pass. You will almost certainly have another chance to bid later and your later actions, if unforced, will tend to deny four hearts. All bids show a normal positive. Bidding their major (here 2♠) is natural showing a 5+ suit. A jump to 3♠ would show a no-trump hand without four hearts and without a spade stop.

If the bidding starts, say, 1♣ : (1♠) : No : (No), opener should almost invariably take some action. You might pass if you were exceptionally strong in spades *and* you considered game was highly unlikely *and* the opponents were vulnerable so that the undertricks you plan to collect are worth 100 each. In other cases, reopen the bidding with a natural bid or a takeout double. Bidding their suit at once is natural. Double first and bid their suit later is artificial and very powerful.

8. GENERAL COMPETITIVE METHODS

NEGATIVE DOUBLES

'Negative Doubles' is an unfortunate choice of nomenclature. They were termed negative as opposed to 'positive' for penalties, not negative as promising a weak hand. They are simply a takeout double by responder. A better choice would be 'Responder's Double' as the double is for takeout and shows responding values, 6+ points.

The main questions to be answered are :

1. To what level should the double of their suit overcall be played for takeout?
2. What suit lengths are promised by responder's double?

Originally the double for takeout was played only at the one- and two-levels. Many top players today play responder's double for takeout up to the four-level (and higher, too!). This needs to be settled within your partnership. As you play double for takeout more and more, the benefits become apparent and most players then wish to extend the range. The only requirement is that as the level increases, so must the strength needed to make the double. Six points or better may be enough to force opener to reply at the one- or two-level, but if your double forces partner to bid at the four-level (say, 1♣ : (3♠) : Double), you should have equivalent to opening points.

The original concept also had the double promising 4+ cards in any unbid major. Thus :

1♣ : (1♠) : Double = 6+ points and 4+ hearts.
1♣ : (2♢) : Double = 6+ points and at least 4-4 in the majors.
1♣ : (1♡) : Double = 6+ points and exactly 4 spades. Therefore :
1♣ : (1♡) : 1♠ = 6+ points and 5+ spades.

The rule was 'Double over major = 4+ in the other major; major suit bid over their major = 5+ in the suit bid.'

1♣ : (1♡) : Double is today played by many top players to deny four spades. The theory is that 1♣ : 1♠ shows 4+ spades and if you can cope with that, it is no more difficult to cope with 1♣ : (1♡) : 1♠ as showing 4+ spades. The double can then be used to show a hand with minor suit lengths, a hand unsuitable for supporting opener, unsuited for a 1NT response and too weak to bid two in the other minor.

After 1◇ : (1♡) : ? each of these hands would be worth a double denying 4+ spades :

♠ AJ5	♠ 62	♠ 5	♠ 876
♡ 974	♡ 9764	♡ 9842	♡ 76
◇ 832	◇ A98	◇ QJ7	◇ 432
♣ Q1063	♣ K952	♣ A9832	♣ AQ983

These are all hands which have no convenient action over 1♡ if the double is not available.

These hands would not be suitable for such a double :

♠ AJ54	♠ 62	♠ 53	♠ 876
♡ 97	♡ K976	♡ 984	♡ Q2
◇ 832	◇ A98	◇ QJ74	◇ AJ2
♣ Q1063	♣ 9562	♣ A983	♣ AQ983
Bid 1♠	Bid 1NT	Bid 2◇	Bid 2♣

This variation of the original usage of the double is eminently sensible. Not so attractive is the use of double to show less than 4-card support for a major in other auctions.

WEST	NORTH	EAST	SOUTH
1◇	2♣	?	

Some players use a double here with no more than 4-3 in the majors. This is unnecessarily risky. Opener may assume a 4-card holding opposite and is entitled to jump to game with sufficient high card strength and a 4-card major. In addition, the auction may become competitive. 4-3 fits are reasonable at the two-level but are risky conveyances at higher levels.

Where both majors have been bid, the double shows both minors.

WEST	NORTH	EAST	SOUTH
1♠	2♡	Dble	

East's double promises 6+ points and at least 4-4 in the minors.

Opener's reply to the double

Opener bids as though responder has bid the promised suit(s) at the one-level. Treat 1♣ : (1♠) : Double as equivalent to 1♣ : 1♡. 1♣ : (1♠) : Double : (No), 3♡ is equal to 1♣ : 1♡, 3♡. It is not a jump shift but rather a jump raise. 1♣ : (1◇) : Double : (No), 3♣ shows the same values as 1♣ : 1♡. 3♣ or 1♣ : 1♠, 3♣.

With a minimum hand, opener bids at the minimum level. With 16-18 points opener should jump bid. With 19 points or more, bid game or if the correct game is not obvious, bid the enemy suit.

Opener should not stretch to make a jump rebid with a borderline 16 point hand. The doubler is expected to bid again with 10 points or better. If you need at least 10 points opposite to make game reasonable, bid at the cheapest level. If the 10 points are there, you will hear from partner.

Responder's rebid

You have made a negative double and opener has bid at the cheapest level. With 6-9 points, you should pass if opener's last action suits you. If not, you may rebid 1NT if available, support one of opener's suits at the two-level or bid a new suit yourself.

WEST	NORTH	EAST	SOUTH
1◇	1♠	Dble	No
2♣	No	2♡	

Double-then-new-suit by the doubler shows 5+ in the suit bid but only 6-9 points. If responder had 10+ points and five or more hearts, responder had a natural 2♡ response available. The double-then-new-suit allows you to take action on a hand like ♠ 54 ♡ QJ7632 ◇ 76 ♣ KJ2 where you would otherwise have to pass (1♠) or overbid greatly with 2♡.

With 10-12 points, responder should invite game. With this strength, responder will normally have a balanced shape or a 4-4-4-1. Responder will not hold 5+ cards in an unbid suit. With such length and 10+ points, take the natural route and bid your long suit. Responder might have 5-card support for opener's minor. After 1♣ : (1♠), double with ♠ 87 ♡ KJ65 ◇ K4 ♣ K9742. If partner rebids 1NT, you are now worth a jump to 3♣. Take one of the kings away and your rebid would be just 2♣.

You show 10-12 points by rebidding 2NT or supporting one of opener's suits to the three-level.

WEST	NORTH	EAST	SOUTH
1◇	1♠	Dble	No
2♣	No	?	

After this beginning, what action should East take on each of the following hands?

1. ♠ KJ6	2. ♠ 763	3. ♠ 862	4. ♠ 6532
♡ KQ65	♡ A762	♡ K762	♡ KQ76
◇ 873	◇ KJ32	◇ Q7	◇ AQ2
♣ Q98	♣ K4	♣ AJ98	♣ 62

Answers :

1. Bid 2NT, promising 10-12 points, balanced shape and a stopper in spades.

2. Bid 3◇.   3. Bid 3♣.   4. Bid 3◇. Best available choice.

With game values, bid the game if it is obvious. If it is not clear which game is best, bid the enemy suit.

♠ A976   If the bidding started 1◇ : (1♠) : Dble : (No), 2♣ : (No),
♡ 8743   you are worth a shot at 3NT. If, however, it went
◇ A8   1◇ : (2♡) : Dble : (No) 3♣ : (No), your best shot is 3♡.
♣ KQJ   Partner may have a stopper in hearts but not primarily a
no-trump hand, perhaps something like ♠ J ♡ A2 ◇ KQ954 ♣ A9532.

Competitive Decisions

WEST	NORTH	EAST	SOUTH
1♣	1♠	Dble	2♠
?			

What should West hold here in order to bid 3♡? How much for a 3♣ rebid? What should West do with these?

1. ♠ Q6	2. ♠ 76	3. ♠ 862	4. ♠ 862
♡ KQ65	♡ A762	♡ K7	♡ K7
◇ 87	◇ KJ	◇ QJ	◇ AJ
♣ AJ982	♣ AK432	♣ AQ9872	♣ AKJ972

If you bid 3♡ on Hand 2, you cannot reasonably bid 3♡ also on Hand 1. Yet you are not worth more than 3♡ on Hand 2.

Likewise, if you bid 3♣ on Hand 4 (and you can hardly do more) you can scarcely justify bidding 3♣ on Hand 3 also. Otherwise, how can responder tell whether to leave it at the three-level and when to push on to a game?

The recommended strategy is for opener to pass in this position with a minimum hand. Treat a rebid at the three-level as having the same strength as a jump to the three-level. In other words, 3♡ by opener here is the same as 1♣ : 1♡, 3♡ and a 3♣ rebid by opener has the same strength as 1♣ : 1♡, 3♣. Responder then knows that opener will have a hand in the 16-18 point range and should be able to make a sensible decision whether to pass or whether to press on.

This does not mean that you let them buy the contract at the two-level. Rather it shifts the responsibility for competing to responder. When 2♠ comes back to responder, some action should be taken even with minimum values. Bid a 5+ suit if available, show support for opener's first suit or double again.

WEST	NORTH	EAST	SOUTH
1♣	1♠	Dble	2♠
No	No	?	

What action should responder take at this stage on these hands?

1. ♠ 87	2. ♠ 87	3. ♠ 87	4. ♠ 852
♡ KQ75	♡ KQ75	♡ QJ9643	♡ AQ32
◇ Q964	◇ 764	◇ K92	◇ KJ762
♣ 764	♣ Q964	♣ 54	♣ 2

Answers :

1. Double. Whatever suit partner bids is fine with you. Partner may have a 5-card club suit.

2. Bid 3♣. Partner knows you have four hearts from the double. With no interest in diamonds, do not use the double.

3. Bid 3♡. This shows long hearts and therefore only 6-9 points.

4. Bid 3◇. 5+ diamonds plus the four hearts already shown.

COMPETING OVER THEIR TAKEOUT DOUBLE

WEST	NORTH	EAST	SOUTH
1♠	Dble	?	

Old style was to redouble on all hands of 10+ HCP and play all other actions as limited, 6-9 points, not forcing.

Modern theory is to retain as much of your normal bidding structure as possible when they intervene. If you believe the methods you play are sound, then why change them because of intervention? Why let the opponents dictate how you should bid?

With this approach, your responses after a takeout double are the same as after a pass except for jump raises, 2NT and the availability of a redouble. Change of suit is natural and forcing, just as though second player had passed. Your raise structure :

2-level = 6-9 points, 9 losers. A little less in HCP is acceptable if the playing strength is correct. On the sequence above you would bid 2♠ with ♠ K963 ♡ 87 ◇ QJ65 ♣ 975 and also with ♠ K963 ♡ 5 ◇ 8753 ♣ 6542. Each has nine losers.

3-level = 6-9 points, 8 losers. The high card values do not change but the playing strength is better than a two-level raise. You would raise to 3♠ with ♠ K963 ♡ 87 ◇ QJ1065 ♣ 54 or with ♠ K963 ♡ 4 ◇ K652 ♣ 8753.

4-level = 6-9 points, 7 losers. This is the same sort of hand on which you would raise to the four-level over a Pass. Bid 4♠ with ♠ K963 ♡ 8 ◇ QJ10652 ♣ 54, a pre-emptive raise with seven losers, or with ♠ Q8752 ♡ – ◇ 652 ♣ K8762.

The aim is to describe your playing strength to opener so that if the opponents bid higher, partner is able to judge whether to sacrifice or whether to defend. Knowing your losers and expecting at most one defensive trick from a direct raise, opener is well placed to gauge the offensive and defensive potential.

2NT = Truscott Convention. This shows 10+ HCP and support for opener's suit. Over a minor opening, 2NT denies holding a major. The aim is to set your territorial claim. 2NT shows that your side has greater high card strength and a good trump fit. It also usually shuts out the doubler's partner.

After a major suit opening, opener may sign off over 2NT in 3-Major (but responder pushes on with 12+ points) or 4-Major (but responder may push on to slam). Opener may also make a trial bid below 3-Major or a cue bid above 3-Major. As the 2NT reply guarantees trump support, it is sensible to treat 3NT by either player as Blackwood.

After a minor suit opening, a new suit at the three-level by either player is a stopper bid for 3NT.

Redouble = 10+ HCP, usually looking for penalties. The redouble denies a fit for opener's suit. With 10+ points and support, choose the 2NT response over the double.

There are two types of hands where the redouble is used. One is a balanced hand with 10+ HCP where you plan to rebid 2NT (10-12) or 3NT (13+) if unable to double them for penalties. This is the kind of hand where you have a stopper in their suit but your trumps are not strong enough for a penalty double.

WEST	NORTH	EAST	SOUTH
1♡	Dble	Rdbl	2◇
No	No	?	

East would bid 2NT with a hand like ♠ Q74 ♡ 73 ◇ K976 ♣ KQ98. Had South bid 2♣, East's trumps are strong enough for a penalty double. Add say the ♡K to the East hand and East would rebid 3NT over 2◇.

The other type is the penalties hand. This hand is short in opener's suit, 10+ points and strong holdings in at least two outside suits. To double them at the one-level or two-level, you need at least four trumps and at least two trump winners in high cards. If partner opens 1♡ and RHO doubles, redouble with ♠ KQ1062 ♡ 7 ◇ AJ92 ♣ J52. You plan to double for penalties if they bid 1♠ or 2◇.

If you have only one long, strong suit you are better off to bid the suit. It is not likely that they will bid that suit and you may as well bid your hand naturally. After 1♡ from opener, Double by RHO, bid 2♣ with ♠ 87 ♡ 63 ◇ K62 ♣ AQJ943.

After the redouble

The advancer should bid just as though third hand had passed. It is no tougher to bid over the redouble than over the pass. With no decent suit, you are allowed to pass the redouble back to partner but psychologically it is still better to bid. Pass advertises profound weakness and makes it more likely that they will double you for penalties. If you bid, you may ward off the double.

Opener should pass a bid by the advancer unless able to make a penalty double (4+ trumps and 2+ trump winners). A bid by opener indicates a sub-minimum and distributional opening. Opener need not bid with a good hand. The redouble promises another bid.

Where advancer's bid is passed back to the redoubler, double is for penalties. All doubles by opener or responder after a penalty redouble are for penalties. Change of suit by the redoubler is forcing for one round.

COUNTERMEASURES BY THE DOUBLING SIDE

After third hand raises to the two-level
Pass = 0-5 points.
Suit bid = 6-9 points.
2NT = 10-12 points, balanced, stopper in their suit, no major suit.
Jump bid in a suit = 10-12 points counting distribution points.
Double = takeout, 6+ points and equal length in the unbid suits of the same rank. See *Responsive Doubles* below.

After third hand raises to the three-level
Suit bid at three-level = 8 losers, generally 10-12 points counting distributional values.
Suit bid at four-level = 7 losers.
3NT = To play, their suit well stopped.
Double = takeout. See *Responsive Doubles* below.

After third hand raises to the four-level
Suit bids = 7 losers or better unless you are sacrificing.
4NT = two-suited takeout.
Double = Co-operative. Shows 10+ points but not necessarily trump winners. Leaves it to partner whether to pass the double (usually best) or whether to bid over their action.

Over their 2NT bid
Suit bid at the three-level = 8 losers
Jump to four-level = 7 losers
Double = For takeout. See *Responsive Doubles*.

RESPONSIVE DOUBLES

Where third hand raises opener's suit over a double, it is best to use Double by fourth player as a takeout double, showing equal length in the unbid suits of equal rank. Such a double by fourth player over the raise is called a 'responsive double'.

WEST	NORTH	EAST	SOUTH
1◇	Dble	2◇	Dble

South's double is responsive and shows equal length in the majors. It solves the problem of which major to bid when holding a hand like ♠ QJ65 ♡ K943 ◇ 872 ♣ J2.

WEST	NORTH	EAST	SOUTH
1♠	Dble	2♠	Dble

South's double is responsive and shows equal length in the minors. Again it solves the problem of which suit to bid when holding something like ♠ 9642 ♡ 7 ◇ KQ65 ♣ KJ92. Allowing partner to choose the minor is better than guessing which one to bid.

It is recommended to use Responsive Doubles at the two-level and at the three-level. Over a three-level raise, you need more strength either in high cards or in playing strength.

WEST	NORTH	EAST	SOUTH
1♣	Dble	3♣	Dble

South's responsive double shows equal length in the majors, perhaps something like ♠ KQ73 ♡ AJ52 ◇ 842 ♣ 65. Partner may bid 3-Major with a minimum or 4-Major with some extra strength.

WEST	NORTH	EAST	SOUTH
1♡	Dble	3♡	Dble

South's responsive double shows equal length in the minors, perhaps a hand such as ♠ 5 ♡ 6532 ◇ AQ96 ♣ KQ75 or perhaps ♠ 7 ♡ 54 ◇ KJ853 ♣ A7642.

If they raise a major, do not make a responsive double with the other major. Simply bid your major. After (1♡) : Double : (3♡), bid 3♠ with ♠ KQ73 ♡ A53 ◇ J872 ♣ 43. Do not double.

WEST	NORTH	EAST	SOUTH
1♠	Dble	2NT	Dble

Where the opponents use 2NT as a strong raise of opener's suit, it is sensible to play Double by fourth hand as responsive. The values may be a bit shaded given the high card values already revealed. South's double here might be suggesting a sacrifice with a hand like ♠ 76 ♡ 8 ◇ QJ872 ♣ Q9854.

The responsive double is not used when third player changes suit. Double then is played as penalties and shows length and strength in the suit doubled. The double is used to expose a likely or a suspected psyche.

WEST	NORTH	EAST	SOUTH
1♡	Dble	1♠	Dble

South's double shows 4+ spades and 6+ points. It indicates South would have bid at least 1♠ and has a respectable hand for that bid. Double with a hand like ♠ KQ974 ♡ 762 ◇ J732 ♣ 5 or ♠ AJ87 ♡ 763 ◇ AQ75 ♣ 62. There is a strong chance that East has bluffed the 1♠ bid with good heart support in reserve. There are many Easts who would try to steal your spade suit with a hand like ♠ 63 ♡ KJ84 ◇ 9864 ♣ 875. After you double, they will run back to hearts sooner or later. You can then bid your spades at whatever level is best or leave it to partner to bid on if you have already shown all your values.

WEST	NORTH	EAST	SOUTH
1♡	Dble	1♠	1NT

South's 1NT promises a stopper in the suit opened, hearts, but does not need a spade stopper. 1NT says 'I would have bid 1NT if third hand had passed.' You are entitled to rely on the doubler to have some cover in the other suits.

COMPETITIVE DOUBLES

With the success and wide appeal of playing doubles by responder for takeout (see *Negative Doubles*, page 95), players turned their attention to other low level double auctions. The old standard was that doubles were for penalties if the bidding had reached the three-level, if the double was of no-trumps or if partner had already bid.

Doubling pre-empts for takeout and doubling for takeout after a raise to the three-level, (1♡) : No : (3♡) : Double, eroded the three-level principle.

WEST	NORTH	EAST	SOUTH
1♡	No	1NT	Dble

Most pairs treat the double of the 1NT response as takeout of the suit opened. South's double is equivalent to (1♡) : Double. This has made inroads into the doubling 1NT = penalties principle.

Competitive doubles follow the principle that all doubles of a suit at the one- or two-level are takeout, regardless of the earlier bidding. The only exceptions arise where your system stipulates that a double is for penalties. A partnership may decide to include as penalty doubles :

- Doubles following a penalty redouble.
- Doubles after an earlier double has been passed for penalties.
- Other specific situations (e.g., doubles after opening 1NT).

All non-stipulated doubles at the one- and two-level are for takeout, regardless of whether the double is by opener, responder or by either defender. Such doubles may occur when an opponent's suit is raised but they are not limited to such cases. Competitive doubles occur far more frequently than the opportunities for a penalty double. They work extremely well in low-level competitive auctions. Even if you missed all your penalties, competitive doubles would be worth adopting. As will be seen later, you may still collect most of your penalties.

West's double in this auction is a competitive double :

WEST	NORTH	EAST	SOUTH
1◇	No	1♡	1♠
Dble			

West is indicating a hand with 3-card support for hearts. It is best to use the competitive double by opener at the one-level to show secondary support for responder's major. This has additional benefits. If opener raises to 2♡ here instead of doubling, responder can be sure of 4-card support. This may be extremely useful if the opponents compete further. In addition, if opener fails to double and fails to raise, responder realises that opener has fewer than three hearts here. A 2◇ or 2♣ rebid by opener would imply 0-2 hearts.

WEST	NORTH	EAST	SOUTH
1◇	No	1♡	1♠
?			

After this start, what action should West take on the following hands?

1. ♠ Q6
   ♡ K65
   ◇ AJ8742
   ♣ K3

2. ♠ 76
   ♡ 43
   ◇ AKJ762
   ♣ A32

3. ♠ 82
   ♡ K72
   ◇ AKJ762
   ♣ AQ

4. ♠ 862
   ♡ Q7
   ◇ AKJ762
   ♣ AK

5. ♠ 6
   ♡ K65
   ◇ AJ874
   ♣ KJ32

6. ♠ 6
   ♡ K653
   ◇ AJ87
   ♣ AJ32

7. ♠ 82
   ♡ 72
   ◇ AKJ76
   ♣ AQ97

8. ♠ 8
   ♡ Q72
   ◇ AKJ76
   ♣ AK85

Answers :

1. Double. Promises 3-card support for responder. The double does not promise extra strength.

2. 2◇. Shows a one-suiter and denies three hearts.

3. Double. Promises 3-card support. Even with a strong hand, double first. If partner take no strong action, you can rebid 3◇ on the next round.

4. 3◇. Shows 16-18 points and a diamond one-suiter. The failure to double denies 3-card support. Consequently a 3♡ rebid by responder would indicate a 6-card suit.

5. Double, showing the 3-card support. If the competitive double were not available, West would be torn between 2♡ and 2♣, with most players opting for 2♡.

6. 2♡. Having the double available means that you do not need the direct raise with 3-card support. Responder can continue, confident that opener has 4-card support for the raise.

7. 2♣. Shows the two-suiter and denies 3-card support for hearts.

8. Double. This is a problem hand without their interference. The hand is too strong for 2♡ but a jump raise to 3♡ would promise 4-card support. Most players rebid 2♣ and hope to be able to show the 3-card support on the next round. The drawback, of course, is that the 2♣ rebid is not forcing in standard methods. Responder is not encouraged to bid on with 6-7 points and preference for clubs. You could find yourself playing in 2♣ with a better (and more valuable) spot available in hearts.

The double solves the problem. The double shows the 3-card support. If partner makes a minimum bid, you can continue with the clubs on the next round. Playing competitive doubles will cause you to welcome rather than fear their interference.

Where the opposition bid comes in at the two-level, opener's competitive double promises shortage in their suit. The ideal holding is secondary support for responder *and* four cards in the unbid suit. However, you may double with either of these holdings. The double of their two-level action therefore does not guarantee 3-card support, although it may be there.

WEST	NORTH	EAST	SOUTH		1.	♠ KJ2	2.	♠ 65
1♦	No	1♠	2♣			♡ 72		♡ AK84
?						♦ AK8632		♦ AJ6532
						♣ J4		♣ 5

Both of these hands are suitable for a double. You need not worry about a heart bid from partner in 1. If partner has four hearts, partner has five spades also, because of the initial 1♠ response. You can convert any heart bid to spades.

Hand 2 is awkward but a 2♦ rebid or Pass could lose the heart suit completely if North produces a club raise. Responder should assume opener has the missing suit rather than 3-card support and bid accordingly. If opener has the 3-card support, opener can revert to responder's suit.

Another advantage of using the competitive double this way arises when opener fails to double. Pass or 2♦ by opener would deny 3-card support for responder and deny four cards in the unbid suit. A 2♦ rebid might be ♠ A ♡ K72 ♦ AQ9854 ♣ 652.

WEST	NORTH	EAST	SOUTH		1.	♠ KJ62	2.	♠ K65
1♡	No	2♣	2♦			♡ AJ963		♡ AKJ842
?						♦ 7		♦ K4
						♣ KJ4		♣ 52

Hand 1 is ideal for the double. You have secondary support for clubs and four spades as well. With Hand 2 you would rebid 2♡. The failure to double denies interest outside hearts.

Responder uses the competitive double freely too.

WEST	NORTH	EAST	SOUTH		1.	♠ KJ962	2.	♠ K6542
1♣	No	1♠	2♦			♡ A862		♡ A9732
No	No	?				♦ 7		♦ 6
						♣ 983		♣ 52

Responder should double on both hands. Neither hand is strong enough for a 2♡ rebid. As a new suit rebid, that would be forcing. The advantage of doubling is that it promises no more strength than your original bid promised. East's double here is comparable to a first round negative double if the bidding had started 1♣ : (2♦). East would double 2♦ on each of these hands.

Competitive doubles may also be used by either defender.

WEST	NORTH	EAST	SOUTH
1◇	1♠	2◇	No
No	Dble		

North's double is for takeout. The failure to double on the first round suggests North has only three hearts. With ♠ KQ762 ♡ AJ76 ◇ 7 ♣ K98, North should double 1◇. However, with ♠ KQ762 ♡ A76 ◇ 7 ♣ KJ98 or with ♠ KQ762 ♡ A76 ◇ J2 ♣ K98, it is better to overcall 1♠ and double 2◇ if the opportunity arises.

WEST	NORTH	EAST	SOUTH
1◇	1♡	2◇	Dble

South's double is for takeout. The expectancy for South is five cards in the other major and tolerance for North's hearts (probably just a doubleton). South may have clubs too, but that is not promised.

WEST	NORTH	EAST	SOUTH
1♠	2♡	2♠	Dble

South's double is for takeout and resembles a double by responder. South should have both minors and tolerance (doubleton) for partner's suit.

WEST	NORTH	EAST	SOUTH
1◇	1♠	2♣	Dble

Where responder changes suit South's double is still for takeout. Here South should have a strong heart suit and no worse than a doubleton in spades. ♠ Q6 ♡ AJ10862 ◇ 543 ♣ 62 would suffice.

It can be seen that negative doubles and responsive doubles at the two-level are just specific cases of the competitive double. There is no reason why the opening side cannot use responsive doubles.

WEST	NORTH	EAST	SOUTH
1♡	1♠	Dble	2♣
Dble			

East's (negative) double was for the minors. West's responsive double implies equal length in the minors (perhaps 0-5-4-4, perhaps 2-5-3-3) and asks responder to choose the minor. There is no need to guess when the double can enlist partner's assistance.

WEST	NORTH	EAST	SOUTH
1♡	1♠	No	2♡
Dble			

Where second player overcalls, fourth player often makes a cue bid of opener's suit to show a strong raise (known as a cue raise or unassuming cue bid – see page 110). How do you play West's double of the cue raise? It could be lead directing but partner would be expected to lead your suit anyway. A sensible use of the double is for takeout of the suit overcalled since RHO's action is a kind of raise. West might hold ♠ – ♡ KQ762 ◇ A873 ♣ KJ62 or ♠ 7 ♡ AJ432 ◇ KQ87 ♣ AQ8.

PLAYING FOR PENALTIES

If the opponents bid and raise a suit to the three-level, it makes sense to play that the double of the suit raised is still for takeout.

WEST	NORTH	EAST	SOUTH
1♠	2♣	No	3♣
Dble			

It is rare to get rich by doubling them when they bid a suit and raise it at once. West's double = takeout.

However, if the raise to the three-level is belated or it is a re-raise to the three-level or it is a new suit at the three-level, it is better to use the double for penalties. In addition if partner has already taken some descriptive action, play double for penalties.

WEST	NORTH	EAST	SOUTH
1♠	Dble	2♠	Dble
3♠	Dble		

North's first double was for takeout. South's double was responsive, showing equal length in the minors. It does not make sense for North to use a further takeout double, given the information about South's hand. North is strongly suggesting penalties.

Pass for penalties

Suppose you wish to play for penalties at the one- or two-level. The method is straightforward. You pass for penalties, hoping partner will reopen the bidding with a takeout double. If partner does double for takeout you leave the double in. Again you pass for penalties.

	WEST	NORTH	EAST	SOUTH
♠ 7		No	1♠	2♦
♡ A3	?			
♦ K10954				
♣ K9832				

The best hands for penalties are those with a shortage in partner's suit, strong trumps and around 9-11 HCP. The West hand is ideal. West should pass 2♦, hoping that East will re-open with a double.

WEST	NORTH	EAST	SOUTH
1♦	1♠	No	No
Dble	2♠	Dble	

East's double is for penalties. East could have doubled 1♠ for takeout. The double of 2♠ implies East would have passed out the double of 1♠ for penalties. Poor North.

	WEST	NORTH	EAST	SOUTH
♠ K87	1♦	No	1♡	2♣
♡ A3	?			
♦ A1095				
♣ K1098				

West should pass. When 2♣ reverts to East, a double will be the most frequent re-opening action if East has less than game values. West passes the double and collects whatever penalties are going.

S.O.S. REDOUBLES

The facts of life are that from time to time the opponents will catch you for penalties. Most of the time you will be able to do nothing about it. You will have to grin and bear it (or bear it without grinning). Occasionally, however, you may be able to find a better spot. In general it does not pay to rescue partner unless the suit to which you are running is at least as strong as partner's is likely to be. A better chance for a rescue is when you have two suits either of which partner may be able to support.

SOUTH	WEST	NORTH	EAST	SOUTH
♠ –	1♡	1♠	No	No
♡ 873	Dble	No	No	?
◇ KJ762				
♣ QJ942				

You were too weak to take any action over 1♠ (and if you did bid, partner may have bid higher in spades). Now your worst fears are realised as East leaves in West's double for penalties. Almost certainly clubs or diamonds will be better for your side than spades, but which one?

The answer is to redouble for rescue, asking partner to choose a suit other than spades.

The redouble of a takeout double normally shows strength. The redouble of a penalty double of a suit is for takeout. The same applies when a takeout double is passed for penalties. The redouble is for takeout.

WEST	NORTH	EAST	SOUTH
1♣	Dble	No	No
Rdbl			

South has passed North's takeout double for penalties. West has redoubled, asking East to pick some spot other than clubs.

How do your play this sequence?

WEST	NORTH	EAST	SOUTH
1◇	2♣	Dble	Rdbl

As the double is for takeout, the redouble is not S.O.S. for rescue. There is no intimation yet that West plans to pass for penalties. It makes no sense however to play the redouble for takeout. East has doubled to show the majors. If South held the majors too, South should pass, eager to defend.

Many pairs use this redouble (partner has overcalled, RHO has doubled for takeout) as promising a top honour in partner's suit. The holding will be a doubleton or longer and it asks partner to lead the suit bid. Partner may have overcalled with a suit headed by the A-Q. Partner will naturally be reluctant to lead such a suit later. Your redouble promises K-x or longer, telling partner that the lead is safe. An immediate raise would deny a top honour and warn partner against making a risky lead in that suit.

LEAD-DIRECTING BIDS

There are many competitive positions where you intend to bid on but where you would not be too pleased to receive the lead of the suit you are bidding. You would much prefer the lead of some other suit. You will often have the chance to tell partner the suit you want led.

	WEST	NORTH	EAST	SOUTH
♠ J107642	1♠	2♣	2♠	No
♡ AKQ	No	3♣	No	No
◇ Q83	?			
♣ 7				

What action should West take now?

You should certainly compete with 3♠ and almost all the time, that will end the bidding. There are some opponents, thank heavens, who do not know when to give up. An incurable North or South may push on to 4♣. Clearly you would rather have a heart lead than a spade. Bid 3♡ asking for that lead. It is not a game try as you passed 2♠. A 3♡ bid over 2♠ would have been a game try. Passing 2♠ and later bidding a new suit asks for that suit to be led.

This situation is most common when you plan to bid on after a competitive auction to game level.

WEST	NORTH	EAST	SOUTH
1♡	1♠	4♡	4♠
?			

If West plans to bid on to 5♡, West can take the opportunity to bid 5♣ or 5◇ to ask for the lead of that suit if they decide to bid on to 5♠.

	WEST	NORTH	EAST	SOUTH
♠ 763	1♠	3◇	4♠	
♡ 76542	5◇	6♠	No	No
◇ KQJ98	?			
♣ —				

Partner lacks two defensive tricks (did not double) and 7◇ will not be expensive. However, you should insure against 7♠. Bid 7♣ en route. That way partner will find the club lead should they try the grand slam.

There is a good case for your bidding 5♣ over 4♠ for the lead. There would be a good case for bidding 7♣ over 6♠ if you held ♠ 763 ♡ 7654 ◇ KQJ98 ♣ 6. The opponents do not know your lead-directing 7♣ is not genuine. They are hardly likely to bid 7♠ when you are advertising you can ruff the first round of clubs.

WEST	NORTH	EAST	SOUTH
1◇	2♠	Dble	?

With ♠ K763 ♡ 54 ◇ 6432 ♣ AKQ, you are worth 4♠. However, bid 3♣ now and follow with 4♠ later and partner will lead clubs if they push on to the five-level.

CUE RAISES OR THE UNASSUMING CUE BID

WEST	NORTH	EAST	SOUTH
1◇	1♠	No	3♠

How do you play South's raise to 3♠? In traditional methods it shows a strong hand, usually opening values, with good support for partner. This approach is not popular among most top players who prefer to use immediate raises of an overcall as pre-emptive. With a strong raise, bid the opposition's suit.

WEST	NORTH	EAST	SOUTH
1◇	1♠	No	2◇

The unassuming cue bid uses this bid as a hand worth a raise to 2♠ based on high card values. Partner can reject the invitation by bidding 2♠ and accept the invitation by bidding a new suit or 3♠ or more.

Cue raises use the two-level cue bid as a two-way bid, either a sound raise of the overcall to the two-level or as a hand worth a game invitation without support for the overcall. The complete structure works like this :

Raise to the two-level (2♠) = Pre-emptive raise, good support but with 9 losers. For example : ♠ KQ98 ♡ 7653 ◇ J7 ♣ 873.

Raise to the three-level (3♠) = Pre-emptive raise, good support and with 8 losers. Something like : ♠ K987 ♡ 7 ◇ 983 ♣ K8743.

Raise to the four-level (4♠) = Pre-emptive, excellent support and 7 losers. Perhaps : ♠ K9872 ♡ 7 ◇ 93 ♣ K8743.

These bids suggest that the value lies in playing the hand rather than defending. If the opponents bid above you, partner knows there is strong support opposite, very little defensive strength (at most one defensive trick) and the promised playing strength. Partner has a sound basis to judge whether to bid higher or defend.

Cue their suit at the four-level (4◇) = Strong raise to game based on high card values and good defence, 6-loser hand.

Cue their suit at the three-level (3◇) = Strong raise to the three-level, based on high cards and good defence, 7-loser hand.

Cue their suit at the two-level (2◇) = Either a strong raise to the two-level based on sound defensive values, 8 loser hand, or a strong all-round hand worth an invitation to game but without support for partner's suit. With a minimum overcall, partner should rebid the overcalled suit. Advancer may pass this or make a natural invitational bid. With a strong overcall, partner should bid a new suit, bid no-trumps or cue the enemy suit in return.

Raising partner's suit via a cue bid indicates the value of the hand probably lies in defending rather than bidding higher if they bid over the level at which you wish to play. The cue raise shows good values outside the trump suit and the trump support tends to be weaker than if a direct raise is made.

9. UNCOMMON BUT EFFECTIVE CONVENTIONS

The conventions in this chapter are not in common use, yet they work very well. You may find that some of them are not permitted in your club or in the lower tournament grades. You will have to curb your enthusiasm to try them until you play at a high enough level, usually national championship grade, where they are accepted.

RCO TWO-OPENINGS

These use the opening bids of 2♡, 2♠ and 2NT to show weak two-suiters. The strength is 6-10 HCP and the patterns are 5-5 at least.

2♡ = Rank. Two suits of the same rank, both majors or minors.
2♠ = Colour. Two suits of the same colour, reds or blacks.
2NT = Odd. Two suits of different colour and different rank, either spades + diamonds or hearts + clubs.

Although these bids are hard to combat, the main purpose in using these bids is to provide a descriptive bid for hands which are powerful in distribution but weakish in high cards. Each of these would be worth a RCO opening.

♠ 5	♠ AJ1063	♠ –	♠ J109764
♡ KQ764	♡ QJ1054	♡ 94	♡ –
◇ QJ8732	◇ 7	◇ KJ8763	◇ KQJ98
♣ 8	♣ 93	♣ KQ763	♣ J5
Open 2♠	Open 2♡	Open 2♡	Open 2NT

RCO, as you have seen, stands for Rank-Colour-Odd or, if you need a memory aid, Responder Can Operate. It is similar to the CRASH openings where 2♡ = Colour, 2♠ = Rank, 2NT = Shape (the pointed suits – spades and diamonds – or the rounded suits – hearts and clubs). RCO has the advantage that with both majors you open 2♡ and can play in hearts at the two-level. Playing CRASH, the opening bid with both majors is 2♠ which compels you to reach 3♡ if that is your fit. If you are lucky enough to own the majors, it is silly to push your side to the three-level when it is just as easy to play RCO and to buy the contract at the two-level. The extra trick is a heavy price to pay for a cute acronym.

Responding to 2♡ or 2♠ with a weak hand

Bid a suit where you have 3+ cards. Usually choose the cheapest option. You may pass if you judge partner has the two-suiter including the suit bid. You may also pass if you have a really weak hand with no inkling which suit partner has.

After a suit bid, opener will 'pass or correct'. Opener passes if holding the suit bid. If not, opener bids the cheaper of the other two suits.

WEST	NORTH	EAST	SOUTH
2♡	No	?	

2♡ = majors or minors. What action should East take with these hands?

1. ♠ K87	2. ♠ 8	3. ♠ 9	4. ♠ 876
♡ 86	♡ K97	♡ K986	♡ Q97
◇ QJ874	◇ QJ874	◇ KJ63	◇ 876
♣ K98	♣ J986	♣ 9872	♣ J752

Answers :

1. Bid 2♠. If partner has the majors, that is where you want to play. If partner has the minors, partner will convert to 3♣ and you can then support the diamonds.

2. Pass. It is highly likely that partner has the majors and it is unnecessary to bid 3◇ and push yourself to 3♡. Yes, partner could have the minors but for the moment, anyway, you ought to pass. If they pass it out and partner does have the minors, you will have to console yourself as you go many down that they were cold for at least game, perhaps slam, in a major.

3. Bid 3◇. If partner has the minors, you prefer the diamonds. If partner has the majors, you are prepared to be at the three-level with a 9-card fit.

4. Pass. You have no idea which suits partner holds but you are so hopelessly weak, you may as well pass and let them try and sort it out. If they double, you will be able to land in one of partner's suits.

Responding to 2NT with a weak hand

Again you bid a suit but 3♣ is not available as that is the strong enquiry. With ♠ 762 ♡ Q94 ◇ KQ986 ♣ A2, bid 3◇. Partner will pass with diamonds-spades and will bid 3♡ with hearts-clubs. With ♠ KQ98 ♡ 5 ◇ KQJ874 ♣ 62, pass 2NT. Partner surely has hearts-clubs and you are in deep trouble. If they double, you will be able to escape into 3◇ (see page 115).

If you have an excellent fit for both options, you may jump to game as an advance sacrifice. Suppose partner has opened 2NT and you have ♠ A9854 ♡ 4 ◇ 76 ♣ KQ874, bid 4♠. Opener will pass with spades-diamonds and convert to 5♣ with clubs-hearts.

Responding to 2♡ or 2♠ with a strong hand

If you have enough for game or at least enough for a game invitation, bid 2NT. This asks opener to show the suits held and whether the hand is a maximum or minimum. Opener bids the cheaper suit if minimum, the higher suit if maximum.

After 2♡ : 2NT relay

3♣ = the minors and minimum.
3♢ = the minors and maximum.
3♡ = the majors and minimum.
3♠ = the majors and maximum.

After 2♠ : 2NT relay

3♣ = clubs + spades and minimum.
3♢ = diamonds + hearts and minimum.
3♡ = diamonds + hearts and maximum.
3♠ = clubs + spades and maximum.

Responding to 2NT with a strong hand

The strong relay is 3♣ which asks opener to show the suits held and the range of the opening. With a minimum, opener bids the cheaper suit held. With a maximum, opener bids the higher suit but bids 3NT if the suits are clubs and hearts.

After 2NT : 3♣ relay

3♢ = diamonds + spades and minimum.
3♡ = clubs + hearts and minimum.
3♠ = diamonds + spades and maximum.
3NT = clubs + hearts and maximum.

After the reply to the strong relay, responder will usually have enough information to place the contract. Any game bid is to play. If opener has shown a minimum hand, responder's bid of one of opener's suits below game is to play. For example,

WEST	EAST	
2♡	2NT	2♡ showed the majors or the minors. In reply to 2NT, opener's 3♡ showed the majors and a minimum.
3♡	3♠	Responder now wishes to play in 3♠.

If opener shows a maximum, the position is game-forcing. If responder now bids a minor at the four-level which opener holds, this sets trumps and asks for key cards. A four-level minor not held by opener sets opener's major suit. For example :

WEST	EAST	
2♡	2NT	3♠ = majors and maximum. Now 4♣ sets hearts and 4♢ sets spades. Opener shows key cards
3♠	?	for the suit set.

DEFENDING AGAINST RCO

The difficulty in defending against RCO is that there is no anchor suit.
You should have a strong hand or a strong suit to enter the auction.
Double = 16+ points, any shape except for the 2NT or 3NT bids.
2NT = 19-21 balanced; 3NT = 22-24 balanced.
Suit bids = Natural but below 16 HCP. At the three-level, a good 6-card
suit and a 6-loser hand is enough.

With other hands, pass initially and if appropriate, make a takeout
double when opener's suits have been clarified.

WEST	NORTH	EAST	SOUTH
2♡	No	2♠	No
No	?		

Treat the position as a weak 2♠
opening, except you know opener is 5-5
in the majors. Any action by you, double
or 2NT or suit bid, will be under 16 HCP.

WEST	NORTH	EAST	SOUTH
2♡	No	2♠	No
3♣	?		

Treat the position as over a 3♣ pre-
empt, except you know opener is 5-5 in
the minors. Any action by you, double
or suit bid, will be under 16 HCP.

In fourth seat, treat any weak action by RHO as their opening. Double
for takeout if short in that suit. With length in that suit, it is likely that
opener has the other suits. You can pass and wait for the correction
before doubling.

In reply to the double in second seat

Pass = strong in the suit doubled.
2♠ if available = weak, not forcing.
2NT = puppet to 3♣ on weak hands. After partner bids 3♣, pass with
clubs or bid your long suit. Partner passes unless very strong or with a
misfit.
Suit bids at the three-level = natural, forcing to game, normally 8 HCP or
better.
3NT in reply to the double = 8-11 points, 4-3-3-3 pattern.
2NT-then-3NT = 12-14 points, 4-3-3-3 pattern.

This is the same defence as against the multi-2♢ where no anchor suit
is known (see page 25). With borderline decisions, it is often best to wait
till opener's suits are clarified and then enter the fray. It is no fun playing
in a suit where opener has five cards.

Bidding over their 2NT opening

Double = 16+ points, any shape.
Suit bids at the three-level = Strong suit, 6 losers.

Over the double use 3♣ puppet to 3♢ with weak hands. Other suit
bids in reply to the double are forcing to game.

COUNTERMEASURES BY THE OPENING SIDE

1. They double the opening

Suit bids = Pass or correct.

Relay bids = Strong enquiry as usual.

Redouble = 'Please make the cheapest bid and then pass my next bid.' This enables responder to escape into a long suit with no fit for either of opener's suits. Suppose partner has opened 2NT, RHO doubles and you hold ♠ KQ98 ♡ 5 ♢ KQJ874 ♣ 62. You know partner has hearts and clubs and if you bid 3♢, opener will correct to 3♡. You then have to bid 4♢ (or 3NT) and blood will flow . . . yours. Best is to redouble, partner will bid 3♣ and you can escape into 3♢. That's the best you can manage on such a misfit. When calamity strikes, cheer up and focus on all the good results the method has brought you.

Pass = 'If this is your suit, this is where I wish to play.'

Suppose partner opens 2♡, double by RHO and you hold ♠ 76 ♡ Q87 ♢ AKJ64 ♣ 762. You should pass. If partner has the majors, this is your best spot. With the minors, opener will remove the double.

If partner opened 2NT, double by RHO, pass by you indicates preference for clubs over hearts. You cannot bid 3♣ as a rescue since 3♣ is the strong relay.

If the double is passed back to the opener, pass if you hold the suit doubled. If not, you can show various hand types with the other suits. It depends on how much space you have.

WEST	NORTH	EAST	SOUTH	
2♡	Dble	No	No	Pass = Both majors. Other bids show both minors :
?				2♠ = Spade fragment, 3-0-5-5.

Redouble = Longer diamonds.

2NT = Longer clubs.

3♣ = Equal length in the minors.

WEST	NORTH	EAST	SOUTH	
2♠	Dble	No	No	Pass = Spades + clubs. Other bids show the red suits.
?				Redouble = Longer hearts.

2NT = Longer diamonds.

3♣ = Club fragment, 0-5-5-3.

3♢ = Equal length in the red suits.

The principle is that redouble shows extra length in the more distant suit. This gives the partnership the best chance of landing in the least expensive contract.

The same principle applies when partner runs to a suit, this is doubled by RHO and you hold the other suits.

WEST	NORTH	EAST	SOUTH	
2♠	Dble	3♣	Dble	**Pass** = Spades + clubs. Other bids show the red suits.
?				Redouble = Red suits, longer hearts.

3◇ = Equal length in the red suits or diamonds longer. Here you do not have room to do everything.

WEST	NORTH	EAST	SOUTH	
2NT	Dble	No	No	**Redouble** = Extra length in the more distant suit. Over 3♣, 3◇ = diamonds + spades with the spades longer.
?				

3♣ = Clubs + hearts with suits equal or clubs longer.

3◇ = Diamonds + spades with suits equal or diamonds longer.

2. They bid a suit over the opening

Double = Takeout at the two-level or three-level with invitational values. It is possible to play the double for takeout or for penalties but experience has shown that takeout doubles work better. It enables you to find a fit when opener has the other suits which is often the case. In reply to the double, opener bids the cheaper suit if minimum, the higher suit if maximum. With 5+ cards in their suit, opener may leave the double in.

A suit bid by responder is still to pass or correct. It suggests less than invitational values. Opener passes or corrects to the cheapest of the other suits. With great playing strength (6-5), opener may raise the suit or make more than a minimum bid.

Double = For penalties at the four-level or higher.

Other competitive decisions

If responder has made a correctable bid and opener has revealed the suits held, double by responder is for penalties.

If responder has made a correctable bid but opener has not had a chance to show the suits held, double by responder says, 'Pass if you hold their suit, otherwise I wish to bid on.'

WEST	NORTH	EAST	SOUTH	
2♡	Dble	3♣	Dble	Opener has shown both minors by passing 3♣. Responder's double of 4♠ is for penalties and opener must pass.
No	3♠	No	4♠	
No	No	Dble		

WEST	NORTH	EAST	SOUTH	
2♡	No	3♣	4♠	Opener's suits are unknown. East's double asks opener to pass with spades or bid 5♣ with the minors.
No	No	Dble		

If responder has used a strong relay, all doubles are penalties.

RCO AS A DEFENCE AGAINST THEIR 1NT OPENING

Most of the methods of competing over 1NT have little scope for showing all or even most of the two-suiter combinations (see Chapter 6, p. 76 onwards). Playing RCO over their 1NT shows all the two-suiters while retaining 2♡ and 2♠ for one-suiters.

After (1NT-weak)

Double = Penalties.

2♡/2♠ = One-suiter.

2♣ = Rank – Two suits of the same rank, majors or minors.

2♢ = Colour – Two suits of the same colour, reds or blacks.

2NT = Odd – Two non-touching suits, spades + diamonds or hearts + clubs.

Against (1NT-strong)

Same as over the weak 1NT except that Double is used for the 'Odd' combinations, the non-touching suits.

These actions are the same in second seat or in fourth seat.

Against a strong NT it is possible to show all two-suiters at the two-level. Using a penalty double against the weak 1NT means the non-touching suits can be shown only at the three-level. It was noted in Chapter 6 (page 78) that if playing the Brozel Double to show any one-suiter, all two-suiter combinations could be shown at the two-level :

2♣ = majors or minors.

2♢ = reds or blacks.

2♡ = hearts + clubs.

2♠ = spades + diamonds.

Bidding over the RCO takeout over their 1NT

After (1NT) : 2♣ or (1NT) : 2♢

With a weak hand, you may pass or bid a suit you can stand at the cheapest level. Partner will pass or correct.

With a strong hand, bid 2NT. Answers are the same as over the 2♡/2♠ RCO openings (see page 113).

After (1NT) : 2NT showing the non-touching suits

Same as over the RCO 2NT opening (see pages 112-113).

After (1NT) : Double showing the non-touching suits

Responder may pass the double, bid a suit with a weak hand on the pass-or-correct basis or bid 2NT as the strong relay (partner's replies follow the same structure as on page 113).

COUNTERMEASURES BY THE 1NT SIDE

These can be found on page 84 dealing with actions where the intervention did not show an anchor suit.

TARTAN TWO BIDS

Tartan twos combine Acol twos in the majors with weak two-suiters including at least one major.

2♡ = Acol Two with long hearts, *or*
      balanced hand of 21-22 points, *or*
      weak two-suiter, hearts and a minor.

2♠ = Acol Two with long spades, *or*
      weak two-suiter, spades and another suit.

2NT = Weak two-suiter in the minors.

Responses to 2♡

2♠ = Relay, need not be a strong hand. Opener rebids 2NT with 21-22 balanced (normal continuations), 3♣/3♢ with the weak two-suiter, 3♡ with the Acol Two or 3♠/4♣/4♢ if you have an Acol Two and this is your second suit.

2NT = Strong relay, game prospects over the weak two-suiter, slam potential opposite one of the strong varieties. Opener rebids as over 2♠ except that 3NT = 21-22 balanced. If opener rebids 3♣ or 3♢, 3♡ by responder is invitational. Any other rebid by responder below game is forcing.

2♡ : 2♠, 3♣/3♢ : 3♡ is to play but 2♡ : 2NT, 3♣/3♢ : 3♡ invites.

3♣/3♢ = To play opposite the weak variety, but enough for game opposite 21-22 balanced. Denies a 4-card major. Does not ask for correction.

3♡ = 3+ hearts, 6-10 points. Pre-emptive opposite the weak variety, forcing over the strong variety. Denies four spades.

4♡ = 3+ hearts, 11-15 points, no ace. To play opposite the weak variety. Worth slam opposite a strong variety. A new suit by opener is a cue bid. Responder cue bids kings in reply. 4NT by opener is to play with the 21-22 balanced hand when two aces are missing.

3NT = 11-15 points, 3+ hearts and including at least one ace. Opener bids 4♡ with the weak two-suiter. With a strong version, 4NT asks for aces, suit bids are cues.

Responses to 2♠

2NT = Relay. Opener bids 3♣/3♢/3♡ to show the second suit or 3♠ with an Acol one-suiter. 4♣/4♢/4♡ = Acol two-suiter.

3♣/3♢/3♡ = To play opposite the weak variety. Does not ask to be corrected.

3♠/4♠/3NT = Same as 3♡/4♡/3NT over the 2♡ opening but with spade support, of course.

Responses to 2NT (both minors)

3♣/3♦ = To play.

4♣/4♦ = Invitational.

3NT/5♣/5♦ = To play. 5♣ or 5♦ is likely to be pre-emptive.

4♡ = Roman Key Card Blackwood with clubs as trumps.

4♠ = Roman Key Card Blackwood with diamonds as trumps.

3♡/3♠ = Natural and forcing, asking for doubleton support. To play in 4♡/4♠, respond 3♡/3♠ and rebid 4♡/4♠.

4NT = Blackwood for aces.

DEFENCE AGAINST TARTAN 2♡ OR 2♠

Adopt the same defence as against a weak two opening (see page 14). Although 2♡ or 2♠ might be a strong opening, it is highly likely if you have a strong hand that opener has the weak two-suiter. Since their opening bid is natural if weak, the same defence as against a weak two reduces memory problems. Whenever one option of a multi is a weak hand including the suit bid, adopt the same defence as against weak twos.

COUNTERMEASURES BY THE OPENING SIDE

After (Double)

No bid = To play opposite the weak variety.

Redouble = For penalties. Like 1♡ : (Double) : Redouble.

Other bids = Usual meanings.

After a suit bid

Double = Penalties

Suit bids = Invitational and correctable.

DEFENCE AGAINST 2NT FOR THE MINORS

Double = Penalties. Double + later double = penalties. No bid + later double = Takeout.

3♡/3♠ = Natural one-suiter, 6 losers.

3♣ = Takeout, both majors, equal length or heart preference.

3♦ = Takeout with both majors, preference for spades.

4♣/4♦ = Strong takeout with both majors and void in the suit bid.

COUNTERMEASURES BY THE OPENING SIDE

Over Double : No bid = For takeout but with no preference for either minor. Redouble = To play (later doubles are penalties).

Other bids have normal meanings.

Over suit bids : Double = penalties. Minor suit bid is invitational.

Other bids have normal meanings.

OPENING 2♣ WHEN PLAYING OTHER TWOS AS MULTIS

There are many methods which use only the 2♣ opening as a strong bid. For example :

2♦ = multi, weak two in either major.

2♥ = weak two-suiter, 5+ hearts and another suit.

2♠ = weak two-suiter, 5+ spades and another suit.

2NT = weak two-suiter in the minors.

Another option is 2♦ Multi and 2♥/2♠/2NT as RCO.

Such methods work best in conjunction with a forcing 1♣ opening. The 1♣ opening need not be strong but as responder must reply (using 1♦ as a negative), opener's rebid can show a powerful hand. For those not using a forcing 1♣, the 2♣ opening has a lot of ground to cover. Those who play many multis are prepared to accept occasional losses from the 2♣ opening (which occur rarely) in exchange for the more frequent profits generated by the far more common multis. Nevertheless, the 2♣ opening can be modified to cover more strong hands than simply those of 23 HCP up or worth a force to game.

Balanced hands of 21-22 HCP can be included in the multi-2♦. Balanced hands of 23 HCP or more come within the 2♣ opening, which also includes hands of 19-22 points and a 6-card suit.

The responses to 2♣ are standard, with 2♦ negative and others as natural and usually 8+ points (see page 17). The variations arise with opener's rebid after a negative response.

After 2♣ : 2♦, opener's rebids are :

3♣/3♦/3♥/3♠ = 19-22, 6+ suit (an Acol two 1-suiter).

3NT = 19-22, solid minor, 9 running tricks.

2NT = 23-24 balanced, not forcing. Usual continuations.

2♠ = Game force with 5+ spades. Standard continuations.

2♥ = Artificial game force without 5+ spades.

After 2♣ : 2♦, 2♥ : ? responder's rebids are :

2♠ = second negative, 0-4 points.

Others = natural, 5-7 points.

After 2♣ : 2♦, 2♥ : 2♠, opener's rebids are :

2NT = 25+ balanced, game-forcing. Normal continuations.

3♣/3♦/3♥ = Natural, game-forcing.

THE KABEL 3NT OPENING

There is little mileage in opening 4NT. If you need to ask for aces, you can always start with some other bid and ask for aces later. Some pairs use 4NT as a specific ace ask. Partner replies 5♣ with no ace, 5◇/5♡/5♠/6♣ with the ace in the suit bid, 5NT with two non-touching aces, 6◇/6♡/6♠ with two aces showing the ace in the bid suit and the ace in the next suit up, with 6NT showing both minor suit aces. The method is reasonable but has the drawback that some answers may come in too high.

Using 3NT as a specific ace ask solves this drawback and gives up little of value. 3NT as a natural strong opening is almost never used. Players prefer to open with some strong 2-opening to leave more room to investigate the best game and possible slams. The Gambling 3NT is a two-edged sword and, because of its inherent danger, is not popular among top players.

Although opening 3NT as an immediate ace ask will not occur often, it works very well when it does occur. If the 3NT opening is not needed in your system, the Kabel 3NT is recommended.

The Kabel 3NT asks partner whether an ace is held.

Responses

4♣ = No ace.
4◇/4♡/4♠/5♣ = Ace in the suit bid.
5◇/5♡/5♠/6♣ = Ace in the suit bid + ace in the next suit along.
4NT = Two non-touching aces.
5NT = Three aces.

After the reply to 3NT, a suit bid is a sign off and 4NT asks for specific kings. If 4NT is not available, 5NT asks for kings.

Replies to 4NT king ask

5♣ = No king.
5◇/5♡/5♠/6♣ = King in the suit bid.
6◇/6♡/6♠ = King in the suit bid + king in the next suit up.
6NT = Kings in both minors.
5NT = Two kings in non-touching suits.
7♣ = Three kings.

Replies to 5NT king ask

6♣ = No king.
6◇/6♡/6♠ = King in the suit bid.
6NT = King of clubs.
7♣ = Two kings.

Examples of the Kabel 3NT opening

Opportunities to ask for specific aces with your first bid are rare. You need a hand of 11 playing tricks or better when finding the correct ace(s) or king(s) solves the problem whether to stop at the five-level, bid six or bid seven. These hands usually have one very long suit or two long suits. One advantage of starting with 3NT is that you will usually not encounter opposition bidding. Starting with artificial strong 2♣ or 2♢ allows destructive intervention at a lower level. Where opener has a very long suit, the opponents often have long suits too. The bidding therefore escalates before opener can describe the hand or discover the information needed for a small slam or a grand slam.

The following hands all arose in tournament play.

WEST	EAST	WEST	EAST
♠ AK	♠ 98643	3NT	4♢
♡ AKQ1098632	♡ 75	4NT	5♣
♢ 32	♢ A64	6♡	No
♣ –	♣ 1098	4♢ = ace of diamonds	
		5♣ = no king	

WEST	EAST	WEST	EAST
♠ KQJ	♠ A8	3NT	4NT
♡ AKQJ9876	♡ 3	7♡	No
♢ KQ	♢ A742	4NT = two aces in non-	
♣ –	♣ J87642	touching suits	

How would you bid this if the bidding started 2♣ : 3♣?

WEST	EAST	WEST	EAST
♠ AKQ	♠ 73	3NT	4♡
♡ K8	♡ AQJ	7♣	No
♢ –	♢ 987642	4♡ = ace of hearts	
♣ AKQJ10965	♣ 32		

WEST	EAST	WEST	EAST
♠ AKQJ98543	♠ 72	3NT	4♣
♡ A	♡ 976	4NT	6♣
♢ A	♢ 52	7NT	No
♣ A2	♣ KJ8743	4♣ = no ace	
		6♣ = king of clubs	

There is no doubt the Kabel 3NT will arise rarely. However, if you do not need 3NT for other purposes, why not use the Kabel 3NT and be well prepared when the giant freak does occur?

5-CARD MAJOR STAYMAN

Many pairs include a 5-card major within their 1NT opening. This enables the strong hand to play the no-trump contracts (otherwise the bidding may well go 1♡ : 1NT or 1♠ : 1NT and the weak hand is the no-trumps declarer). The 2♣ enquiry then asks whether a 5-card major is held.

Simple replies to 2♣

2♡/2♠ = 5-card suit.
2♢ = No 5-card major.

After 1NT : 2♣, 2♢ : ?

2♡ = Four hearts, may have four spades. Not forcing. Opener may pass or raise to 3♡, bid 2♠ or 2NT with no major.
2♠ = Four spades, denies four hearts. Not forcing. Opener may pass or raise to 3♠, or bid 2NT without support for spades.
2NT = No 4-card major. Invites 3NT.
3♣ = Natural, not forcing, not encouraging.
3♢ = Artificial, forcing, asks for 4-card majors (Stayman). Opener bids 3♡ with hearts or both majors, 3♠ with spades or 3NT with no 4-card major. Over 3♡, responder can bid 3NT with four spades, allowing opener to bid 4♠ when holding both majors. The 3♢ rebid by responder guarantees at least one 4-card major.
3♡/3♠ = Forcing with 5+ major.

The Lavings extension

After 1NT : 2♣,

2♢ = Minimum, no 5-card major.
2♡/2♠ = Minimum, 5-card suit.
2NT = Maximum, no 5-card suit.
3♣/3♢/3♡/3♠ = Maximum, 5-card suit.

After 2♢ or 2NT, 3♢ is Stayman, asking for 4-card majors. After 2♢ or 2NT, 3♣ is Baron, asking for 4-card suits up-the-line. It is sensible to use the 3♢ Stayman enquiry to say 'Bid a major unless you are 4-3-3-3. Bid 3NT if you are 4-3-3-3.' The 3♣ enquiry can be used to reach a major even if opener is 4-3-3-3.

OPENER 1	OPENER 2	RESPONDER
♠ 972	♠ 97	♠ 843
♡ AQ84	♡ AQ84	♡ KJ63
♢ AK8	♢ AK82	♢ 954
♣ KJ4	♣ KJ4	♣ AQ7

After 1NT : 2♣, 2NT : 3♢ opener 1 bids 3NT, the best spot, while opener 2 bids 3♡ and reaches 4♡, also the best spot.

5-card major Stayman over 2NT

It is quite common to open 2NT with a 5-card major, especially when the partnership methods do not provide for another way of showing a balanced 21-22 count with a 5-card major. It is useful to play 3♣ to ask whether opener does have a 5-card major.

Simple replies to 3♣

3◇ = No 5-card major.
3♡/3♠ = 5-card suit.

Over 3◇, responder can bid a 4-card major, forcing. If responder bids 3♡, opener bids 3♠ if holding four spades.

The drawback to this is that responder plays many of the 4-4 major fits.

Puppet Stayman extension

This ensures opener ends up as declarer as often as possible.

After 2NT : 3♣

3◇ = No 5-card major but at least one 4-card major.
3♡/3♠ = 5-card suit.
3NT = No 5-card major, no 4-card major.

Over 3◇, if responder is interested in a 4-card major, responder bids the major in which there is no interest :

2NT : 3♣, 3◇ : 3♡ = Four spades.
2NT : 3♣, 3◇ : 3♠ = Four hearts.
Opener bids 4-Major with support for the major shown, otherwise 3NT.
2NT : 3♣, 3◇ : 4◇ = Responder is 4-4 in the majors.

Responder should use the 3♣ route when holding a 4-card major or 3-card support for either major (unless responder has a 4-3-3-3 pattern and judges it preferable to stay in no-trumps). However, with a 5-card major, including 5-3 in the majors, responder should choose a transfer sequence.

2NT : 3◇ = Transfer to hearts with 5+ hearts (and perhaps 4 spades as well). Opener will bid 3♡ almost all of the time. With five spades and two hearts, opener bids 3♠. Responder may raise to 4♠, bid 3NT or transfer to hearts via 4◇.

2NT : 3♡ = Transfer to spades with 5+ spades (but not 4 hearts). Opener bids 3♠ almost all of the time. With five hearts and two spades, opener bids 3NT. Responder may pass, transfer to hearts via 4◇ or transfer to spades via 4♡.

The only loss is the rare occasion when opener is 5-2 in the majors and the partnership cannot stop in a 3-Major sign-off.

2NT : 3♠ = Responder has 5 spades and 4 hearts.

TWO-WAY TRIAL BIDS

After 1♡ : 2♡ or 1♠ : 2♠, one may play long suit trials or short suit trials (see pages 48-50). Each method has its merits. If one had to choose one approach over the other, long suit trials are useful more often. However, if you are prepared to forego the natural use of 2NT, it is possible to play both long suit trials and short suit trials.

After 1♡ : 2♡
2♠ = Artificial, meaning 'I am about to make a short suit trial.'
2NT = Long suit trial in spades.
3♣/3♢ = Long suit trial in the suit bid.
3♡ = General invitation to game. Asks responder to pass if minimum and bid 4♡ if maximum.

After 1♡ : 2♡, 2♠
Responder bids 2NT to ask for the short suit and opener rebids :
3♣ = Short in clubs.
3♢ = Short in diamonds.
3♡ = Short in spades.

   If responder has a short suit, responder may show the shortage rather than ask via 2NT. Responder's 3♣/3♢/3♡ bids over 2♠ show the same shortages as opener's 3♣/3♢/3♡ bids over 2NT.

After 1♠ : 2♠
2NT = Artificial, meaning 'I am about to make a short suit trial.'
3♣/3♢/3♡ = Long suit trial in the suit bid.
3♠ = General invitation to game. Asks responder to pass if minimum and bid 4♠ if maximum.

After 1♠ : 2♠, 2NT
Responder bids 3♣ to ask for the short suit and opener rebids :
3♢ = Short in diamonds.
3♡ = Short in hearts.
3♠ = Short in clubs.

   When showing the short suit, a new suit shows the shortage in the suit bid and 3-Major shows the shortage in the suit that is not available at the three-level.

   Responder may show a shortage rather than ask via 3♣.

DEFENCES AND COUNTERMEASURES

Same as against long suit and short suit trials (pages 48-50).

SLAM-ASKING BIDS

If a partnership is able to find out key cards at a low level, it makes sense to use asking bids to locate key honours in suits other than trumps. 3NT as Roman Key Card Blackwood (see page 61) allows plenty of space after key cards and the trump queen have been located. Even 4NT RKCB may leave you with room to make a six-level ask for a king or queen outside trumps.

Systems such as Precision provide plenty of space for slam exploration since a game force can be implemented and a trump suit agreed by the two- or three-level. In its original version, sequences such as 1♣ : 1♡, 2♡ or 1♣ : 1♠, 2♠ asked about the trump suit. A useful variation would be to treat these as RKCB. Likewise, there were asking bids available after starts such as 1♣ : 2♣, 2♠ or 1♣ : 1♠, 2♡. Again, it makes sense to reply to these with Step 1 = no support and Steps 2 onwards showing support and giving key card replies.

Control Asks

Often you may be missing one key card and be concerned whether a critical suit may be unguarded. After the key cards and the trump queen have been located, a new suit is a control ask. After the reply to RKCB showing 0/3 or 1/4 aces, a new suit other than the trump queen ask is a control ask. The answers :

Step 1 = No control (first or second round).
Step 2 = King.
Step 3 = Singleton.
Step 4 = Ace.
Step 5 = Void.
Step 6 = A + K.
Step 7 = A + K + Q.

If a singleton or void is impossible, the other steps simply drop down one or two notches. If you hold king singleton or ace singleton, show the honour, not the singleton. Partner can make a repeat control ask for third round control or to locate a singleton king or singleton ace.

WEST	EAST	WEST	EAST
♠ K1074	♠ AQJ52	1♢	1♠
♡ 652	♡ QJ98	3♠	3NT
♢ AKJ82	♢ 94	4♣	4♡
♣ A	♣ KQ	4♠	No

3NT = RKCB, 4♣ = 0 or 3 key cards, obviously 3 on the bidding.
4♡ = control ask. 4♠ = no control in hearts.

Repeat control asks

After the answer to a control ask, a repeat ask in the same suit asks for third round control.

Step 1 = No third round control.
Step 2 = Q.
Step 3 = Doubleton.
Step 4 = Q-doubleton.
Step 5 = Singleton (if the first answer showed the ace or king).

WEST	EAST	WEST	EAST
♠ K1074	♠ AQJ652	1◇	1♠
♡ Q3	♡ AKJ54	3♠	3NT
◇ AQJ82	◇ 9	4♣	4♡
♣ A5	♣ 6	4♠	5♡
		6◇	7NT

3NT = RKCB, 4♣ = 0 or 3 key cards, obviously 3 on the bidding.
4♡ = control ask. 4♠ = no control in hearts. 5♡ = repeat ask.
6◇ = queen doubleton. At teams or rubber, 7♠ would be safer.

Asking bids beyond five of the agreed suit

Since an asking bid higher than five of your suit commits you to the six-level anyway, it is assumed there is no key card missing. The asker knows about the ace in the suit asked from the answer to RKCB. The answers therefore deal only with the king and queen in the asked suit.

Step 1 = No Q, no K.
Step 2 = Q but no K.
Step 3 = K but no Q.
Step 4 = K + Q.

Singleton ask

Where partner is known to hold a singleton (e.g., after a splinter), you can ask by bidding the singleton suit.

Step 1 = 10 or worse.
Step 2 = J. Step 3 = Q. Step 4 = K. Step 5 = A. Step 6 = Void.

WEST	EAST	WEST	EAST
♠ KJ107	♠ AQ8652	1◇	1♠
♡ J	♡ AKQ105	4♡	4NT
◇ AQJ82	◇ 9	5♣	5♡
♣ AQ6	♣ 2	5NT	7NT

4♡ = splinter raise to 4♠. 4NT = RKCB. 5♣ = 0 or 3 key cards, obviously 3 on the bidding. 5♡ = singleton ask. 5NT = jack.

Key card control asks

If the bidding has started, say, 1◇ : 1♠, 2♠ and 3NT now would be RKCB, what would a bid of 4♣ mean? If you play this as a cue bid, fine. If, however, you are not using cue bids, a new suit instead of RKCB can be played as a Key Card Control Ask. The KCCA = 'Do you have first or second round control in this suit?'

Step 1 = No control in this suit.
Steps 2 on = Control in the suit asked plus RKCB answers.

WEST	EAST	WEST	EAST
♠ K1074	♠ AQJ52	1◇	1♠
♡ A	♡ KQJ	3♠	4♣
◇ AKJ82	◇ Q4	4◇	4♠
♣ 987	♣ J63	No	

4♣ = Key Card Control Ask. 4◇ = no control in clubs.

Weak key card answers

Where partner is known to hold a poor hand, there is no value in the weak hand using the whole key card range for holdings that cannot possibly be held. For example, after 2♣ : 2◇, 2♠ : 3♠ responder has at most 7 points. If opener bids 3NT RKCB, even two key cards would be too much to expect.

For a known weak hand, the key card responses are :

Step 1 = No key card, no queen of trumps.
Step 2 = Queen of trumps but no key card.
Step 3 = One key card, no trump queen.
Step 4 = One key card + the trump queen.
Step 5 = Two key cards, no trump queen.
Step 6 = Two key cards + the trump queen.
Step 7 = Three key cards.

A weak hand is one known to be below opening hand strength. The maximum possible holding for a hand of 12 HCP or less is three key cards.

WEST	EAST	WEST	EAST
♠ AKJ84	♠ Q75	2♣	2◇
♡ AKQ	♡ 762	2♠	3♣
◇ –	◇ 9432	3NT	4◇
♣ AJ873	♣ KQ5	5♣	5♡
		6♣	6♡
		7♠	No

3NT = RKCB, 4◇ = weak reply, trump queen but no key cards.
5♣ = control ask, 5♡ = ♣ K; 6♣ = repeat control ask, 6♡ = ♣ Q.

NEGATIVE FREE BIDS

Partner opens 1♠, RHO bids 2♡. What action do you take with :
♠ 52 ♡ 43 ◇ 863 ♣ AKJ975?

In standard methods, you would have to pass. The hand is not strong
enough for a forcing change of suit at the three-level. Pairs playing
negative free bids allow responder to make a non-forcing change of suit
after intervention by second hand. This usually applies only at the two- or
three-level. For example, after 1◇ : (2♣), a negative free bid would be
an ideal description for ♠ KQ9872 ♡ 8 ◇ 872 ♣ KJ4. Responder would
normally have a 6+ suit and 8-11 HCP. The suit should conform to the
Suit Quality Test (see page 9).

Opener will usually pass with a minimum opening. With support or
with extra values, opener should bid on. A raise is invitational, new suit is
forcing, a rebid of opener's suit is encouraging and a bid of the enemy
suit below 3NT asks for a stopper for 3NT. Play responder to hold a
6-card suit and a seven loser hand, about the same as a maximum weak
two opening.

Negative free bids work well for the situation for which they were
created. However, you need to be able to deal with the strong responding
hands, too. The bidding has started 1♠ : (2♡) to you. What do you do
with ♠ 52 ♡ 43 ◇ AJ3 ♣ AKJ975, given that 3♣ is not forcing?

The strong hands are slotted into responder's double. Double followed
by a change of suit is forcing (unlike the weak treatment of this sequence
in standard negative doubles). With the given hand, you start with a
double. If partner bids 2♠, you can follow with 3♣, forcing. If partner
bids 2NT you can choose 3♣ forcing or 3NT. If partner bids 3◇, you can
bid 3♡, asking for a stopper in hearts.

Similarly, after 1◇ : (1♠) responder needs to start with a double with
♠ 62 ♡ AQ9872 ◇ K4 ♣ AJ2 as 2♡ would not be forcing. Assuming
opener does not bid hearts, responder can bid hearts next and this rebid
will be forcing below game.

Opener needs to be more circumspect than usual in replying to a
negative double and cannot assume responder has support for all unbid
suits. If opener has the values for game, opener may need to bid the
enemy suit rather jump to game.

WEST	NORTH	EAST	SOUTH
1◇	2♣	Dble	No
?			

With ♠ KQJ3 ♡ A4 ◇ AKJ86 ♣ 92,
opener should rebid 3♣ rather than 4♠.
Playing negative free bids, there is no
guarantee that responder has spades.

ROMAN JUMP OVERCALLS

These show two-suiters, normally 5-5 at least. The strength is usually weak, especially when advancer is allowed to pass. The strength for a 5-5 is in the 8-12 point range. For a 6-5 shape, 6-7 points is permissible and any strength is acceptable for a 6-6.

The jump bid in a new suit shows the suit bid and the next suit along, excluding the suit shown by the opponents. The bid of the opponents' suit shows the non-touching pair (excluding their suit again).

Over (1♠) : ?
3♣ = clubs and diamonds.
3♦ = diamonds and hearts.
2♠ = clubs and hearts, the non-touching pair.

Over (1♡) : ?
2♠ = spades and clubs.
3♣ = clubs and diamonds.
2♡ = spades and diamonds, the non-touching pair.

Over (1♦) : ?
2♡ = hearts and spades.
2♠ = spades and clubs.
2♦ = hearts and clubs, the non-touching pair.

Over (1♣) : ?
2♦ = diamonds and hearts.
2♡ = hearts and spades.
2♣ = diamonds and spades, the non-touching pair.

In this scheme, you would use a jump bid in the enemy minor, (1♣) : 3♣ or (1♦) : 3♦ as natural, intermediate strength (about 11 to 15 HCP with a 6+ suit). If you wish to retain (1♣) : 2♣ as natural and (1♦) : 2♦ as natural, you would use (1♣) : 2♠ as spades and diamonds, and (1♦) : 3♣ as clubs and hearts.

(1♣) : 2NT and (1♦) : 2NT can be played as 5-5 at least in the minors. If this is not wanted, the 2NT can be used as a powerful two-suiter (4-loser or better) excluding the suit bid.

(1-Major) : 2NT can be used to show a 6-5 pattern with six in the other major and a 5-card minor. This is a useful variation, since with the Michaels Cue Bid (see page 71) it is often difficult for the overcaller to show a 6-card major.

Otherwise, the (1-Major) : 2NT overcall can be harnessed as a powerful two-suiter, 4 losers or better.

Single jump overcalls which are not needed as Roman jumps can be played as intermediate jumps, 11-15 HCP and a 6+ suit. For example, (1♡) : 3◇ is not needed for diamonds + spades as that is shown via (1♡) : 2♡ which keeps the bidding lower. (1♡) : 3◇ can therefore be used as natural, intermediate.

Similarly, (1♠) : 3♡ is not needed for hearts + clubs, as that could take you to the four-level. Use (1♠) : 2♠ for hearts + clubs. (1♠) : 3♡ can be played as an intermediate jump.

One advantage of this approach is that it eliminates the ambiguity in (1♠) : 2♠ and (1♡) : 2♡. There must be occasions when the bidding starts (1♠) : 2♠ : (4♠) – where 2♠ is Michaels – when advancer may be prepared to sacrifice in one minor but dares not bid lest partner holds the other minor. Suppose you have ♠ 8642 ♡ 43 ◇ A ♣ KJ8762 and the bidding has been (1♠) : 2♠ : (4♠). How much better off you are playing Roman where partner is showing hearts + clubs than playing Michaels where partner is showing hearts and a minor (where it would usually be suicidal to take action and hit partner with hearts + diamonds).

After a Roman jump to the two-level

Bids of the suits shown are to play (jumps are pre-emptive). With a hand worth an invitation to game or better, advancer bids 2NT, asking for clarification. 3♣ shows any minimum. Bidding one of the suits shows extra length. The cheapest bid, excluding 3♣ and a shown suit, indicates a maximum with equal length in the two suits. For example :

After (1♣) : 2♡ showing both majors : (No) : 2NT, (No) : ?

3♣ = Minimum values.
3◇ = Maximum values, equal length in the majors.
3♡ = Maximum, hearts longer.
3♠ = Maximum, spades longer.

After (1♡) : 2♠ showing spades + clubs : (No) : 2NT, (No) : ?

3♣ = Minimum values.
3◇ = Maximum with equal length.
3♡ = Maximum with clubs longer.
3♠ = Maximum with spades longer. Implies a 5-4 pattern if you are using (1♡) : 2NT to show the 6-major + 5-minor hand.

It is also possible to play (1♡) : 2NT to show 6 spades-5 clubs, and (1♡) : 3◇ to show 6 spades-5 diamonds (rather than intermediate). Likewise, you could use (1♠) : 2NT as 6 hearts-5 clubs and (1♠) : 3♡ as 6 hearts-5 diamonds.

After (1♡) : 2NT or (1♠) : 2NT where 2NT shows 6-major + 5-either-minor

3♣/3◇/4♣/4◇/5♣/5◇/6♣ = To play if that is partner's minor. If not, partner corrects to the other minor.

Partner's major or 3NT = To play.

Opener's suit = Game-force, needs to know opener's minor.

If advancer attempts to sign off and partner bids on, partner is showing a hand of great playing strength, normally 3-4 losers.

WEST	NORTH	EAST	SOUTH	WEST	NORTH	EAST	SOUTH
1♡	2NT	No	3♣	1♡	2NT	No	3♣
No	3♠			No	4♠/4♣		

North has nine playing tricks. North has ten playing tricks.

After a Roman jump to the three-level

Bids of the suits shown = To play.

Bidding the unbid suit = Natural, forcing, 6+ suit.

Bidding the enemy suit = Game force.

DEFENCE AGAINST SPECIFIC MICHAELS CUES

Where they bid opener's major

Use the same defence as against the Michaels Cue Bid (see page 72) since this is a specific version of the major-minor two-suiter. A bid of the minor shown by the overcaller asks for a stopper in that suit for 3NT. Double = looking for penalties. Bidding the enemy major suit is used as a limit raise or better and promises support for opener's major.

Where they bid opener's minor

After 1♣ : (2♣) showing diamonds and spades : ?

Double = Aiming for penalties.

2◇ = 10+ HCP with hearts.

2♡ = Natural but not forcing.

2♠ = Limit raise or better in clubs.

3♣ = Sound raise to 2♣.

2NT or 3NT = To play.

3◇ or 3♠ = Splinter raise in clubs with singleton or void in the suit bid. 3♠ would imply a stopper in diamonds so that opener can bid 3NT with the spades well covered.

After 1◇ : (2◇) showing hearts and clubs : ?

Use a similar approach, with Double for penalties, 2♡ as 10+ HCP with spades, 2♠ as natural and not forcing, 3♣ as a limit raise or better in diamonds, 3◇ as a sound raise to 2◇ and jumps to 3♡ and 4♣ as splinters. You can play a jump to 3♠ as a splinter if you normally do, or as a powerful one-suiter otherwise.

COUNTERMEASURES BY THE OVERCALLING SIDE

Bids of the suits shown are to play. Redouble = 'Make the cheapest bid and pass my next bid.' Double of their bid = penalties.

DEFENCE AGAINST 1-MAJOR : (2NT) – 6+ OTHER MAJOR PLUS A MINOR

Double = Aiming for penalties.
3-Major = Sound raise to the two-level.
1♠ : (2NT) : 3♡ = Limit raise or better in spades.
1♡ : (2NT) : 3♣ = Artificial, limit raise or better in hearts.
1♡ : (2NT) : 3♠ = Splinter, game-force in hearts.
Other suit bids at the three-level = Natural, forcing.
Jumps to 4♣/4♢ = Splinters.
1♠ : (2NT) : 4♡ = Splinter.

COUNTERMEASURES BY THE OVERCALLING SIDE

Bid of the major shown is to play. Redouble = 'Bid 3♣ and then pass my next bid.' Any minor suit bid is correctable. Passing the double allows partner to show the minor or to redouble to show far better playing strength in the 6+ major.

DEFENCE AGAINST ROMAN JUMPS SHOWING THE SUIT BID AND THE NEXT SUIT ALONG

WEST	NORTH	EAST	SOUTH
1♢	2♠	?	

North's 2♠ shows spades + clubs.
After a jump to the two-level :
Double = Takeout. Then 3♡ over opener's 3♢ rebid is not forcing.
Supporting opener's suit (3♢) = Sound raise to the two-level.
3♣ = Limit raise or stronger. 3♣, then 3♠ over 3♢ = stopper ask.
3♠ or 4♣ = splinter.
The missing suit (3♡) = Natural and forcing.
2NT or 3NT = natural, not forcing.

WEST	NORTH	EAST	SOUTH
1♡	3♣	?	

North's 3♣ = clubs + diamonds.
After a jump to the three-level :
Double = Takeout.
Bidding their other suit (3♢) = Limit raise or better.
Unbid suit (3♠) = Natural and forcing.
Their suit at the four-level (4♣ or 4♢) = Splinter.

COUNTERMEASURES BY THE OVERCALLING SIDE

Bidding the other suit is to play. Bidding opener's suit is a stopper ask for 3NT. Raises are invitational.

Roman jump overcalls over Precision 2♣

Here there is no incentive to bid their suit in any natural sense as opener has 5+ clubs. You can play overcalls at the two-level as 10-15 HCP (if stronger, double first) and jumps to the three-level as two-suiters.

(2♣) : 3◇ = diamonds + hearts.

(2♣) : 3♡ = hearts + spades.

(2♣) : 3♣ = diamonds + spades, the non-touching suits.

(2♣) : 3♠ can be played as natural (a strong one-suiter) or as a two-suiter with spades + diamonds including 6+ spades.

Roman jump overcalls over weak twos

These still show two-suiters in the usual way but the hands will be strong playing hands, normally five losers or better. This follows the principle of 'Bid strongly over their weak bids.'

(2♡) : 3♠ = spades + clubs.

(2♡) : 4♣ = clubs + diamonds.

(2♡) : 3♡ = spades + diamonds, the non-touching suits. This is better than (2♡) : 4◇ as you can stop in 3♠.

(2♠) : 4♣ = clubs + diamonds.

(2♠) : 4◇ = diamonds + hearts.

(2♠) : 3♠ = hearts + clubs, the non-touching combination.

Roman jump overcalls over multis

Over 2◇ where 2◇ = a weak two in one of the majors

(2◇) : 3♡ = hearts + a minor.

(2◇) : 3♠ = spades + a minor.

(2◇) : 4♣ = clubs + diamonds.

Over 2♡ or 2♠ where these show the suit bid.

Use the same defence as against weak twos (see above).

Over RCO or CRASH two-suited openings

The jump shows the suit bid + the companion which is not a suit held by the opener. It would not be too bright to jump with a two-suiter where the opener is bound to have one of those suits.

(2♡-Rank) : 4♣ = clubs + diamonds

(2♡-Rank) : 3♠ = spades + hearts, strong enough to stand 4♡.

(2♠-Colour) : 4♣ = clubs + spades.

(2♠-Colour) : 4◇ = diamonds + hearts.

(2NT-Odd) : 4♣ = clubs + hearts.

(2NT-Odd) : 4◇ = diamonds + spades.

In each case, you should hold a strong two-suiter, at least 5-5 and no worse than five losers.

EXTENDED USES FOR LEBENSOHL

The Lebensohl Convention, the use of a 2NT reply as a puppet to 3♣, was first devised to counter interference over a 1NT opening (see pages 80-82). It was extended to replying to a takeout double to a weak two opening (see page 15). There are other auctions where the concept is eminently playable.

WEST	NORTH	EAST	SOUTH
1♠	No	2♠	Dble
No	?		

In this auction, North can be stuck with a blizzard or North can have a fairly useful collection. Given that they have bid and raised a suit, the need for a natural 2NT is slight. It makes sense to use Lebensohl to distinguish advancer's hopeless hands from the worthwhile ones.

2NT = 'Please bid 3♣. I have a useless collection and wish to sign off.' After partner bids 3♣, advancer passes with clubs or bids the suit held. With a powerful hand, doubler can reject 3♣. Any other bid implies a strong suit, no worse than a 5-loser hand.

3♣/3◇/3♡ = Advancer's preferred suit and a fair hand, about 7-9 points. It would be uncommon for advancer to have more than this, given the values revealed by the other calls. Should the advancer have 10+ points, give a jump reply to the double. With 13+ points (clearly someone has psyched and you have to trust your partner), bid the enemy suit.

WEST	NORTH	EAST	SOUTH
1♡	No	2♡	Dble
No	?		

In this sequence, 2♠ is a weak call and 2NT would be used only for a weak takeout into clubs or diamonds. The jump to 3♠ is about 7-10 points with five spades. 2NT by advancer followed by a 3♠ rebid over 3♣ would show 7-10 points but only four spades.

WEST	NORTH	EAST	SOUTH
1♠	Dble	2♠	?

Lebensohl 2NT does not apply if RHO bids over partner's double. In this case, advancer need not bid at all. With a worthless hand, pass. Therefore 2NT is not needed to differentiate between hands of no merit and those with some merit. In this sequence, advancer's 2NT should be played as natural, about 10-12 points.

2NT in this sequence is not needed to show both minors. The responsive double caters for that (see pages 101-102).

WEST	NORTH	EAST	SOUTH
1♠	No	2♠	No
No	Dble	No	2NT

2NT in reply to a delayed double is not played as Lebensohl either. In a delayed double auction, there is little need for 2NT natural or to distinguish poor hands from good ones as you are merely contesting the partscore. 2NT here shows both minors, something like ♠ 873 ♡ 54 ◇ KJ65 ♣ K984.

WEST	NORTH	EAST	SOUTH
1◇	2♠	No	No
Dble	No	?	

How would you play 2NT by responder in this sequence?

There is a case for using 2NT as natural (spade stopper, 7-9 points) but there is a much stronger case for using Lebensohl. In this situation, East can have a worthless hand or some fair values. West can also have a minimum opening short in spades or can have a very powerful hand. It can be vital for West to know whether East's hand is next to useless or whether it does contain something of value.

It is not likely that East has some values with 4+ hearts, because of the failure to double. However, even if playing negative free bids, there are many hands where East would not take action at the three-level on hands with 7-10 points. East ought to pass 2♠ on each of these :

♠ 7653	♠ 97	♠ Q5	♠ 9743
♡ 42	♡ AK	♡ A93	♡ K72
◇ A2	◇ 632	◇ K2	◇ A72
♣ KJ752	♣ J85432	♣ 875432	♣ Q43

In reply to the double, East should bid 3♣ on the first three examples. This shows reasonable values and 4+ clubs. With a poor hand (0-5 points), East would use 2NT and pass 3♣ or convert to 3◇ or 3♡.

The last hand with no suit to call poses a problem. The values are reasonable but there is no genuine suit. Recommended is to bid 3◇ in reply to the double. This would not make sense to show reasonable values with diamond support. With that, you would have bid 3◇ at once over 2♠. The delayed bid showing support and values should therefore indicate this type of hand : real values but not real support.

Likewise a bid of 3♡ here cannot show both values and a heart suit. With that, East would have doubled 2♠.

WEST	NORTH	EAST	SOUTH
1◇	2♠	No	No
Dble	No	?	

Bid 3♡ at once with long hearts and about 4-5 HCP, something like :
♠ 652 ♡ KQ8743 ◇ 43 ♣ 62.

WEST	NORTH	EAST	SOUTH
1◇	2♠	No	No
Dble	No	2NT	No
3♣	No	3♡	

Use the Lebensohl 2NT route to 3♡ with a woeful hand, perhaps with
♠ 7652 ♡ J8743 ◇ 5 ♣ 653 or with
♠ 876 ♡ Q98532 ◇ 32 ♣ 54.

10. CONVENTIONS IN CARD PLAY

LEADING THIRDS AND FIFTHS

The standard lead from a long suit without a sequence is fourth highest.
However, many top players prefer to lead third highest from a 4-card suit
and fifth highest from 5-card or 6-card suits. Playing this approach the
card to lead is underlined :

KJ<u>7</u>3   KJ73<u>2</u>   KJ76<u>3</u>2   Q7<u>2</u>   87<u>2</u>   98<u>5</u>2

Playing fourth highest leads, you would lead the 2 from Q-8-4-2 and also
from Q-4-2. The bottom card can be from a 4-card or a 3-card holding.
You would also lead the 3 from K-J-6-3 or from K-J-6-3-2, a 4-card or a
5-card holding. With a difference of only one card between such holdings,
it is usually impossible for partner to diagnose the actual length with the
leader.

   Playing thirds and fifths, there is a two card difference when the bottom
card is led. If partner leads the 2, this will be from a 3-card suit or a
5-card suit normally. You will be able to tell more often which of these is
the actual holding. If partner is leading an unbid suit against no-trumps, it
is almost a sure thing that the bottom card indicates a 5-card suit.

   The advantage of knowing the exact number of cards can be useful,
even essential, in a trump contract. This is particularly so when the
problem is a cash out situation.

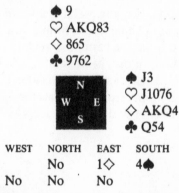

♠ 9
♡ AKQ83
◇ 865
♣ 9762

		♠ J3
		♡ J1076
		◇ AKQ4
		♣ Q54

WEST	NORTH	EAST	SOUTH
	No	1◇	4♠
No	No	No	

West leads the 3 of diamonds. South plays the 10 under East's queen.
How should East continue?

♠ 9
♡ AKQ83
◇ 865
♣ 9762

♠ J3
♡ J1076
◇ AKQ4
♣ Q54

Against 4♠, West leads the 3 of diamonds and South drops the 10 under East's queen. Playing fourth highest, West's 3 could be from J-9-3, J-9-7-3 or J-9-7-3-2. If South has a singleton, it may be vital to switch to clubs at trick 2, leading the queen and playing South for
♠ AKQxxxx ♡ xx ◇ 10 ♣ Kxx.

However, if South has a second diamond, it is safe enough for East to cash a second round and then switch to clubs. In that case a low club is best. That will defeat the game if South has K-x or K-10-x and gives South a guess with K-J in clubs.

Playing fourth highest, East has no idea which to try. Thirds and fifths make some of these decisions easier. From J-9-7-3-2, West would lead the 2. The 3 lead therefore cannot be from five diamonds. It might be from J-9-3, J-7-3, J-9-3-2 or J-7-3-2. In any case, it is safe for East to cash a second diamond. With a 3-card holding, West will play the higher card next (and East can then cash a third diamond). With four, West follows with the lower card and East can then switch to a club.

Thirds and fifths do not eliminate all ambiguities. West's lead of the 2 could be from three or five. However, it is easier for East to contend with two possibilities than three. Given South's jump to 4♠ it is more likely that South has a singleton diamond than three cards in a suit bid by the opposition.

Thirds and fifths are particularly useful in no-trumps when you wish to know whether partner's opening lead is from a 4-card or a 5-card suit. If it is only a 4-card suit, it may be better to switch to some other suit. If it is known to be a 5-card suit, it may be preferable to return partner's lead. Playing fourth highest usually leaves third hand in a quandary. Playing thirds and fifths, the bottom card lead reveals the 5-card holding and places third hand in a better position to decide whether to switch or to return partner's lead.

Thirds and fifths have a drawback in leading the bottom card from three rags. In standard methods, the bottom card is led only from three or four cards headed by an honour. From three or four rags, middle-up-down is the preferred leads approach. Playing thirds and fifths, you lead the same card from K-3-2 and 4-3-2.

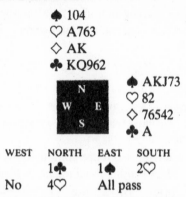

```
            ♠ 104
            ♡ A763
            ◇ AK
            ♣ KQ962
                           ♠ AKJ73
              N            ♡ 82
          W       E        ◇ 76542
              S            ♣ A
```

WEST	NORTH	EAST	SOUTH
	1♣	1♠	2♡
No	4♡	All pass	

West leads the 2 of spades. How should East defend?

Playing standard methods, it is easy for East to win the ♠K, cash the ace of clubs and return a low spade. West's lead of the two promises an honour (it must be the queen) or a singleton. In either case, West will win and return a club for East to ruff.

Playing thirds and fifths, West's lead could be from 8-6-2 just as easily as Q-6-2. It would look silly for East to return a low spade and find South scoring the queen of spades. At imps or rubber, that does not matter. There is hardly any other chance to defeat the contract than to play West to win the second spade. At pairs, however, the overtrick may give you a bottom board.

The answer is that you accept the drawbacks that your methods entail. If they give you good results most of the time and a poor result every now and again, that is no reason to decry those methods. Whether it is your bidding system or your leads and signals, no method works well all of the time. Still, West can give a suit preference signal on the ace of clubs, high club if holding the ♠Q, lowest if not.

Players who do use thirds and fifths believe that the information as to partner's length in the suit led is more valuable than the information about partner's honour card holding in that suit. If you do adopt thirds and fifths, you follow the same approach to leads later in the defence when shifting to a new suit. However, when switching, top of nothing is common when you hold a worthless suit. A high card *switch* implies little interest in the suit led, a low card *switch* is interested in having the same suit returned.

UNDERLEADING HONOURS (RUSINOW LEADS)

Playing standard, the top card is led from sequence holdings. When underleading honours, the second card of the touching honours is led from almost all sequence combinations where the top card of the touching honours is led in standard. The card to lead when playing Rusinow is underlined :

AK̲J7   KQ̲J4   KQ̲107   KQ̲2   QJ̲105   QJ̲93   QJ̲7

J10̲94   J10̲82   J10̲5   10̲985   10̲972   10̲95

AQJ̲63*   AJ10̲52*   A10̲98*   KJ10̲7   K10̲98   Q10̲98

*Against no-trumps only. With these holdings against a trump contract, you should not lead the suit at all or, if you must, start with the ace.

The top card is still led from sequence combinations when leading partner's bid suit or when leading touching honours doubleton.

A̲K   K̲Q   Q̲J   J̲10   10̲9

Rusinow removes the ambiguity of the king lead from A-K-x holdings (lead the king) and from K-Q-x holdings as well (lead the queen). Leading ace from A-K-suits and king from K-Q-suits does that also, although there is a slight ambiguity in trump contacts with the ace lead which may be from an A-K suit or from a suit headed by the ace without the king. Since it is unattractive to lead from an ace-high suit lacking the king, this is not a common problem for overleaders.

   One clear advantage from Rusinow leads is that third hand can tell when the lead is from two touching honours doubleton.

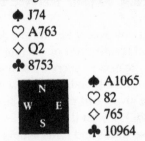

♠ J74
♡ A763
◇ Q2
♣ 8753

N W E S

♠ A1065
♡ 82
◇ 765
♣ 10964

South opened 1♡ and rebid 4♡ over North's 2♡. West leads the king of spades followed by the queen of spades. How should East defend?

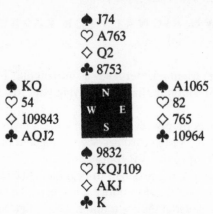

♠ J74
♥ A763
♦ Q2
♣ 8753

♠ KQ
♥ 54
♦ 109843
♣ AQJ2

♠ A1065
♥ 82
♦ 765
♣ 10964

♠ 9832
♥ KQJ109
♦ AKJ
♣ K

In standard methods it would usually be a colossal blunder for East to overtake the second round of spades. Playing Rusinow, East knows when West leads the king-then-queen, that West started with K-Q doubleton. East knows enough to overtake the queen with the ace and return a spade for West to ruff. Otherwise, East-West may never come to a third trick in spades.

The negative side of Rusinow leads occurs when the opening lead is the nine. This could be from a doubleton or from holdings such as 10-9-x, 10-9-8-x, Q-10-9-x or K-10-9-x. In standard methods, the 9 lead is bound to be from a doubleton (or specifically K-J-9). In Rusinow the ambiguity cannot be clarified until the second trick.

The Rusinow ambiguity of honour leads from 3-card holdings or from two honours doubleton can also cause problems.

NORTH
♣ Q762

EAST
♣ AK94

Against 4♥, West leads the 10 and declarer plays low from dummy. Which card should East play?

If West is leading from 10-doubleton, East should win, cash the other winner and give West a third round ruff. This would not be an enterprising start for the defence if West has in fact led from J-10-x! However, if East plays low and West has led from 10-x, the defence misses the ruff. South scores the jack and perhaps South can manage to discard the other losers in this suit. East needs to be clairvoyant to know what is going on.

UPSIDE-DOWN SIGNALS (OR REVERSE SIGNALS)

In standard methods, when partner leads a suit you play high-low to encourage partner to continue that suit. Playing your lowest asks partner to shift.

Upside-down signals simply reverse this process. Playing your lowest is the encouraging signal. A high card is discouraging and high-then-low indicates no desire to have the suit continued.

Standard high-encouraging is taught to beginners because at their infant stage, beginners tend not to notice a low card. Drop a 10 or a 9, however, and you may catch their attention. Thus, high-low encouraging is ingrained early in a bridge player's life.

Upside-down signals are technically superior. The theory is that if you want a suit continued you may not be able to afford a high card but you can always spare your lowest. Conversely, if you do not wish the suit continued you can easily afford to play a highest card. You are always bound by the cards you hold, but when you do wish to encourage, you will always have a lowest card.

	♠ J762	
♠ AK5		♠ Q1043
	♠ 98	

West leads the ace. East cannot afford the 10. In standard, East would have to signal with the 4, a card that West may well misread. Upside-down, East plays the 3. The lowest card is the most encouraging. West continues with the king and a third one and East still has Q-10 sitting over J-7. Playing upside-down you never have to squander your high cards.

If you play upside-down signals and, hoping for a ruff, you wish to encourage a suit where you hold a doubleton, you again reverse the normal order of play. Low-high asks for the suit to be continued.

	♠ J762	
♠ AK54		♠ 93
	♠ Q108	

West leads the ace. If East wishes to encourage, East drops the 3. If East does not want the suit continued, East drops the 9.

If you are signalling count in a suit, the order here is reversed, too. You play bottom from an even number and high-low with an odd number. Again, you can always afford the bottom from a doubleton (but not always the top) and with three cards you can usually afford the middle or the top card to start the high-low.

Upside-down discards

The same theory applies to discards. In standard, high discard asks for the suit to be led, lowest indicates no interest. Upside-down discards mean that a high discard shows no interest while discarding lowest asks for that suit to be led. Again this works better than standard since the lowest card in the suit you want is at least as affordable as a higher one and often more affordable. Likewise, if you have no interest in a suit, you can usually spare a highish card in that suit.

Odd-even discards

This method provides you with the maximum flexibility in your discarding. You can signal within a suit that you want that suit led. You can tell partner you have no interest in a particular suit and at the same time indicate to partner the suit that you do want played.

Odd discards are encouraging. If you discard a 3, 5, 7 or 9 you are asking partner to lead the suit discarded.

Even discards are discouraging. If you discard a 2, 4, 6, 8 or 10, you do not want partner to lead that suit.

Even discards carry a suit preference message.

A low even discard asks partner to lead the lower outside suit. One suit you do not hold and the even card discourages the suit thrown. That leaves only two suits. If you discard the 2, you are asking partner to shift to the lower outside suit.

A high even discard asks partner to lead the higher outside suit. Discard a 10 or an 8 and you are asking partner to switch to the higher of the remaining suits.

You are always bound by the cards you have been dealt. With odd-even discards, you usually have a wide range from which to choose to carry the intended message to partner.

If you have the opportunity to make two discards and you have no suitable discards available, you can play high-then-low with odd cards. High odd card followed by low odd card in the same suit = 'Please disregard the encouraging message.'

Note that odd-even applies only to discards and not to following suit, whether it is partner's suit or declarer's. There are usually too few choices to use the method when following suit.

11. And The Beat Goes On . . .

FORCING MINOR SUIT RAISES

Strong hands with no major suit but with support for opener's minor are notoriously difficult to bid. A popular solution is to treat the simple raise in a minor as forcing and the jump raise as a weaker action. Thus:

WEST	EAST	
1♣	3♣	Responder has 6-9 points, support for opener's minor
or		and no major suit. If opener wishes to bid further, a new
1♢	3♢	suit at the three-level is a stopper bid for 3NT.

Defence: Double for takeout, suit bids are natural.
Countermeasures: All bids retain the normal meaning.

WEST	EAST	
1♣	2♣	Responder has 10+ points, support for opener's minor
or		and no major suit. The bid is forcing for one round. The
1♢	2♢	weakest action for opener is to re-raise the minor to the
		three-level. If minimum, responder will pass this.

If responder bids again after opener's 3-minor, the position is game-forcing. A suit at the three-level is a stopper bid while a jump in a new suit (1♣ : 2♣, 3♣ : 4♠) would be a splinter bid (see page 43).

Strong actions after 1♣ : 2♣ or 1♢ : 2♢

A new suit by opener shows game interest. The new suit may be genuine or may be just a stopper. If responder then bids 3-minor, this shows a minimum (10-11 points) and can be passed. If opener bids a new suit and responder also bids a new suit (stopper bid) or 2NT, the situation is game-forcing.

A 2NT rebid by opener is forcing to game and confirms stoppers in the unbid suits. Lacking a stopper in one of the suits, start with a new suit stopper bid. A new suit by responder over 2NT shows a shortage and concern for 3NT unless opener has the suit well-covered.

A jump-bid by opener over 2-minor is a splinter (1♢ : 2♢, 3♡) and is forcing to game. Responder can bid 3NT if strong in the short suit. With slam ambitions, responder can cue-bid or bid 4-minor as an ask for key-cards (see page 63).

Defence: Double 2-minor for takeout; 2NT = 5-5 hearts, and the other minor; jumps bids are pre-emptive.
Countermeasures: Redouble to suggest penalties; doubles of 2NT or suit bids are for penalties.

BERGEN RAISES

These are very popular among experts who play 5-Card Majors but they can also be used if you open 4-card suits.

The theory here, as well as for Forcing Minor Suit Raises, is that in strong competition you will not be allowed to play in your suit after a simple raise to the two-level. Competitive strategy demands action almost invariably if they bid and raise a suit to the two-level and are prepared to pass it out there. Since you will not be able to play at the two-level when you have a good trump fit, you may as well grasp the nettle and commit yourself to the three-level at once.

WEST	EAST	6-9 points with 3-card support, or 4-card support if the
1♥	2♥	hand pattern is 4-3-3-3.
or		**Defence:** Double for takeout, suit bids are natural.
1♠	2♠	**Countermeasures:** All bids retain the normal meaning.

WEST	EAST	0-5 points with 4+ support and some shape (at least a
1♥	3♥	4-4-3-2 pattern). The jump-raise is wholly pre-emptive
or		and opener needs a very powerful hand to bid game.
1♠	3♠	**Defence:** Double for takeout, suit bids are natural.
		Countermeasures: All bids retain the normal meaning.

WEST	EAST	6-9 points with 4+ support and some shape (at least a
1♥/1♠	3♣	4-4-3-2 pattern). A constructive raise.

Opener can sign off in 3-agreed-major or bid game. A new suit below 3-major is a trial bid (see page 48). A new suit beyond 3-major is a slam try. This is a rarity and opener mostly bids 3-major or 4-major.

WEST	EAST	10-12 points with 4+ support. This is a limit raise with
1♥/1♠	3♦	an expectancy of 8 losers.

Opener can sign off in 3-agreed-major or bid game. Any new suit is a cue bid and a slam try.

With 13+ points or 7 losers, the hand is too strong for 3♦. With no shortage, travel via Jacoby 2NT (page 40). With a singleton or a void and 4+ support, use a splinter response (page 43).

Defence to the Bergen 3♣ and 3♦ responses

Double shows the minor suit doubled and is also lead-directing. It may be a one-suiter or the first step in showing a two-suiter (by bidding the other suit on the next round). Bidding opener's major shows the other major and the unbid minor. 3NT is to play (long, running minor and a stopper in their major), while 4NT is both minors with about 4 losers.

Countermeasures: Over double, redouble is a trial bid in the minor suit doubled. Other bids have their normal meaning. After any other action by the opponents, double indicates a desire for penalties.

FIT-SHOWING JUMPS

These are jump bids which promise a strong 5+ suit and support for partner's suit as well. The side-suit should be K-Q-x-x-x or better (perhaps A-J-10-x-x at the very worst). The aim is to discover whether a double fit exists. If so, the partnership can often make at least one trick more than points or the loser count might suggest. For example:

WEST	EAST	WEST	EAST
♠ A63	♠ 52	No	
♡ KQJ862	♡ A743	1♡	3♣ – fit-showing
◇ 5	◇ 98	4NT	5♡
♣ KJ4	♣ AQ853	6♡	No

West has six losers, East seven. That suggests the limit is eleven tricks. Likewise, point count does not indicate slam potential, yet twelve tricks should be child's play. The explanation lies in the power of the double fit.

Fit-showing jumps are also commonly used in competitive auctions such as after an opponent's takeout double, after their weak jump-overcall or after partner has made an overcall. The last bid in each of these auctions would be fit-showing (but regular partnerships need to agree on these):

W	N	E	S		W	N	E	S		W	N	E	S
1◇	Dble	2♡	...		1◇	2♡	3♠	...		1◇	1♡	1♠	3♣

FIT-SHOWING JUMP-SHIFTS (incompatible with Bergen Raises)

These show a strong 5+ suit and support for opener's suit. The strength is either that of a limit raise or a hand with slam potential. Hands which are worth game but no more are shown by a change of suit and the delayed game raise. After the jump-shift, opener can sign off in his suit or bid a new suit as a cue bid to show slam interest.

(a) ♠ 96   (b) ♠ AJ   Each of these qualifies for a fit-showing
    ♡ K1082   ♡ AJ43   jump to 3◇ after partner's 1♡ opening.
    ◇ KQ632   ◇ AQJ95
    ♣ 85   ♣ 95

With (a) you would pass if opener rebids 3♡, and sign off in 4♡ if opener makes a cue bid. With (b) if opener bids 3♡ or 4♡ you would continue with a cue bid in spades. Slam is still possible opposite a minimum opening.

Defence to fit-showing jumps or jump-shifts

Double shows the unbid suit(s); new suit bid is natural; bid of their suit shows a highly distributional hand in the other suits.

Countermeasures: Over double, redouble suggests penalties. Otherwise, double = desire for penalties and other bids have their normal meaning.

MORE ON MINI-SPLINTERS (incompatible with Bergen Raises, Fit-showing Jump-Shifts or Standard Strong Jump-Shifts – see also page 30)

Mini-splinter jump-shift responses show the values for a limit raise or stronger and show a shortage in the suit bid. They are useful in being able to distinguish singletons from voids when responder has enough for game or more.

WEST	EAST	
1♡	3♣	East has a singleton club, 4+ support for hearts and is strong enough for at least 3♡. East is allowed to have a void in clubs but only if the hand is a limit raise.

Responder will have a limit raise with a singleton or a void OR enough for game or slam with a singleton. In the above auction, opener can sign off in 3♡ or 4♡ or bid a new suit as a cue bid with slam interest.

If opener signs off in 3♡, responder passes with the limit raise, bids game with extra values and cue bids or asks for aces with slam potential.

WEST	EAST	
1♡	4♣	If playing mini-splinters, a double jump splinter shows a void in the suit bid, 4+ support and game values. If opener signs off in game and responder continues with 4NT, opener ignores the ace of the void suit in replying.

WEST	EAST	
1♢	2♠	Mini-splinters can also be played in a major suit after a minor suit opening. East's 2♠ might be a limit raise to 3♢ with a singleton or void in spades OR a hand with game or slam potential with specifically a singleton spade.
1♢	3♠	The double jump splinter is game-forcing with a void in the suit bid.

WEST	EAST	WEST	EAST	
♠ 32	♠ 8765	1♡	3♣ – mini-splinter	
♡ AQJ86	♡ K743	4♡	No	
♢ KQ4	♢ A973	(After 1♡ : 3♡, West would pass.		
♣ 875	♣ 10	Interchange West's minors and West would bid 3♡ over 3♣.)		

Defence to mini-splinters

Bids are natural. Double a splinter for the lead of the short suit has little value. Use the double to show strength in the higher-ranking unbid suit (as a lead-directing bid or suggesting a sacrifice – see also page 46).

WEST	NORTH	EAST	SOUTH	
1♡	No	3♣	Dble	South's double shows strength in spades, the higher unbid suit.

Countermeasures: All actions retain normal meanings. Redouble suggests penalties – see page 47.

MAJOR-OVER-MAJOR AS A GAME-FORCE IN STAYMAN AUCTIONS

When responder has slam potential and receives a favourable reply to Stayman, there is no cheap, convenient way in standard methods to set opener's major as trumps and start a cue bidding sequence.

WEST	EAST	
1NT	2♣	Standard style, 3♡ by East would be invitational and 4♡ is a sign-off. Some play a jump to 4♣ as Gerber,
2♡	?	others as a splinter. Even if 4♣ were a cue bid, responder may not have a cheap cue bid available.

A solution to this problem is possible by utilising a bid of 3-in-the-other-major by responder.

WEST	EAST	
1NT	2♣	After a major suit reply to Stayman, 3-other-major is a game-force raise in opener's major and suggests slam
2♡	3♠ . . .	possibilities. Opened is asked to start cue bidding.

WEST	EAST	Whether you play transfers or not, there is no need
1NT	2♣	to bid 3-other-major as a natural move.
2♠	3♡ . . .	A fringe benefit is that 1NT : 2♣, 2♡/2♠ : 4NT must be a quantitative raise (else bid 3-other-major first and Blackwood later).

The same concept can be applied after a 2NT opening:

WEST	EAST	
2NT	3♣	3♠ here sets hearts as trumps and indicates slam potential. (With four spades, East bids 3NT with game
3♡	3♠ . . .	values only, 4NT with slam interest and 5NT to insist on slam. With 4-4 in the majors, opener can now show the spades.)

WEST	EAST	
2NT	3♣	4♡ here sets spades as trumps. If minimum, opener bids 4♠ (responder can continue with 4NT or a cue
3♠	4♡ . . .	bid). With a maximum, opener can cue bid or ask for aces/key-cards with 4NT.

WEST	EAST	WEST	EAST
♠ AK52	♠ QJ104	2NT	3♣
♡ Q96	♡ AK	3♠	4♡ – sets spades
◇ AQ	◇ 962	5♣ – cue	5♡ – cue
♣ AK85	♣ J742	6♣ – cue	6♠ – no grand slam interest
		No	

Defence to artificial bid of the other major
Double is lead-directing.

Countermeasure
Redouble as a cue bid in the suit doubled.

POWER 2♣ AND 2◇ RESPONSES TO A MAJOR SUIT OPENING

These artificial strong responses indicate the partnership objective at once and thereby free other responses for weaker responding hands.

WEST	EAST	
1♡/1♠	2◇	The 2◇ response is artificial and forcing to game. It covers all game-force hands other than a splinter raise.

WEST	EAST	
1♡/1♠	2♣	2♣ is an artificial game-try, c. 10-12 points. In reply, opener shows a minimum (11-13 HCP) with an artificial 2◇ rebid. Higher rebids force to game.

WEST	EAST	
1♠	2♡	The 2♡ response to 1♠ shows 6+ hearts and invites game. With a minimum and no significant fit for hearts, opener is expected to pass. With 4-5 hearts and 10-12 points, bid 2♣ first and rebid 2♡ over 2◇.

After 1♡/1♠ : 2◇, bidding continues along natural lines. Playing 4-card suits, opener's first duty would be to show a 5-card major, except that a 3♣ or 3◇ rebid by opener would show at least a 5-5 pattern.

Raises to game show a minimum hand. Raises below game show extra values and slam interest. After 1♡ : 2◇, 2♡ : 3♡ is stronger than 4♡.

If you are playing a 12-14 1NT, it follows that a 2◇ rebid by opener after 1♡/1♠, 2♣ will not be a balanced hand.

After 1♡/1♠ : 2♣, 2◇ (minimum opener), bidding proceeds on natural lines looking for the best part-score.

Since 2♣ and 2◇ cover the strong hands, jump-raises and jump-shifts show weak hands. 1♡/1♠ : 2NT can show a weak hand with the minors.

WEST	EAST	WEST	EAST
♠ AQJ72	♠ 4	1♠	2♡
♡ 96	♡ KQ8732	No	
◇ KQ	◇ A84	A natural sequence is likely to	
♣ 8532	♣ J74	reach the riskier 3♡.	

WEST	EAST	WEST	EAST
♠ AJ864	♠ KQ92	1♠	2♣
♡ KQJ	♡ A32	2◇	2♠
◇ Q2	◇ J84	No	
♣ 843	♣ J105	(2♣ allows you to stop low.)	

For more information, see *Power Acol* in the Master Bridge Series.

Defence to Power 2♣ and 2◇ responses

Doubling the artificial minor is lead-directing.

Countermeasure

Pass denies a stopper in the minor doubled. Bids promise a stopper. Redouble is a suggestion to play in the minor suit redoubled.

MULTI-CUES

In multi-cue bidding, the first set of cue bids can show first or second
round control. Bypassing a suit denies first *and* second round control.
One benefit is that an uncontrolled suit is quickly located, allowing the
partnership to stop at game-level. After cue bidding has confirmed that
all suits are controlled, 4NT RKCB (page 59) can be used to make sure
you are not missing two key cards.

Standard cue bidding in which only first round controls are shown initially
can strike problems when controls cannot be shown economically. With
multi-cues, more controls are available for the first cue bid and an
uneconomic step is highly descriptive by the denial of controls.

WEST	EAST	WEST	EAST
♠ A972	♠ KJ1084	1♡	1♠
♡ AQJ103	♡ K8	3♠	4◇
◇ KQ	◇ AJ3	4♠	No
♣ 85	♣ QJ4	5♠ might make but 4♠ is safer.	

East's 4◇ denied club control and so West signed off in 4♠.

WEST	EAST	WEST	EAST
♠ A972	♠ KQ1084	1♡	1♠
♡ AQJ103	♡ K8	3♠	4♣ (1)
◇ K8	◇ A3	4◇ (2)	4♡ (3)
♣ Q5	♣ A432	4NT (4)	5♣ (5)
		5♠ (6)	6♠ (7)
		7♠ (8)	No

(1) Shows 1st or 2nd round club control.
(2) 1st or 2nd round diamond control.
(3) Shows the ♡K or ♡A. West knows it must be ♡K. Do not cue bid a
singleton or void as your first cue in a suit where partner has length.
(4) Roman Key Card Blackwood.   (5) 0 or 3 key cards.
(6) Signs off in case it is 0. East could have 15 HCP but no key cards.
After the sign-off, partner must bid again with 3 (see page 60).
(7) 3 key cards + the trump queen and no outside king or source of
tricks.
(8) If West could be sure that East had five spades, West would bid 7NT
but the thirteenth trick may have to come from a ruff.

Defence to Multi-Cues

Doubles are lead-directing.

Countermeasures

Redouble = First round control of this suit. Pass allows partner to
redouble with no worries in the doubled suit. Bids = Normal meaning.

LACKWOOD (OR VOIDWOOD OR EXCLUSION BLACKWOOD)

How can you handle a void after you have agreed on a trump suit? Asking for key cards will not help unless partner's reply reveals that all the key cards are held. You could start cue bidding but partner might be unable to tell whether you are cue bidding an ace or a void. One solution is to use Lackwood, a jump bid in a new suit after trump agreement.

WEST	EAST	The 4♡ rebid shows slam interest with a void in
1♠	2♣	hearts. One style allows opener to cue bid with 4♠, ask
3♣	4♡ . . .	for key cards with 4NT or even sign off in 5♣ with
		significant wastage in hearts.

However, the preferred approach is for partner to show key cards by the usual steps in reply to Lackwood (also known as Voidwood) but ignoring the ace in the void suit in the reply.

WEST	EAST	WEST	EAST
♠ AQ7	♠ K109843	1♡	1♠
♡ AJ832	♡ KQ4	2♣	4♣ (1)
◇ 5	◇ AKQ2	4NT (2)	7♠ (3)
♣ J532	♣ –	No	

(1) Lackwood: void in clubs and asking for key cards outside clubs.
(2) Step 4 = two key cards plus the trump queen.
(3) East knows West has ♡A, ♠A, ♠Q. That is enough to bid 7♠.

WEST	EAST	WEST	EAST
♠ 8762	♠ KJ10943	1♡	1♠
♡ QJ1083	♡ K4	2♣	4♣ (1)
◇ J	◇ AKQ52	4◇ (2)	4♠ (3)
♣ AKQ	♣ –	No	

(1) Lackwood.   (2) Step 1 = 0 or 3 key cards.
(3) East knows that West cannot have three key cards outside clubs and, unlikely though it might seem, the ♡A and ♠A must be missing.

WEST	EAST	WEST	EAST
♠ A9842	♠ KJ	1♠	2♣
♡ KQ2	♡ –	4♣	5♡ (1)
◇ 9	◇ AKQ62	5♠ (2)	7♣ (3)
♣ AK93	♣ QJ8762	No	

(1) Lackwood.   (2) Step 1 = 0 or 3 key cards.
(3) East knows it must be 3.

Defence: Double of the Lackwood bid asks for the lead of the higher non-trump, non-void suit.

Countermeasures: All bids retain their normal meaning.

KICKBACK

This space-saving method of asking for key cards was expounded by Jeff Rubens in an article in *The Bridge World*. After a trump suit has been agreed, the bid immediately above four of the agreed suit is Roman Key Card Blackwood. Thus, if clubs are trumps, 4◇ is RKCB; for diamonds, 4♡ is the ask, and for hearts the ask is 4♠. If spades is the agreed suit, the usual 4NT RKCB applies. The method has a great advantage for the minor suits as a lack of key cards can be located without the risk of bidding beyond game (see also page 63).

WEST	EAST		WEST	EAST
♠ KQJ53	♠ 2		1♠	2◇
♡ Q75	♡ 4		4◇	4♡ (1)
◇ AJ86	◇ KQ97542		5♣ (2)	5◇ (3)
♣ A	♣ KQ72		No	

(1) Kickback. (2) 2 key cards, no trump queen.
(3) As two key cards are missing, East signs off.

Note that if East had to use 4NT to ask for key cards or aces, the 5♡ reply would be most unwelcome.

If Kickback is available without a jump bid, then 4NT operates as a cue bid in the Kickback suit:

WEST	EAST		
1♠	2◇		As 4♡ would be Kickback (and 4♠ would suggest
4◇	4NT . . .		playing there), 4NT is a cue bid in hearts, with
			diamonds as the agreed suit.

If the Kickback bid is a jump, how can it be distinguished from Lackwood?

WEST	EAST		
1♠	2♣		Should 4◇ be Kickback or Lackwood?
3♣	4◇ . . .		As Kickback is much more valuable than Lackwood,
			it is best to play 4◇ here as Kickback.

WEST	EAST		
1♠	2♣		4NT can then be used as Lackwood in diamonds.
3♣	4NT . . .		The only risk in this area is a memory problem, so be
			sure that you and partner are on the same wavelength.

Defence

Double of the Kickback suggests a sacrifice (not lead-directing, as you will be on lead). Double of the reply to Kickback is lead-directing.

Countermeasures

Whether Kickback or the reply to Kickback is doubled, further bids are normal. Pass denies 1st and 2nd round control in the doubled suit. After Pass, partner can sign off while other bids retain the usual meaning.

RELAYS OVER WEAK TWOS

Relays can be useful when responder has slam ambitions but limited support for opener's major. It is possible to enjoy all the benefits of the Ogust Convention (see page 12) and also relay to find opener's exact shape. Assuming the weak two opener has a 6-3-2-2 or 6-3-3-1 pattern or a 6-4-2-1 where the 4-suit is a minor, the following structure is suitable. If your partnership opens a weak two with a void or perhaps with just a 5-card suit, you will need to make your own adjustments.

2♡ : 2♠ = relay: see below. Used mainly for slam hands or with game values where the fit for opener's major is poor.

2♡ : 2NT = Ogust. Standard rebids. Used for game invitational or game/slam hands with a decent fit for opener's suit.

2♠ : 2NT = relay: see below.

2♠ : 3♣ = Ogust. Rebids: 3♢ = minimum, good or bad suit.
                      3♡/3♠/3NT : standard maximums.

After 3♢, 3♠ is a sign-off while 3♡ asks for clarification:
    Then 3♠ = 1 top honour; 3NT = 2 top honours.
    Normal continuations apply after the reply to Ogust.

In reply to the relay, the hand patterns are shown in steps:

Step 1 = 6-3-3-1
Step 2 = 6-3-2-2
Others = 6-4s

Thus:

2♡ : 2♠ (relay)
?   2NT = some 6-3-3-1
    3♣ = some 6-3-2-2
    3♢ = 1-6-2-4
    3♡ = 1-6-4-2
    3♠ = 2-6-1-4
    3NT = 2-6-4-1

Shortages are shown in rank order, high shortage first, and so complete patterns come out in numerical order, as for 3♢ through 3NT above.

After 2♡ : 2♠, 2NT (6-3-3-1) : 3♣ asks for the singleton. Similarly this is shown in rank order from the top, so:

    3♢ = 1-6-3-3
    3♡ = 3-6-1-3
    3♠ = 3-6-3-1 (Again note the numerical order)

After 2♡ : 2♠, 3♣ (6-3-2-2) : 3♢ asks for the 3-card suit:

    3♡ = 2-6-2-3
    3♠ = 2-6-3-2
    3NT = 3-6-2-2 (in numerical order)

After a weak two opening in spades:

2♠ : 2NT (relay)

?   3♣ = some 6-3-3-1

     3♦ = some 6-3-2-2

     3♥ = 6-1-2-4 or 6-2-1-4: (if you need to know which, 3♠ asks and
                                 3NT = 6-1-2-4, 4♣ = 6-2-1-4)

     3♠ = 6-1-4-2

     3NT = 6-2-4-1

After 2♠ : 2NT, 3♣ (6-3-3-1) : 3♦ asks for the singleton:

     3♥ = 6-1-3-3

     3♠ = 6-3-1-3

     3NT = 6-3-3-1

After 2♠ : 2NT, 3♦ (6-3-2-2) : 3♥ asks for the 3-card suit:

     3♠ = 6-2-2-3

     3NT = 6-2-3-2

     4♣ = 6-3-2-2

(3NT is bypassed here only when the 3-card suit is hearts. If this is undesirable, do not use the 3♥ relay.)

After the shape is known, 3NT is to play while 4♦ is a puppet to 4♥ *en route* to terminating the auction. Otherwise, step 1 (the cheapest available bid) sets opener's major as trumps and asks for key cards. If the ask is below 4♠, the cheapest reply shows a minimum hand and responder needs to ask again for key cards if still interested.

Suits other than opener's major can also be set. Step 2 (excluding always 3NT and the 4♦ puppet) sets the next longest suit, Step 3 the next longest and Step 4 the shortest suit. Where suits have equal length, a major precedes a minor and clubs precede diamonds.

Some examples:

WEST	EAST	WEST	EAST
♠ K87	♠ AQJ5	2♥	2♠ – relay
♥ AJ10874	♥ 3	2NT (1)	3♣ – relay
♦ J52	♦ AKQ764	3♠ (2)	4♠ (3)
♣ 8	♣ A6	5♣ (4)	5♠ (5)
		6♦ (6)	7♦

(1) Some 6-3-3-1.   (2) Precisely 3-6-3-1.

(3) RKCB with diamonds set as trumps.   (4) One key card.

(5) Asking bid in spades.

(6) ♠K but no ♠Q (see page 127 for answers to control asks).

WEST	EAST	WEST	EAST
♠ A109843	♠ K5	2♠	2NT – relay
♡ 4	♡ A76	3♡ (1)	3♠ – relay
◇ J5	◇ K8	3NT (2)	4♡ (3)
♣ K1083	♣ AQJ652	5◇ (4)	6♣

(1) 6-1-2-4 OR 6-2-1-4.   (2) Precisely 6-1-2-4.
(3) RKCB with clubs set as trumps.
(4) Maximum values (7 losers) and two key cards for clubs, no ♣Q.

WEST	EAST	WEST	EAST
♠ AJ10762	♠ –	2♠	2NT – relay
♡ K54	♡ A76	3♣ (1)	3◇ – relay
◇ 2	◇ AJ1053	3♠ (2)	4◇ (3)
♣ 952	♣ AK643	4♡ (4)	5♣ (5)

(1) Some 6-3-3-1 pattern.   (2) Precisely 6-3-1-3.
(3) Puppet to terminate the auction.
(4) Forced.   (5) After the 4◇ puppet, responder's next bid is terminal.

Other than the relay and Ogust enquiry, change of suit is natural and not forcing. Opener's jump-shift 2♠ : 4♣/4◇/4♡ or 2♡ : 3♠/4♣/4◇ shows a strong suit missing one of the top three honours, either a single-suited hand or a strong suit + support for opener's suit. This is particularly useful if responder has a void. For example:

WEST	EAST	WEST	EAST
♠ A109762	♠ KQ	2♠	4♣ (1)
♡ 98	♡ AKQJ	4♡ (2)	7♣ (3)
◇ 1094	◇ –		
♣ K8	♣ AQJ7643		

(1) Powerful club suit missing one of the top three honours.
(2) Shows the missing club honour but a minimum hand. If maximum, opener shows key cards when holding the missing honour, so that 4♠ would be a maximum with 0 key cards, 4NT = 1 key card, etc.
(3) Safe as long as the 2♠ opening must be better than a jack-high suit.

Defence

Double of an artificial bid is lead-directing.

Countermeasures

Pass denies 1st and 2nd round control in the suit doubled. Bids retain the normal meaning but promise 1st or 2nd round control of the doubled suit.

SOAP – SYSTEM OVER ARTIFICIAL PRE-EMPTION

This method of dealing with artificial low-level openings was developed by Paul Marston, one of the world's leading bidding theorists. You are not likely to encounter such openings in your day-to-day club games but unusual methods are more common at championship level.

1. *If their artificial opening bid shows a suit or suits*

Double is for takeout of the suit(s) *shown*. Other bids have their natural meaning. For example, if they use transfer openings and start with 1♢, showing hearts, double is takeout of hearts while 2♢ and 3♢ are natural bids. You could use a bid of 1♡ as natural and 2♡ as Michaels or use 1♡ and 2♡ both as Michaels, 1♡ to show spades + clubs and 2♡ for spades + diamonds.

Since they have shown at least one specific suit, you do not need exotic methods to deal with it. Most of the time their methods will give you more space than if they had started with a natural bid.

2. *If their artificial opening bid does not show a specific suit*

Since no suit has been shown, you may wish to play in any suit. Marston draws an analogy with competing over their 1NT opening where likewise you may wish to play in any of the four suits.

(a) *Their artificial start is Pass, One Club or One Diamond*

Either major can be bid at the one-level, and a bid of either minor is also natural. Double is for takeout over 1♣ or 1♢ as though their bid were natural. Over a Strong Pass, 1♣ is for takeout. Other bids are natural.

(b) *Their artificial start is One Heart or One Spade*

Now you need something more sophisticated. The Marston model resembles a defence to a 1NT opening.

Over 1♡ (which does not show any specific suit):
Double = 16+ points, any shape. In reply, 1♣ is an artificial negative reply, 0-7 points. Other bids are natural, 8+ points, forcing to game.
1♠ = 11-15 points, 4+ spades. May have a longer outside suit.
1NT = 13-15 balanced.
2♣ = 11-15 points with 5+ hearts.
2♢ = 11-15 points with 5+ diamonds, no 4+ major.
2♡ = 11-15 points, 4 hearts and a longer minor.
2♠ = 11-15 points with 6+ spades.
2NT = 11-15 points, both minors, at least 5-5.
3♣ = 11-15 points with 6+ clubs.

Higher bids are natural and pre-emptive.

If their artificial opening is 1♠ or 1NT, the approach is the same except that 2♢ shows 5+ spades, and 2♠ shows 4 spades and a longer minor, while in reply to Double, 2♣ is the negative.

The hand types fall into three categories, those with 16+ points (start with Double), those in the 0-10 point range (pass unless suitable for a pre-emptive bid) and those of 11-15 points which warrant action. A key rule is that the cheapest bids always show the most important features, major suits.

One of the benefits of SOAP is that it can be used at any level, such as over RCO two-openings (see page 111), a 2NT opening showing a weak pre-empt in any suit, the Gambling 3NT (see page 29) and so on.

If their artificial opening is in a minor suit at the two-level or higher, no artificial structure is needed as the major suits can be bid at the same level. Over any high level artificial bid, Marston recommends passing with length in the suit bid and playing all doubles for takeout (with shortage in the suit bid).

ANOTHER DEFENCE AGAINST CRASH OR RCO OPENINGS

When an opponent opens with an artificial bid showing a two-suiter but no anchor suit is promised (as in CRASH or RCO, page 111 *et seq*), it is important to be able to show your own two-suiter in order to locate the best fit for your side. Avon Wilsmore has put forward a clever scheme:

Double = the matching two-suiter including clubs.
3♣ = the matching two-suiter without clubs.
Other bids are natural.

For example, if they open 2♡ showing majors or minors, Double would show the minors (the pair including clubs) and 3♣ would show the majors (the pair not including clubs). If their opening was 2♠ (red suits or black suits), Double = clubs and spades (the pair including clubs) and 3♣ = hearts and diamonds (the pair without clubs). Over their 2NT opening (odd suits, spades + diamonds OR hearts + clubs), Double shows clubs and hearts, while 3♣ = spades and diamonds.

As 3♣ is forcing (since it figures to be one of their 5+ suits), it can be used with varying strengths from 6 losers or better. You would be most unlucky to find that your two-suiter has the same two suits as opener.

DEFENCE AGAINST NATURAL WEAK TWO-SUITERS

Where administrators in some countries have barred RCO and CRASH openings except at the highest levels, players have switched to natural weak two-suited openings such as 2♡ for 5+ hearts and a second 4+ suit (possibly spades) and 2♠ for 5+ spades and a 4+ minor. Recommended defence against these openings is the same as against a natural weak two opening (which is usually a one-suiter). See pages 14-15.

THE 2NT OPENING FOR THE MINORS

Opening 2NT to show a weak hand with both minors is even more effective than the Unusual 2NT overcall since neither opponent has yet made a bid. The continuations are as after the 2NT overcall (page 68). A response of 3♡ or 3♠ is forcing, showing a strong hand and a 6+ suit.

Defence

3♡ or 3♠ is natural. 3♣ and 3♢ are artificial, showing both majors. 3♣ indicates preference for hearts, 3♢ emphasises spades. A jump to 4♣ or 4♢ is at least 5-5 in the majors with a shortage (singleton or void in the minor bid). Double shows a strong balanced hand and suggests penalties if partner has a decent 4+ holding in the minor they bid.

Countermeasures

Use the same as after a 2NT overcall – see page 69.

THE 2♣ OR 2♢ OPENING SHOWING BOTH MAJORS

An opening to show a weak two-suiter in the majors is often used by pairs who use the 2♡ and 2♠ openings for major-minor two-suiters. The hand pattern can be 5-5, 5-4, 4-4-4-1 and, for the heroic contingent, even 4-4-3-2 is acceptable. Any response in a major is to play. 2NT is the strong enquiry asking for clarification of shape. A minor suit reply to 2NT is natural (4- or 5-card suit) while a major shows a 5+ suit.

Defence

2NT is 16-18 balanced, Double is takeout (minors) or 19+ balanced. 2♡ or 2♠ is natural (expectancy is a strong 6+ suit) while 3♡ or 3♠ is a stopper ask for 3NT, presumably with a long, running minor.

Countermeasures

Doubles are for penalties. A major suit at the 3-level is invitational.

EXTENDED DEFENCE TO NATURAL WEAK TWOS

Over a weak two, 4NT shows both minors and about 4 losers (page 14). A jump to four of their suit – (2♡) : 4♡ shows both minors with 2-3 losers but no loser in their suit (void, ace singleton or A-K doubleton).

Bidding their suit, (2♠) : 3♠, was recommended as Michaels (see page 14). The strength should be around 4-5 losers. With a stronger Michaels type hand, around the 3-loser mark, bid 4♣ (5+ clubs and the other major) or 4♢ (5+ diamonds and the other major).

If you have a powerful one-suiter in a minor, too strong for 3♣ or 3♢, start with a double. If partner bids 2NT (Lebensohl, see page 15), bid 3♢ or 4♣ to show the strength and the minor held.

TAKEOUT DOUBLES OVER PRE-EMPTS AT THE FOUR-LEVEL

Over high-level pre-empts, it is more efficient to play Double for takeout than for penalties or as a general all-round hand. You may miss some penalties but you can cater far more effectively for the more common hands with a shortage in their suit.

After (4♡) : Double, 4NT from advancer is for takeout with both minors, at least 4-4. After (4♠) : Double, 4NT shows a hand that is playable in at least two suits. Finding the best strain and the right game is more important than slam considerations. See also page 30.

DEFENCES AGAINST THEIR 1NT OPENING

BERGEN (also known as DONT : DISTURBING OPPONENT'S NT)
Devised by Marty Bergen, the structure is

Double = a one-suiter, usually not spades
 (2♣ from the advancer asks the doubler to pass or bid his suit)
♣ = Clubs and another suit
♢ = Diamonds and a major (denies clubs)
♡ = Both majors
♠ = Natural, one-suiter in spades

The same approach can be used if they double your 1NT opening (with redouble showing the one-suiter) or if they overcall 1NT.

POTTAGE (Great Britain) OR CAPPELLETTI/HAMILTON (USA)
Double = Penalties
♣ = Any one-suiter
♢ = Both majors
♡ = Hearts and a minor
♠ = Spades and a minor

TRASH (TRAnsfer or two Suits Higher)
A suit bid shows either 5+ cards in the next ranking suit *or* the other two suits.

(1NT) : 2♣ = Transfer to diamonds *or* both majors. If advancer bids 2♢, partner's 2♡ bid then confirms both majors, while other suit bids show the suit bid plus diamonds (2♠ = spades + diamonds; 3♣ = clubs + diamonds and 2NT = hearts + diamonds)

(1NT) : 2♢ = transfer to hearts *or* spades + clubs, and so on.

Countermeasures by the 1NT side
These can be found on pages 80–86.

12. MODERN TIMES

Bridge continues to evolve. New ideas are tested and played for some time. They are then either discarded, become part of mainstream bridge or are adopted by a significant number of top players. The material in this chapter covers, by and large, the most recent developments in bridge bidding. They may give you ideas for inclusion in your regular partnerships. Be sure to discuss them fully with your partner(s).

BANZAI POINTS

The 4-3-2-1 count is pretty much entrenched among bridge players, but it is easy to see that, as a trick-taking measure, this count is inadequate. Consider these examples:

Dummy	1. 4 3 2	2. 4 3 2	3. 4 3 2	4. 4 3 2
Declarer	A Q 6	K Q J	A K 7	A Q J

#1 and #2 both have 6 points, but #2 has two sure tricks, while #1 has a 50% chance of two tricks. #3 and #4 have 7 points, but #3 has two tricks and no more, while #3, with sufficient entries to dummy has a 50% chance of three tricks.

The 4-3-2-1 count makes no allowance for the presence of tens, but a ten might provide an extra trick or a much better chance for an extra trick.

Dummy	5. 7 2	6. 7 2	7. 6 4 2	8. 6 4 2
Declarer	K Q J 6	K Q J 10	A J 7	A J 10

#5 and #6 both count six points, but #6 has three sure tricks, while #5 will make only two tricks most of the time. #7 and #8 both measure five points, but given enough entries to dummy, #8 has a 75% chance of two tricks, while #7 has only a 25% chance of two tricks.

A ten can be particularly useful when attached to higher honours, but this need not be so.

Dummy	9. 10 2	10. 7 2	11. 10 4 2	12. 6 4 2
Declarer	K Q J 6	K Q J 10	Q J 7	Q J 5

In #9 and #10, you have three tricks, whether the ten is on its own or with the higher honours. In #11 you have a trick even though the ten is by itself. Without the ten, #12 has a 75% chance of scoring a trick.

The conclusion to be drawn from this is that some allowance should be made when your hand includes one or more tens. Some advocate adding half a point for a ten. A different solution was proposed in *Better Balanced Bidding* where David (Banzai) Jackson suggested a return to a previous valuation method, the 5-4-3-2-1 count (A = 5, K = 4, Q = 3, J = 2 and 10 = 1) for balanced hands. With this method, #1 measures 8 points and #2 = 9 points, indicating that #2 is more valuable than #1. Likewise, #4 (10 points) is better than #3 (9 points). Adding1 point for a ten also goes some way to estimating the potential value of holding that card.

The total number of points in the pack when using the 4-3-2-1 count is 40. When using 5-4-3-2-1, the total is 60. It is thus easy to change a range in 4-3-2-1 to 5-4-3-2-1 by simply adding 50%. Thus, a 12-14 1NT = an 18-21 1NT in Banzai Points (BPs). A 15-17 1NT = 22-25 BPs, while a 20-22 2NT = 30-33 BPs.

A requirement of 25 HCP to bid 3NT = 37.5 BPs, so at least 37 and preferably 38. Similarly, 33 points for 6NT becomes 49.5 BPs. When using the 5-4-3-2-1 count for balanced hands, it is sensible to add extra points for a 5-card suit in a 5-3-3-2 pattern. A reasonable allowance is 2 points for a 5-card with two honours or fewer and 3 points for a 5-card suit that include three or more honours.

SPLINTERS AFTER A 1NT OPENING

WEST 1	EAST 1	WEST 2	EAST 2
♠ K 3	♠ A Q 5 4	♠ K 3	♠ A Q 5 4
♡ J 8 7	♡ 6	♡ A Q J 5	♡ 6
♢ A Q J 4 3	♢ K 8 7 6	♢ Q J 4 3	♢ K 8 7 6
♣ Q 9 8	♣ A 7 6 3	♣ 9 8 4	♣ A 7 6 3

How should East proceed after West opens a weak 1NT? Clearly W1-E1 should avoid 3NT, while 3NT is fine for W2-E2. Stayman 2♣ will not solve the problem. Even if West 1 had a fourth low heart, 3NT would still be in some jeopardy, while 5♢ is a fine contract. The same would apply to a strong 1NT (swap the ♢J for the ♢K).

If East can show the shortage, West should be able to judge whether 3NT is a sensible spot. This can be achieved via 1NT : 3♣ / 3♢ / 3♡ / 3♠ = a void or a singleton in the suit bid. Responder should not have a 5-card major. Common patterns would be 4-4-4-1 and 5-4-3-1, but a long minor is feasible. If opener rejects 3NT, responder can bid 5-minor.

After the splinter, opener can choose 3NT or bid a suit to seek support there. W1-E1 would bid 1NT : 3♥, 4◇ : 5◇, Pass. W2-E2 would bid 1NT : 3♥, 3NT, Pass.

An auction like 1NT : 3◇, 3♥ : 3♠ would imply responder had 4 spades, but only 3 hearts. If opener bids a suit and responder has support and slam ambitions, responder can bid the short suit or bid 4NT for key cards.

DEFENCE

Double to ask partner to lead dummy's short suit.

COUNTERMEASURES

(1) Note the double and take action accordingly.

(2) Change the splinter approach to:

SUBMARINE SPLINTERS AFTER A 1NT OPENING

In this method, you bid the suit below your short suit. 1NT : 3♣ = short diamonds, 3◇ = short hearts, 3♥ = short spades, 3♠ = short clubs. This virtually eliminates the lead-directing double. It also gives opener an extra bid, the cheapest bid, i.e., the short suit.

With the short suit well-stopped and no interest in another contract, opener bids 3NT. With no intention of playing in 3NT, opener bids the short suit. Bidding then continues naturally to the best spot. For example:

1NT : 3◇, 3♥ : 3♠, 3NT . . . 3◇ = short hearts, 3♥ = not keen on 3NT, 3♠ = I have four spades (the splinter denies a 5+ major), 3NT denies four spades and lets responder continue the dialogue. Responder can now bid a 5-card minor or bid 4♥ if 4-1-4-4.

If opener bids a suit other than the short suit but below 3NT, opener has four cards in that suit and also at least one stopper in the short suit. If no major suit fit is found, the partnership can subside in 3NT. For example, 1NT : 3♣, 3♠ : 3NT . . . 3♣ = short diamonds, 3♠ = four spades, not four hearts and the short suit stopped, 3NT = not four spades. Similarly, in 1NT : 3♣, 3♥ : 3♠, 3NT : Pass, opener has four hearts, responder has four spades and not four hearts and opener does not have four spades.

After opener or responder has bid a natural suit, bidding the short suit shows slam interest. Opener's jump to 4-major after the short suit was revealed shows a 5-card major and wastage in the short suit. Bidding the short suit and later showing a 5-card major = no wastage in the short suit.

WRINKLES AFTER SOUTH AFRICAN TEXAS

After the 1NT : 4♣ and 1NT : 4◇ transfers to 4♡ and 4♠ respectively (see page 36), opener can use the in-between step to deny interest in being declarer and let responder become declarer. For example, opener holds:

♠ K Q J   ♡ A K   ◇ 8 7 6 2   ♣ 9 8 7 3

If it goes 1NT : 4◇ transfer to spades, there is no benefit for opener being declarer and so opener should bid 4♡, 'Please play it yourself'. If playing a strong 1NT, add an ace to the hand above and the same strategy applies.

After opener does take the transfer, 1NT : 4♣, 4♡ or 1NT : 4◇, 4♠, responder can use this route to ask for key cards. The other transfer paths, 1NT : 2◇, 2♡ : 4NT or 1NT : 2♡, 2♠ : 4NT can be used as quantitative.

MORE ON 5-CARD MAJOR STAYMAN AFTER 1NT

5-card Major Stayman after 1NT was introduced on page 123. If you have 5-3 in the majors and enough for game, you can use 1NT : 2♣ to ask and still use transfers after opener denies a 5-card major. This is an attractive structure:

After 1NT : 2♣, 2◇ – no 5-major, responder could pass (weak hand with, say, a 3-3-5-2 pattern), bid 2♡ , 2♠ or 2NT, natural, not forcing. Higher rebids by responder are forcing to game:
3♣ = 4-card major Stayman
3◇ = transfer to hearts
3♡ = transfer to spades
3♠ = both minors, some slam interest

After 3♣, opener rebids 3♡ or 3♠ (4-card major and some 4-4-3-2 pattern), 3NT (no 4-card major and not 4-3-3-3) or 3◇ (any 4-3-3-3 pattern). Over 3♡, responder's 3NT would show four spades, but responder could also bid 3♠ with four spades and slam prospects or with a desire to be declarer. Over 3◇, responder can still show a 4-card major, but opener's 4-3-3-3 pattern may encourage responder simply to bid 3NT.

WEST	EAST	WEST	EAST
♠ K J 8	♠ Q 4	1NT	2♣
♡ A 7 6 3	♡ 9 8 5 4	2◇	3♣
◇ Q J 4	◇ A K 8 7	3◇	3NT
♣ Q 9 8	♣ K J 6	Pass	

4♡ is a terrible spot. If using a strong 1NT, interchange the ◇4 and ◇K.

After 3♢, transfer to hearts, and 3♡, transfer to spades, opener bids the major with 3- or 4-card support or 3NT otherwise. Once opener shows support, responder can sign-off or start cue-bidding or ask for key cards.

After 3♠, opener can bid 3NT (no interest in either minor) or bid 4♣ or 4♢ to set that minor as trumps and start cue-bidding. One could also play, after 4♣ or 4♢, that the cheapest bid is asking for key cards rather than a cue-bid. Another option, after 3♠, is for opener to bid 4♡ (sets clubs) or 4♠ (sets diamonds) to ask for key cards.

MORE ON BIDDING AFTER A 2NT OPENING

The basic responses to 2NT appear on page 37 and Puppet Stayman after 2NT is on page 124. There have been considerable developments in this area and you should find the following structure more comprehensive.

After 2NT:

3♣ = 5-card Major Stayman. Opener bids 3♡ or 3♠ (5-card major), 3♢ (no 5-major, but at least one 4-card major or three spades) or 3NT (no 5-card major, no 4-card major and not three spades).

3♢ = transfer to hearts and 3♡ = transfer to spades

3♠ = both minors, likely to have slam interest

4♣ and 4♢ = natural, 6+ suit, slam interest. Opener should cue-bid.

3NT, 4♡ or 4♠ = natural, to play

After 2NT : 3♣, 3♢, if you have memory problems, you can play 3♡ = four hearts and 3♠ = four spades. The downside of this, of course, is that the much stronger hand might become dummy. Most experts prefer Puppet Stayman after this beginning where 3♡ = four spades, 3♠ = four hearts and 3NT = no 4-card major.

What does responder do with 4-4 in the majors? One approach, after the 3♢ rebid by opener, is to play 4♣ = 4-4 majors, slam interest, and 4♢ = 4-4 majors, no slam interest.

If memory is not a problem for you or partner, try this approach:

3♡ = four spades *OR* no major (opener bids 3♠ with 4 spades, else 3NT)

3♠ = four hearts (opener can bid 4♡ or cue-bid to show heart support and a strong hand if responder has slam interest)

3NT = 4-4 majors, no slam interest
4NT = 4-4 majors, slam inviting
5NT = 4-4 majors, pick a slam.

4♣ = 4-4-1-4 singleton diamond
4♦ = 4-4-4-1, singleton club

Opener can now show support for a major, raise responder's minor or bid the short suit to set opener's minor and suggest slam potential.

4♥ = 5 spades – 4 hearts, no slam interest. Opener passes or bids 4♠.
4♠ = 5 spades – 4 hearts and slam potential. Opener bids 4NT, key card for hearts, or 5♣, key card for spades. Because the 3♦ bid promised three spades or one major or both majors, responder is guaranteed to find a fit with the 4♥ or 4♠ bid.

The memory-aid for this method is that, after 2NT : 3♣, 3♦, every bid from 3NT onwards shows at least 4-4 in the majors. The danger is that either partner or both partners forget that 2NT : 3♣, 3♦ : 3NT (natural sounding) shows both majors and you end up in 3NT instead of 4-major.

One of the benefits is that responder can show a hand with slam potential and a 5-card minor via 2NT : 3♣, 3♦ : 3♥, 3♠ or 3NT, 4♣ or 4♦. The 3♥ rebid said, 'spades or no major'. Whether opener rebids 3♠ or 3NT, opener's 4-minor shows a 5+ suit and slam interest. Opener will cue-bid with support for the minor or bid 4NT (minimum) or 5NT (maximum) without support. If opener bids 3♠ over 3♥ and responder has 4 spades, responder can bid 4♠ (to play) or 4♥ (slam interest with spade support).

After 2NT : 3♦ transfer, opener can simply accept the transfer or use one of several options to super-accept. This one covers many hands:

2NT : 3♦, 3♠ = good heart support and a source of tricks outside. To find the source-of-tricks suit, responder bids 3NT and opener bids 4♣ or 4♦, to show the suit, or 4♥ if the suit is spades. Source of tricks is a suit of K-Q-J-x-x or better.

2NT : 3♦, 3NT / 4♣ / 4♦ = cheapest cue-bid, with good heart support and a maximum 2NT. Opener's 3NT = cue-bid in spades. After any of the super-accept rebids, 4♦ if available is a re-transfer to hearts.

2NT : 3♦, 4♥ = 4+ support, maximum 2NT and control in every suit.

Analogous sequences apply after 2NT : 3♥ transfer, with 3NT = outside source of tricks (4♣ asks and 4♦ / 4♥ = that suit and 4♠ = source of tricks in clubs), 4♣ / 4♦ / 4♥ = cheapest cue-bid with good spade support and 4♠ = 4+ spade support, control in every suit and a maximum 2NT. 4♥ if available is a re-transfer to 4♠.

After 2NT : 3♠, opener rebids 3NT (no minor support), 4♣ or 4♦ to set the minor or 4♥ (clubs) / 4♠ (diamonds) as a key card ask in the suit set.

Special responses

2NT : 5♡ or 5♠ = 7-card suit to the K-Q or A-Q and an outside king. Opener can pass, raise to six or bid 5NT to ask for the king. For example:

WEST	EAST	WEST	EAST
♠ A 10 9	♠ 6 4 3	2NT	5♡
♡ A 7 3	♡ K Q 9 8 5 4 2	5NT	6♣
◇ A Q 4	◇ 3	7NT	Pass
♣ A Q J 3	♣ K 2		

2NT : 3◇, 3♡ : 5♡ or 2NT : 3♡ : 3♠, 5♠ = 7-card suit to the K-Q or A-Q and an outside ace. Opener should be able to place the contract.

X – Y – Z

While the Benjamin 2♣ and 2◇ openings (see page 20) have lost much of their popularity, 2♣ and 2◇ have come into vogue in another area. It originated with auctions which began 1X : 1Y, 1NT. After that start, 2♣ is a puppet to 2◇. Opener has no option but to bid 2◇. Responder might then pass (sign-off with length in diamonds or support for opener's diamonds) or rebid to show a hand worth a game-invitation. For example:

(1)	(2)	(3)	(4)
♠ Q J 9 7 6 3	♠ A J 9 8 3	♠ A J 9 8 3	♠ A J 9 8 3
♡ 7 3	♡ J 2	♡ Q J 9 8	♡ Q J 9 8
◇ Q J 7	◇ K Q 8	◇ 4 3 2	◇ K 2
♣ 9 3	♣ 8 7 3	♣ 8	♣ 9 2

After 1♣ : 1♠, 1NT (12-14): Hand (1) bids 2♠, a sign-off. Hand (2) bids 2♣ : 2◇, 2♠ to invite game with five spades. Hand (3) bids 2♡ to show 5+ spades, 4+ hearts and no interest in game. Opener should pass or revert to 2♠. Hand (4) bids 2♣ : 2◇, 2♡ to invite game with five spades – four hearts. Opener can pass, bid 2♠ or 2NT, counter-invite with 3♡ or 3♠ or jump to 3NT, 4♡ or 4♠. You can adjust the strength of responder's hand for these sequences if your 1NT rebid shows 15-16 or 15-17 points.

There are other invitational options after 1X : 1Y, 1NT : 2♣, 2◇. Thus, 3X = invitational in opener's suit and 3Y = 6+ suit and invitational in responder's suit. 2Y would invite game in responder's suit, but suggest no more than a 5-card suit. 3-new suit = invitational with length in that suit (for example, 1◇ : 1♠, 1NT : 2♣, 2◇ : 3♣ = invitational with club length) and 2NT = inviting 3NT. For 1X : 1Y, 1NT : 2NT, see page 168.

After 1X : 1Y, 1NT, responder's rebid of 2♦ is artificial and forcing to game. There are other rebids that force to game, but these have more extreme shape than those that travel via 2♦. The huge benefit of the 2♦ rebid is that the partnership can explore game prospects and know that the bidding will not be dropped below game. In addition it provides plenty of room for slam investigation.

Bidding after 2♦ is natural. A suit bypassed denies the relevant holding in that suit. For example, after 1♣ : 1♥, 1NT : 2♦, 2♥ = 3-card support, 2♠ = four spades and denies three hearts, 2NT = not four spades and not three hearts, 3♣ = five clubs and not three hearts and 3♦ = four diamonds and four clubs, not three hearts, and so a 3-2-4-4 pattern.

Players that adopt X-Y-Z usually play that a rebid in a suit at the one-level shows an unbalanced hand and a 1NT rebid may bypass a 4-card major. For example, for 1♦ : 1♥, 1NT, opener could have four spades. This might occasionally lead to an inferior part-score, where responder has four spades, but is too weak to invite game, but the benefits of knowing opener has unbalanced shape more than compensates for this. Thus, 1♦ : 1♥, 1♠ = 5+ diamonds, 4 spades or have a 4-1-4-4 pattern, 1♣ : 1♦, 1♥ = 5+ clubs, 4 hearts or 4-4-1-4, while 1♣ : 1♦, 1♠ or 1♣ : 1♥, 1♠ = 5+ clubs and 4 spades. Open 1♦ if 4-1-4-4.

With X-Y-Z, it is also common after 1♣ to show a 4-card major ahead of a longer minor, unless the hand clearly has game values or slam potential. With weaker hands, responder can show the major and, after opener's 1NT, sign off in diamonds via 2♣ : 2♦, Pass or invite game with length in diamonds via 2♣ : 2♦, 3♦. This can have a benefit of disclosing less to the opponents if a major-suit fit is found and the diamond suit has not been mentioned.

OTHER CONTINUATIONS AFTER 1NT

Responder's reverse is forcing to game and shows at least a 6-4 pattern. For example, 1♣ : 1♦, 1NT : 2♥ = 4 hearts and 6+ diamonds. With a 4-5 holding, responder uses the 2♦ rebid as a game-force.

Jumps to the three-level are forcing to game and if the jump is not in responder's suit, it promises at least a 5-5 pattern (1♣ : 1♠, 1NT : 3♥ or 1♣ : 1♠, 1NT : 3♣). A jump to game in responder's suit is to play. 1♣ : 1♠, 1NT : 4♥ offers opener the choice of game and has no slam interest, otherwise responder would have rebid 3♥. A jump to three-of-responder's-suit sets that suit as trumps, indicates slam prospects and asks opener to start cue-bidding.

THE 2NT REBID AFTER 1NT

With 1X : 1Y, 1NT : 2♣ artificial, puppet to 2◇, and 1X : 1Y, 1NT : 3♣ forcing to game with a 5-5 pattern, how can responder sign off in clubs? Since 1X : 1Y, 1NT : 2♣, 2◇ : 2NT is the route to invite game in 3NT, the sequence 1X : 1Y, 1NT : 2NT is free for other purposes. One of these is to sign off in clubs. Just as you cannot sign off in 2♣ after a 1NT opening, so that is also not available with X-Y-Z. In any event, if you did try to sign off in 2♣ in natural methods, competent opponents would almost invariably compete and push you to 3♣ anyway.

The 2NT rebid forces opener to bid 3♣. With the weak sign-off hand, responder passes. If responder does bid again, it is game-forcing and shows four cards in responder's first suit and 5-card club support. Thus, after 1♣ : 1♡, 1NT : 2NT, 3♣, for example, responder's actions are:

Pass = weak, a sign-off

3◇ = a 1-4-3-5 pattern

3♡ = 2-4-2-5 and poor doubletons, offering a choice of contracts

3♠ = a 3-4-1-5 pattern

3NT = 2-4-2-5, strong doubletons, but still offering a choice of contract

GOING FURTHER WITH X-Y-Z

When X-Y-Z became popular after a 1NT rebid from opener, players soon decided to apply it also after a one-level suit rebid. This eliminated the need for fourth-suit forcing here since a 2◇ rebid was always available to force to game, regardless of the suit opened. For example, 1♣ : 1♡, 1♠ : 2♣ = puppet to 2◇ and 1♣ : 1♡, 1♠ : 2◇ = artificial, forcing to game and coincidentally the same bid as fourth-suit forcing. Likewise, 1◇ : 1♡, 1♠ : 2◇ = artificial, forcing to game, even though the opening bid was 1◇. To sign off in diamonds, responder would bid 2♣ over 1♠ as a puppet to 2◇ and then pass. To invite game with diamond support after opener's 1♠ rebid, responder bids 2♣ : 2◇, 3◇.

The only difference when opener rebids in a suit at the one-level rather than 1NT is that opener might have a very strong hand. When responder rebids 2♣, opener might not be prepared to bid 2◇ and risk being passed out there. After 1♣ : 1♡, 1♠ : 2♣ or similar sequences, if opener has about 17+ points and is prepared to look for game opposite 6-9 points, then opener rejects the 2◇ puppet and makes any natural bid. Any bid by opener other than 2◇ over 2♣ shows such a hand.

TRANSFERS AFTER 1♣

Suppose you open 1♣ and partner responds 1♡. What do you do with:

♠ A Q J   ♡ Q 7 2   ◇ 7 6   ♣ A 8 7 3 2

If you rebid 1NT, responder is normally disinclined to repeat a 5-card suit and 2♡ might easily be better than 1NT. On the other hand, if you raise to 2♡, responder might have a poor-to-modest 4-card suit and 1NT is where you want to be. Most of the time 1NT will be preferable to playing in a 4-3 fit at the two-level.

Because transfers work so well after a 1NT or 2NT opening, many experts have adopted them after a 1♣ opening. Thus:

1♣ : 1◇ = 4+ hearts

1♣ : 1♡ = 4+ spades

1♣ : 1♠ = 4+ diamonds, no 4-card major unless worth a game-force

Some play that 1♣ : 1♠ = no major, balanced, but not ideal for a no-trump bid, or diamonds, while others play it as simply no 4+ major. You and partner can choose, but if you have not used these transfers before, the recommendation is to use 1♣ : 1♠ = 4+ diamonds as above.

After the transfer response, there are different treatments for opener's rebids. The most common is:

1♣ : 1◇, 1♡ = exactly three hearts, but not a hand that fits a 2NT rebid

1♣ : 1◇, 2♡ = minimum opening with 4-card support

1♣ : 1◇, 3♡ = 4-card support, extra values, like a natural 1♣ : 1♡, 3♡

1♣ : 1◇, 1♠ or 1NT or 2♣ or 2◇ = natural rebids that deny three hearts (the 2◇ rebid is a natural reverse).

You would show support and game values as you already do, via splinters or other methods. The bidding follows analogous lines for the 1♣ : 1♡ (4+ spades) sequences, with 1♣ : 1♡, 1♠ showing exactly three spades.

Most play 1♣ : 1◇, 1♡ and 1♣ : 1♡, 1♠ as forcing and that is the recommended approach. Some play these as non-forcing and will choose some other action (reverse, jump-shift) with very strong hands and show the 3-card support on the next round.

One of the great benefits of these transfers is that responder instantly knows whether an 8-card trump fit exists or not. That does not apply to this variation, where opener's acceptance of the transfer = 2 or 3 trumps:

1♣ : 1◊, 1♡ = 2 or 3 hearts and 1♣ : 1♡, 1♠ = 2 or 3 spades, typically a weak 1NT opening. With enough to invite game or force to game, responder can use X-Y-Z to clarify the degree of support. A benefit here is that 1♣ : 1◊, 1NT or 1♣ : 1♡, 1NT = 18-19 points, balanced.

The next two approaches work very well, allowing you to stop low in some cases and giving you more room to explore slam in other cases:

1♣ : 1◊, 1♡ = 3 hearts or 4 hearts, but only 4 hearts if minimum

1♣ : 1♡, 1♠ = 3 spades or 4 spades, but only 4 spades if minimum

Other rebids:

(A) 1♣ : 1◊, 2♡ and 1♣ : 1♡, 2♠ = 4-card support, 18-19 points and balanced or a 5-4-2-2 pattern. Responder can unravel the shape of opener's hand via the cheapest bid as a relay.

1♣ : 1◊, 2♡ : 2♠ = asking. Opener bids 2NT = 3-4-3-3, 3♣ with some 4-4-3-2 and 3◊ if 2-4-2-5. After 2NT, responder can set the contract or set a trump suit and start cue-bidding. After 3◊, responder can bid game or start cue-bidding or ask for key cards. After 3♣, responder can set hearts with 3♡ and start cue-bidding or clarify opener's pattern with a 3◊ relay. Opener rebids in steps: 3♡ = 2-4-3-4, 3♠ = 3-4-2-4 and 3NT = 4-4-2-3. The order is high-shortage-first: 2 spades / 3 spades / 4 spades.

The continuations are analogous after 1♣ : 1♡, 2♠, with 2NT the relay bid. Opener's rebids are the same as for hearts above, except that the bid to show the 4-3-3-3 is 3NT and the high-shortage refers to hearts.

1♣ : 1◊, 3♡ and 1♣ : 1♡, 3♠ = 4-card support, 15-17 points, just like a natural 1♣ : 1♡, 3♡ and 1♣ : 1♠, 3♠ sequence.

(B) Reversing the above auctions, so that 1♣ : 1◊, 2♡ and 1♣ : 1♡, 2♠ = 4-card support and 15-17 points, just like natural 1♣ : 1♡, 3♡ and 1♣ : 1♠, 3♠ sequences. This will keep you lower if responder has a poor hand and also allow responder to make a trial bid with mild game interest.

1♣ : 1◊, 3♡ and 1♣ : 1♡, 3♠ = 4-card support, 18-19 points and balanced or a 5-4-2-2 pattern. Responder does not have room to discover opener's exact pattern.

In both approaches, the stronger hand becomes declarer. You and partner need to determine whether to adopt (A) or (B).

After 1♣ : 1◊, 1♡ and 1♣ : 1♡, 1♠, responder can continue with 1NT, 6-9 points, not forcing, or with X-Y-Z or 2NT (pages 166-168).

After 1♣ : 1◇, 1♡, responder might rebid 1♠. This will show four spades with 6-9 points and normally denies 5+ hearts. With more points, responder would continue with the 2♣ puppet (10-12 points) or the 2◇ game force (with 13+ points). After 1♣ : 1◇, 1♡ : 1♠, opener can revert to 2♡, raise spades or rebid naturally (1NT or 2♣ if minimum).

X-Y-Z after a transfer response

Where 1♣ : 1◇, 1♡ or 1♣ : 1♡, 1♠ = 3-card support or, if minimum, 4-card support, then after the 2♣ puppet, opener bids 2◇ with 3-card support only and below 17 HCP, 2-Major with 4-card support and balanced shape, 3-Major with four trumps, a 4-4-3-2 pattern and 14 points, or a very good 13, or 2NT with four trumps and a 4-3-3-3 pattern and 14 points (or 13 very good points). Other bids would be natural and show 3-card support only and 17+ points.

After opener's action after 2♣, responder's continuation should not be difficult. A useful sequence for responder after 2♣ : 2◇ is a 3NT rebid (1♣ : 1◇, 1♡ : 2♣, 2◇ : 3NT or 1♣ : 1♡, 1♠ : 2♣, 2◇ : 3NT). This shows the minimum values for game with a 5-card major and a 5-3-3-2 pattern. Opener is given the choice of 4-Major or 3NT. With a 4-3-3-3 pattern, it will often be best for opener to pass 3NT. With other shapes, it is usually preferable for opener to choose 4-Major.

If responder bids 2◇ (artificial game-force) after 1♣ : 1◇, 1♡ or 1♠ (3-card support or, if minimum, 4-card support), opener will bid 2-Major with a balanced 11-14, 3-Major with a 5-4-2-2 pattern, not strong enough for a jump-bid to show that shape, or 2NT with a 4-3-3-3 pattern. After 2NT, responder can ask for the 4-card suit with 3♣. Opener shows the 4-card major held or bids 3◇ to show four clubs. Opener's other rebids deny four hearts, with 3NT showing 5 clubs and 3 hearts in a 5-3-3-2 pattern and 3♣ showing 6+ clubs and 3 hearts.

Splinters are available after a transfer response just as they would be after a natural response. A possible approach would be:

1♣ : 1◇, 2♠ / 3◇ = four hearts, 0-1 spade / diamond, 15-17 points

1♣ : 1♡, 3◇ / 3♡ = four spades, 0-1 diamond/ heart, 15-17 points

1♣ : 1◇, 3♠ / 4◇ = four hearts, 0-1 spade / diamond, 18+ points

1♣ : 1♡, 4◇ / 4♡ = four spades, 0-1 diamond/ heart, 18+ points

After 1♣ : 1◇, 1♡ : 2◇ and 1♣ : 1♡, 1♠ : 2◇, opener's jump-bid in a new suit would also be a splinter with 4-card support, about 11-14 points, not strong enough to justify one of the above splinter rebids.

After 1♣ : 1♠ (4+ diamonds), opener can rebid 1NT with a minimum hand. It might be off-shape: 4-4-1-4, 3-4-1-5 and 4-3-1-5 patterns are possible. With support for diamonds, opener can bid 2◇ (minimum) or 3◇ (stronger, 15-17 points) or splinter with 3♡ or 3♠ (stronger still, about 18+ points). Without support and unsuitable for a 1NT rebid, opener can bid 2♣ (minimum), 3♣ (better, 15-17 points) or 2♡ / 2♠ as a natural reverse.

After 1♣ : 1♠, 2♣, responder can bid 2◇ to play or 2NT or 3◇ to invite game. 1♣ : 1♠, 2♣ : 2♡ / 2♠ = game-force, 4-card suit or game-inviting or better and showing a stopper in the bid suit. With four cards in the major bid, opener raises to the three-level, otherwise treats it as a stopper auction, looking for 3NT.

ONE-LEVEL COMPETITION AND TRANSFERS

If the opponents intervene cheaply, you do not need to lose transfers. Double and redouble can be harnessed to carry out the transfers.

After 1♣ : (Double) . . .

● Redouble = 4+ diamonds.

● 1◇ = 4+ hearts

● 1♡ = 4+ spades

● 1♠ = no-trump hand, but unsuitable for a no-trump bid

● Higher bids have their normal meaning, ignoring the double.

After 1♣ : (1◇) . . .

● Double = 4+ hearts

● 1♡ = 4+ spades

● 1♠ = no-trump hand, but unsuitable for a no-trump bid

● Higher bids have their normal meaning, ignoring the double. Most would play 2◇ as a limit raise or better in clubs.

After 1♣ : (1♡) . . .

● Double = 4+ spades

● 1♠ = diamonds, but not strong enough to bid 2◇, natural, forcing

● Higher bids have their normal meaning, ignoring the double. Most would play 2♡ as a limit raise or better in clubs.

After 1♣ : (1♠) or higher, transfers are off and your usual methods apply.

If opener accepts the transfer or rebids elsewhere at the one-level, then X-Y-Z and opener's other systemic rebids will apply, as usual.

After 1 ◇ : (Double) . . .

• Redouble = 4+ hearts

• 1 ♡ = 4+ spades

• 1 ♠ = clubs, but not strong enough to bid 2 ♣, natural, forcing

• Higher bids have their normal meaning, ignoring the double.

After 1 ◇ : (1 ♡) . . .

• Double = 4+ spades

• 1 ♠ = clubs, but not strong enough to bid 2 ♣, natural, forcing

• Higher bids have their normal meaning, ignoring the double. Most would play 2 ♡ as a limit raise or better in diamonds.

After 1 ◇ : (1 ♠) or higher, transfers are off and your usual methods apply.

After 1 ♡ : (Double) . . .

• Redouble = 4+ spades

• 1 ♠ = 6-9 points, unsuitable for 1NT, both minors or one long minor. If opener rebids 1NT, responder can bid 2 ♣ or 2 ◇, natural and not forcing. If stronger, responder would have chosen a stronger bid initially.

• Higher bids have their normal meaning, ignoring the double. Most would play 2 ♠ as a limit raise or better in hearts.

After an opening bid of 1 ♠, transfers do not apply, whether there is opposition bidding or not.

TRANSFER REBIDS AFTER 1X : 1Y, 2NT

Because transfers are so beneficial after a 1NT or 2NT opening, players are eager to introduce them in other auctions. This works particularly well after opener's jump-rebid of 2NT, balanced and 18-19 points or so.

(A) After 1X : 1Y, 2NT . . .

• 3 ♣ = transfer to diamonds

• 3 ◇ = transfer to hearts

• 3 ♡ = transfer to spades

• 3 ♠ = transfer to clubs

Examples:

1♣ : 1♡ (natural), 2NT : 3◇ = 5+ hearts. Opener is expected to bid 3♡.

1♣ : 1♡ (natural), 2NT : 3♡ = transfer to spades, showing 4 hearts and 4 spades, asks opener to choose the contract. With four spades, opener would normally bid 3♠, which would be stronger than 4♠ (fast arrival).

1♣ : 1♠ (natural), 2NT : 3♡ = 5+ spades. Opener is expected to bid 3♠.

1♣ : 1♠ (natural), 2NT : 3◇ = transfer to hearts, 5+ spades, 4+ hearts. Opener can support hearts, prefer spades or rebid 3NT without support for either major. If opener cue-bids 4♣ or 4◇ over 3◇, that should show strong support for hearts. After 4♣, 4◇ is a re-transfer to 4♡.

1◇ : 1♡ (natural), 2NT : 3♠ = transfer to clubs. Here opener is not obliged to bid 4♣. If opener does not have support for clubs or does not wish to support clubs, opener simply rebids 3NT. There is an inference here that responder has only four hearts and longer clubs. With five hearts and 4+ clubs, responder would have bid 3◇ over 2NT (five hearts) and after 3♡, responder can bid 4♣ to show clubs.

(B) In this approach, 3◇, 3♡ and 3♠ are still transfers, but 3♣ over 2NT is a puppet to 3◇. It does not promise a diamond suit or extra diamonds. It depends on responder's continuation. Benefits from this approach are that responder can show 5-5 patterns as opposed to 5-4 and, with slam potential, responder can set a trump suit and start cue-bidding.

Examples:

1♣ : 1♠ (natural), 2NT : 3◇ = 5+ spades and exactly four hearts

1♣ : 1♠ (natural), 2NT : 3♣, 3◇ : 3♡ = 5+ spades and five hearts. Opener can now support hearts, prefer spades or rebid 3NT. A cue-bid of 4♣ or 4◇ agrees hearts as trumps and is stronger than a raise to 4♡.

1♣ : 1♠ (natural), 2NT : 3♡ = 5+ spades. Opener should bid 3♠. Responder might then bid 3NT, choice of contracts, or 4♣ or 4◇, second suit, forcing and exactly four cards in the minor. Responder might even pass 3♠ with a hand that was not really worth an initial response.

1♣ : 1♠ (natural), 2NT : 3♣, 3◇ : 3♠ sets spades as trumps and starts cue-bidding. Responder has long spades and ambitions for slam.

1♣ : 1♠ (natural), 2NT : 3♠ = exactly four spades (no transfer to spades) and 5+ clubs. Opener should cue-bid.

1♣ : 1♠ (natural), 2NT : 3♣, 3◇ : 4♣ = 5 spades, 5 clubs, slam interest

1♣ : 1◇, 2NT : 3♣, 3◇ : 3NT = mild slam invitation, 5+ diamonds

1♣ : 1◇, 2NT : 3♣, 3◇ : 4◇ sets diamonds as trumps, asks for cue-bid

1♣ : 1◇, 2NT : 4NT = quantitative

1♣ : 1◇, 2NT : 3♣, 3◇ : 4NT = quantitative with five diamonds

1♣ : 1◇, 2NT : 3♣, 3◇ : 5NT = five diamonds, pick a slam

1♣ : 1◇, 2NT : 3♠ = 4 diamonds, 4 clubs, slam interest

1♣ : 1◇, 2NT : 4♣ = 4 diamonds, 5 clubs, slam interest

1♣ : 1◇, 2NT : 3♣, 3◇ : 4♣ = 5 diamonds, 5 clubs, slam interest

Method (B) provides significant benefits and is recommended.

TRANSFER RESPONSES AND 1X : 1Y, 2NT

The transfer rebids after 2NT are as in the previous section. You can apply Method (A) or Method (B). Because the initial response was a transfer, the strong hand will become declarer most of the time.

1♣ : 1◇ (♡s), 2NT : 3◇ = five hearts. Opener is expected to bid 3♡.

1♣ : 1◇ (♡s), 2NT : 3♡ = transfer and so four hearts and four spades

1♣ : 1◇ (♡s), 2NT : 3◇, 3♡ : 3♠ = five hearts and four spades

1♣ : 1◇ (♡s), 2NT : 3♣ (puppet), 3◇, 3♠ = six hearts and five spades

1♣ : 1◇ (♡s), 2NT : 3♣ (puppet), 3◇ : 3♡ sets hearts as trumps and starts cue-bidding.

1♣ : 1◇ (♡s), 2NT : 3♣ (puppet), 3◇ : 3NT = 4 hearts, 4 diamonds and mild slam interest. 4NT after 3◇ would be the same, but a stronger slam invitation.

1♣ : 1◇ (♡s), 2NT : 3◇, 3♡ : 4◇ = 5 hearts, 4 diamonds, slam interest

1♣ : 1◇ (♡s), 2NT : 4◇ = 4 hearts, 5+ diamonds, slam potential

1♣ : 1◇ (♡s), 2NT : 3♣ (puppet), 3◇ : 4◇ = 5 hearts, 5 diamonds and slam interest

Analogous sequences apply after it starts 1♣ : 1♡ (spades), 2NT and also after 1♣ : 1♠, (diamonds) 2NT. If responder then transfers to a major, this will be very strong, as a major is shown first below 13 points.

OPENING BIDS AND TRANSFERS

Because transfers after the 1♣ opening have become so popular, players have changed the opening structure to give themselves more opportunities to use transfers. One approach is that all balanced hands outside the 1NT and 2NT range or stronger are opened 1♣. Thus an opening of 1♣ might have four diamonds and two clubs and even a 5-3-3-2 pattern with five diamonds and 2-3 clubs. It can also be an unbalanced hand with 5+ clubs or a 4-4-1-4 pattern. Opening 1◊ promises an unbalanced hand with five diamonds or a 4-4-4-1 pattern with four diamonds.

Benefits can arise after a transfer response, from keeping the shape less disclosed if the 1♣ opener becomes declarer, and knowing that the 1◊ opening must be an unbalanced hand. Downsides after a 1♣ opening include difficulty in raising clubs and partner choosing an opening lead when the opponents win the contract and the 1♣ opener could have five clubs and two diamonds or five diamonds and two clubs.

Another approach is to open 1◊ with 4+ diamonds and an unbalanced hand or any balanced hand of 12-14 points. The 1♣ opening shows 4+ clubs in an unbalanced hand or 18-19 points balanced (with 1NT 15-17). Here, too, opener might have five diamonds and two clubs or five clubs and two diamonds for each of the minor-suit openings. The transfer responses to 1♣ allow the strong, balanced hand to become declarer if a trump fit exists. After a 1◊ opening, there is less need for a balanced 12-14 hand to be declarer.

The ideas are interesting, but the jury is out whether these methods will stand the test of time.

2-OVER-1 GAME-FORCE

Growing in popularity, and especially espoused in the USA, are methods where a two-over-one response is forcing to game, rather than the 10+ points and forcing for one round, as part of Acol or standard American. The plus side is that after a two-over-one, there is plenty of room to locate the best game or slam contract. There are several downsides:

• The 1NT response is forcing and so you cannot play in 1NT (a serious loss at match-points).

• The 1NT response is wide-ranging, 6-12 points. That can make the later bidding very difficult to judge. Suppose it starts 1♠ : 1NT, 2♠. Do you bid or pass with a singleton spade, a 6-card suit and 10-11 points?

• After the forcing 1NT, if opener does not have 6+ cards in the major and does not have four hearts after opening 1♠, opener is expected to bid a 3-card minor.

• After the forcing 1NT, if opener has four spades – five hearts and 2-2 in the minors in a hand too weak to reverse, opener is expected to rebid 2♣. Some use the Flannery 2◇ opening to include this hand type, but that takes up a whole opening bid to cover a disadvantage of the forcing 1NT response. Others simply accept the loss and bid 2♣ with the 4-5-2-2. Thus, pairs give preference to the major suit with a doubleton, even when holding 4-card support for the minor. Thus they can be playing in a 5-2 major-suit fit when a 4-4 or 5-4 fit in the minor is available.

In any event, there are plenty of books available on Two-over-One Forcing to Game. Tackle one of those if the method appeals to you.

1♡ / 1♠ : MULTI-2♣ RESPONSE

After a 5-card major opening, pairs that play Jacoby 2NT (page 40) and Bergen Raises (page 145) often use conventional limit raises with 3-card support for the major via a jump-shift in the other major. Thus, 1♡ : 2♠ = a 3-card limit raise of hearts and 1♠ : 3♡ = a 3-card limit raise of spades. While this might be well and good, these responses take you to the three-level and this can sometimes be too high.

There are methods that show these values, but enable the partnership to stop at the safer two-level. One of these is the multi-2♣ response to a major when playing 5-card majors.

1♡ or 1♠ : 2♣ = 4+ clubs, unbalanced game-force *OR* any balanced game-force *OR* a limit raise with 3-card support *OR* a minimum limit raise with 4-card support and poor shape, typically a 4-3-3-3 pattern.

1♡ : 2♣, 2♡ and 1♠ : 2♣, 2♠ = 'I would not accept a limit raise.' With the limit raise hand, responder passes. Mission accomplished. The partnership has been able to stop at the two-level.

After 1♡ : 2♣, 2♡ and 1♠ : 2♣, 2♠, responder can rebid with the strong hands. A new suit would show 5+ clubs and the suit bid. 2NT = a big balanced hand, allowing opener to set the major with a 6-card suit. Raising to 3-major = strong, balanced, 3-card support, forcing.

After 1♡ or 1♠ : 2♣, 2◇ = 'I would accept a limit raise.' Responder rebids 2♡ / 2♠ with the limit raise, 2NT if balanced, a new suit = clubs and that suit and 3♡ / 3♠ with the strong, balanced hand and three trumps.

1♡ : 2♣ / 2◇ AND 1♠ : 2♣ / 2◇ ARTIFICIAL

One such approach can be found on page 149. This is a more modern and more comprehensive approach for these methods. The idea is to establish the aim early and then proceed to locate the best spot.

1♡ / 1♠ : 1NT = 6-9 points, not forcing

1♡ / 1♠ : 2♣ = artificial, game-inviting, c. 10-12 points. 1♡ : 2♣ denies 4+ spades. Can be 13 points if holding 3-card support for the major.

1♡ / 1♠ : 2◇ = artificial, game-force, usually 13+ points, not 5+ spades

1♠ : 2♡ = game-force with 6+ hearts or with 5 hearts and a 5-card minor. Other game-forcing hands with 5+ hearts travel via 2◇.

1♡ / 1♠ : 2NT = 4+ support and 6-13 points.

After 1♡ / 1♠ : 2NT, opener can sign off in 3-Major or 4-Major, bid 3◇ as a very mild game invitation, bid 3♣ to ask for responder's range or show a shortage by bidding a new suit beyond 3◇. To start cue-bidding, opener must first ask with 3♣. After the 3♣ ask, responder bids 3-Major (weakest hand, 6-7 points), 3◇ (8-9 points) or the cheapest cue (10-13).

After 1♠ : 2♡, opener can support hearts (3♡ strong, 4♡ weaker) or via a splinter jump to 4♣ or 4◇, bid 3♣ or 3◇ to show a 5-5, including a doubleton heart, 2NT to confirm a doubleton heart (responder bids 3♡ to set hearts or 3-minor to show the 5-5), 3♠ to set spades as trumps or 2♠ if none of the previous rebids apply. After 2♠, responder bids 2NT (six hearts, no 5-minor), 3♡ (seven hearts) or 3♣ / 3◇ with a 5-card minor.

After 1♡ : 2◇ (artificial game-force), opener rebids 3♠ (0-5-4-4), 3♡ to set hearts as trumps and start cues, 3-minor (5-5 pattern), 2NT (18-19 balanced), 2♠ (4 cards in the other major) or 2♡ for all the other holdings (6+ major or minimum balanced or 4-card minor). The same structure applies after 1♠ : 2◇ except that 3♠ sets spades and 3♡ = 5-0-4-4.

After 1♡ : 2◇, 2♠ (4-other-major), responder can bid 2NT to seek further information (extra length in a major or 3-4 card minor suit residue), set either major as trumps or bid 3-minor with a 6+ suit.

After 1♡ : 2◇, 2♡, responder can bid 2♠ (relay for more information), bid 2NT to show a doubleton in opener's major (opener rebids 3NT with minimum, balanced, 3-major to set the suit as trumps or 3-minor to show the 4-card suit), raise to 3-major to set trumps or bid 3-minor (6+ suit). After 1♡ : 2◇, 2♡ : 2♠ (relay) opener rebids 2NT (minimum, balanced), 3-minor (4-card suit only), 3-major (6+ suit, not 3 in the other major) or 3-other-major with three cards in that major and 6+ in the major opened.

The same structure applies after 1♠ : 2◇ except that the relevant suit is spades and 1♠ : 2◇, 2♠ = 5+ spades and 4+ hearts (the other major).

After 1♡ / 1♠ : 2♣ (artificial, about 10-12 points), opener bids 2◇ with a minimum opening hand (11-13 points) and primarily denying interest in game. Opener's rebids of 2♡ and higher show 14+ points, are forcing to game and have the same meaning as those bids after 1♡ / 1♠ : 2◇ (see opposite page). 1♡ / 1♠ : 2◇, 2♡ : 2NT = balanced, exactly 14 points or a downgraded 15 points.

After 1♡ / 1♠ : 2♣, 2◇ (any minimum), bidding is essentially natural. Responder may support opener at the 2-level (10-11 points), at the 3-level (good 11-12 points) or at game-level (good 12-13 points). Thus, with an ordinary limit raise, the partnership can stop at the 2-level. If the auction goes 1♡ : 2♣, 2◇ : 2♠, this cannot be natural as 1♡ : 2♣ denies 4+ spades. It is used to show both minors and deny support for hearts.

This is a difficult hand for standard bidders:

West dealer : N-S vulnerable

WEST	EAST	WEST	EAST
♠ 7 3 2	♠ Q 8	1♡	2♣
♡ K Q 8 7 4	♡ 9	2◇	2♠
◇ Q 6	◇ K J 8 5 3	3♣	Pass
♣ A 7 3	♣ K Q 9 6 2		

The deal arose in a National Swiss Pairs in 2016. Out of 73 tables, six pairs managed to play in 3♣, sixteen failed at game level and seventeen went minus in the wrong part-score. As you can see from the auction on the right above, after 2♠ shows boths minors, West has an easy sign-off in 3♣.

After 1♡ / 1♠ : 1NT, bidding is natural (with one exception). A new suit can be expected to have at least four cards. A reverse is forcing for one round. A jump-shift to the 3-level in a lower suit is forcing to game and shows at least a 5-5 pattern. This is very useful and is available because 1♡ / 1♠ : 1NT, 2NT is artificial and forcing to game. Playing a 15-17 1NT opening means that opener does not need an invitational 2NT raise. With 18-19 HCP, you are prepared to insist on game.

After 1♠ : 1NT, 2NT responder will usually rebid 3♣, waiting. Opener then shows the nature of the hand. A new suit will be four cards only, repeat of the major = six cards and 3NT = five spades and four clubs. If, instead of 3♣, responder bids 3◇ or 3♡, that would be a 5-card suit, while 3NT from responder shows 6+ clubs and denies two spades.

The same applies after 1♡ : 1NT, 2NT except that 1♡ : 1NT, 2NT : 3♠ shows both minors and denies two hearts. With doubleton support for the major, it is better to rebid 3♣ over 2NT in case opener has a 6-card major.

GAZZILLI

This is an articial 2♣ rebid by opener after it starts 1♡ : 1♠, 1♡ : 1NT or 1♠ : 1NT. The 2♣ rebid covers any hand of 17+ points, 11-16 points with 5-major and 4+ clubs or if playing a weak 1NT, a 5-3-3-2 hand with 15-17 points. Opener's rebids at the 2-level other than 2♣ are natural with 11-16 points. This means responder need not strive to keep the bidding alive with 8-9 points and false preference.

After 1♡ : 1♠, opener's rebids are 1NT (balanced, 12-14), 2♣ = Gazzilli, (mostly 17+ points), 2◇ = natural (4+ diamonds 11-16 points), 2♡ = 6+ hearts, 11-14 points, 2♠ = 3 or 4 spades, 11-14 points, 2NT = 14-16 points and either a splinter with 4 spades or 3 spades and 6 hearts. The 3♣ relay discovers which it is or responder can sign off in 3♡ or 3♠. Opener's rebids at the 3-level all show 14-16 points: 3♣ / 3◇ = 5-5 shape, 3♡ = 6+ suit, not 3 spades, and 3♠ = 4-5-2-2. Opener's jump to 4♣ / 4◇ = six hearts, four spades and singleton or void in the bid minor.

Followers of Gazzilli play a 1NT response as forcing by an unpassed hand, but not forcing by a passed hand. After 1♡ : 1NT, opener rebids as follows: 2♣ = Gazzilli, 2◇ = natural (4+ diamonds 11-16 points), 2♡ = 6+ hearts, 11-14 points, 2♠ = 4+ spades, 5+ hearts, 17+ points (natural reverse), and 2NT = 17+ points, 6 hearts and any 4-card second suit. Responder can attempt to sign off in 3♡ or bid 3♣, game-forcing, to ask for the second suit. Opener's 3♠ rebid = five spades, six hearts. Other rebids at the 3-level show 14-16 points: 3♣ / 3◇ = 5-5 shape and 3♡ = 6+ suit. 4♣ / 4◇ = six hearts, five in the bid minor and 14-16 points.

The bidding is analogous after 1♠ : 1NT, with spades the dominant suit. Opener's 2♡ rebid = 5 spades, 4 hearts, 11-16 points, 3♡ = 5 spades – 5 hearts, 14-16 points and 4♡ = 6 spades, 5 hearts, 14-16 points.

After the Gazzilli 2♣ rebid, responder can bid 2◇, artificial, 7+ points, forcing to game if opener subsequently shows a hand with 17+ points. Other rebids by responder are natural and show a weaker hand, with a 2NT rebid being artificial and showing 5-5 in the minors. After responder's 2◇ rebid, if opener rebids the major, this shows 5-major, 4 clubs, 11-16 points and is not forcing. Responder takes suitable action. Opener's rebid of 2NT = 5-3-3-2 and 15-17 if that is feasible, 18-20 balanced otherwise. Opener's other rebids are natural, 17+ points. Further bidding is natural.

MORE ON 1♡ : 2NT / 1♠ : 2NT JACOBY

An early version of the Jacoby 2NT Convention appears on page 40. There have been developments in this area. The 2NT response to a major still shows 4+ support and is game-forcing. Modern rebids include:

3♣ = any minimum opening

3♢ = extra strength and a singleton or void somewhere. Expectation for extra strength would normally be 14/15 HCP or more.

3-agreed-major = extra strength and a 6+ suit, no shortage

3NT = extra strength and a 5-card suit, no shortage

3-other-major or 4♣ / 4♢ = a sound opening bid and a second suit as a source of tricks. The second suit will be K-Q-x-x-x or better. It follows that 1♡ : 2NT, 3♠ will show 6 hearts and 5 spades.

West dealer : N-S vulnerable

WEST	EAST	WEST	EAST
♠ A J	♠ 8 5	1♡	2NT
♡ A 8 7 4 3	♡ K Q 9 6 2	4♣	4NT
♢ 6	♢ A 3 2	5♡	7♡
♣ K Q 9 6 2	♣ A J 3	Pass	

4♣ showed the secondary suit and 5♡ showed two key cards, no ♡Q. East can expect to pitch the spade loser or the diamond losers on the clubs and ruff any loser in the other suit in the West hand. East could ask 5NT for kings and bid 7NT if West shows a king. Note that it is more valuable for East to know the source of tricks than the shortage in diamonds.

After 3-agreed major or 3NT, responder will cue-bid or ask for key cards.

After 3♢, responder can ask for the shortage via 3♡. Opener rebids 3♠ (the shortage is a void) or 3NT (singleton in the other major) / 4♣ / 4♢ (singleton in the bid suit). After 3♠ (void somewhere), responder asks with 3NT and opener bids 4♣ / 4♢ (void in the bid suit) / 4♡ (void in the other major).

The advantage of the 3♣ minimum opening is that responder can jump to 4-major with a minimum 2NT response and opener's shape has not been disclosed. If responder has slam interest even opposite a minimum opening, responder can bid 3♢ to inquire. Opener rebids 3-other major, shortage somewhere and step asks for the short suit, 3-major and 3NT as above, and 4♣ / 4♢ / 4♡ (other major) = hand with a source of tricks.

MORE ON SPLINTERS

The basic material on splinters can be found on pages 43-47. Further developments have appeared.

Some play 1-Major : 3NT as a raise to 4-Major with no singleton or void and 12 to a poor 14 points. A splinter is used for hands with 10-13 points. It follows that 1-Major : 2NT Jacoby will show a good 14 points or better and 14-15 points would now be the range for 1-Major : 2NT, 3♣ minimum.

Others use a splinter with a wider range and it can obviously be useful to determine whether the splinter is a singleton or void and whether it has minimum strength or extras. There are a number of ways to achieve that.

After a splinter bid, the cheapest bid that is not a sign-off asks for range. The next step = minimum, next is extras and singleton and the third step is extras and void. For example, after 1♣ : 3♡ splinter, 3♠ asks and 3NT = minimum, 4♣ = extras with a singleton spade and 4♢ = extras with a void in spades.

After extras have been shown, the cheapest bid other than a sign-off asks for key cards. Where a minimum was shown, cheapest bid asks and then Step 1 = singleton, Step 2 = void. After the reply, the cheapest step, not a sign-off, asks for key cards.

Another approach after a splinter and the cheapest bid as an inquiry is to use Step 1 = minimum, Step 2 = extras + singleton, Steps 3-6 = extras + void and key cards at the same time. After Step 1 minimum, cheapest bid (not a sign-off) asks and then Step 1 = singleton, Steps 2-5 = void and key cards. After singleton shown, the next step asks for key cards.

It is recommended that when the inquiry for a splinter is 4♣ or higher, then Step 1 minimum should be omitted. Use Step 1 = singleton and Steps 2-5 = void and key cards.

If this clarification of the splinter appeals, then it becomes awkward when the bidding starts 1♡ : 4♢ splinter or 1♠ : 4♡ splinter. There is no convenient inquiry because you run out of space. It is better to use 4NT as a key-card ask (and 4♠ as the key-card when hearts are agreed – see later) than as a clarification inquiry. To create space for the inquiry, you can play 1♠ : 3NT = heart splinter and 1♠ : 4♡ = natural. 4♣ over 3NT becomes the inquiry bid. You can also play 1♡ : 3NT = diamond splinter (4♣ inquiry) and 1♡ : 4♢ = 5 hearts and no diamonds. These uses for 3NT are incompatible, of course, with 3NT as a strong, balanced raise.

MORE ON 2-LEVEL OPENINGS

(1) The 2♣ Opening

The standard approach can be found on page 17. Here are two modern approaches, which are used by experts.

Kokish 2♣

After the standard 2♣ : 2◇ reply, negative or waiting, opener's 2♡ rebid shows 5+ hearts or a balanced game-force. Responder inquires with 2♠ and if opener rebids 2NT, it shows a balanced game-force (continue as after a 2NT opening). Any rebid by opener other than 2NT is natural and promises 5+ hearts. 3♡ would, of course, show 6+ hearts. Opener's rebids other than 2♣ : 2◇, 2♡ have their normal meaning, with 2NT 23-24 balanced and a suit bid promising a 5-card suit or longer.

Maxi 2♣

Hands with around nine playing tricks are hard to show. They are not quite worth a game-force, but to open at the 1-level risks partner passing and a game might be missed. This 2♣ version allows opener to show such hands.

2♣ : 2◇ = usual negative or waiting, up to a balanced hand of 9 points.

Suit responses other than 2◇ = normal positive meaning. 2♣ : 2NT = 10+ points balanced. Continue as after a 2NT opening. Slam is highly likely.

After 2♣ : 2◇ . . .

2♡ = artificial, any game-force without five spades

2♠ = game-force, 5+ spades. Bidding continues naturally.

2NT = 23-24 balanced. Continue as after a 2NT opening.

3♣ / 3◇ / 3♡ / 3♠ = 6+ suit, one-suiter, nine playing tricks. Responder can take appropriate action.

3NT = 9+ playing tricks, to play in 3NT with a long, solid suit

4♣ / 4◇ sets the suit as trumps and asks for a cue-bid. Responder bids an ace OR 4NT with no ace, but one or more kings OR raises the minor with no ace, no king.

4♡ / 4♠ = long, strong, one-suiter, 9½ or 10 playing tricks, three losers

After 2♣ : 2◇, 2♡ ...

2♠ = second negative, including balanced hands up to 7 points

2NT = balanced 8-9 points. Continue as after a 2NT opening.

3♣ / 3◇ / 3♡ / 3♠ = about 5-8/9 points, 5+ suit. In the upper range, the suit quality is probably not good enough for an immediate positive.

3NT = 10+ points, some 4-4-4-1, 4♣ asks for the singleton. In reply, 4NT shows a singleton club.

After 2♣ : 2◇, 2♡ : 2♠ ...

2NT = balanced, game force. Continue as after a 2NT opening.

3♣ / 3◇ / 3♡ = natural, 5+ suit, game-force. Natural continuations.

3♠ = 4 spades, 5+ hearts, game-force. 2♣ : 2◇, 2♠ would have shown 5+ spades and a game-force and so 3♠ here is not needed for that.

(2) The 2◇ Opening

The multi 2◇ appeared on page 23 and the defence to it on page 25. Since then various defences to the multi 2◇ have been suggested. This one is particularly effective:

(2◇) : Double = 'I have an overcall in hearts or in spades.' This will, from time to time, enable you to inflict a severe penalty on the opponents instead of bidding 2♡ or 2♠ and walking into their 6-card suit. If next hand passes, partner can pass the double for penalties, bid 2♡ or 2♠, pass or correct or bid 2NT as a strong action to ask for your major. In reply, 3♣ = 5 hearts, 3◇ = five spades, 3♡ = six hearts, 3♠ = six spades.

(2◇) : 2♡ or 2♠ = takeout of the suit bid or very strong. If third hand passes, continue as though partner has made a takeout double of the bid suit. Lebensohl applies, if you normally use it, and the strong actions remain the same: 2NT then 3NT = stopper in the suit partner bid and 4 cards in the other major, 2NT then 3 in the suit partner bid = 4 cards in the other major and no stopper in the suit partner bid, 3NT at once = stopper in the suit partner bid, but not 4 cards in the other major and 3 in the suit partner bid = no stopper in that suit and not 4 cards in the other major.

(2◇) : 2NT = 15-18, balanced, stoppers in both majors. Continue as after a 2NT opening.

(2◇) : 3♣ or 3◇ = normal overcall

(2♢) : 3♡ or 3♠ = 6+ suit, good hand, six losers. With a 6-card suit and five losers, double first and bid 3-Major next. With a strong 6+ suit and four losers, double first and and bid 4-Major next.

(2♢) : 4♣ or 4♢ = Leaping Michaels, 5+ in the bid minor and 5 cards in one of the majors, five losers or fewer. It is best played as forcing.

After (2♢) : 4♣, 4♢ asks for the major and 4♡ / 4♠ = natural.

After (2♢) : 4♢, 4♡ / 4♠ = pass or correct.

After one of these 4-level two-suiters commits you to game and an opponent bids, double is penalties, pass is forcing, a 5-level bid invites slam. Pass and later remove partner's double is merely to play or 'pass or correct'.

They	You	They	You
2♢	Double	2♡	Pass
Pass	?		

Double is for takeout with 5+ spades. Partner can pass for penalties.

They	You	They	You
2♢	Double	2♠	Pass
Pass	?		

Double is for takeout with 5+ hearts. Partner can pass for penalties.

They	You	They	You
2♢	Double	2♡	Pass
2♠	?		

Double is for takeout with 5+ hearts. Partner can pass for penalties. As partner is known to be very weak (no double and no action), you can also pass 2♡ or 2♠ rather than double in the above sequences.

They	You	They	You
2♢	Double	Pass	Pass
2♡/2♠	?		

Double is for takeout with 5+ cards in the other major. Bids = natural and include the other major. If your suit is also the opener's major, pass and await a takeout double from partner, just as you would if they had opened 2-Major originally.

They	You	They	You
2♢	Double	2♡/2♠	?

Double = pass or correct. Sufficient strength to compete to the 3-level.

They	You	They	You
2◇	Double	2♡	Double
Pass	?		

Pass = penalties ('I have a 2♡ overcall.'). 2♠ = natural, a minimum 2♠ overcall. 3♣ / 3◇ = 4+ suit, good overcall in spades. 3♡ = stopper ask for 3NT, strong spade overcall. 3♠ = good hand, 6-card suit, 5 losers.

They	You	They	You
2◇	Double	2♠	Double
Pass	?		

Pass = penalties ('I have a 2♠ overcall.'). 3♣ / 3◇ = 4+ suit, good 2♡ overcall, need not have extras. 3♡ = 2♡ overcall, need not have 6 hearts. 3♠ = stopper ask for 3NT, strong 2♡ overcall. 4♡ = strong, 6+ suit.

They	You	They	You
2◇	Double	2♡	Double
2♠	?		

Double = penalties. Pass = a 2♡ overcall, but without significant extras. (Then double by partner = penalties.) 3♣ / 3◇ = 4+ suit, good overcall in hearts. 3♡ = 6+ hearts, good hand, about five losers. 3♠ = stopper ask for 3NT, strong heart overcall. 4♡ = strong 6+ suit and extras.

They	You	They	You
2◇	Double	3♡ / 3♠	?

Double = pass or correct.

They	You	They	You
2◇	Pass	2♡ / 2♠	?

Double = takeout of the bid suit. Normal continuations.

(2◇) : 3NT = offer to play, long, running suit or 19+ points

(2◇) : 4NT = at least 6-5 in the minors

They	You	They	You
2◇	3♣ / 3◇	Pass	?

A new suit here is natural, including either major. Then a new suit by the 3♣ / 3◇ bidder is also natural.

They	You	They	You
2◇	Pass	2♡	Pass
2♠	?		

2NT = minors. Double = takeout of spades.

A DIFFERENT 2◇ OPENING

The 2NT opening with 20-22 points works pretty well and tends to inhibit the opponents. Opening balanced hands of 18-19 points with a 1-opening allows the opponents in cheaply. To obviate this, some pairs adopted a 2♣ opening for balanced hands of (17+) / 18-19 / (20-) points and used a 2◇ opening for the game-force hands. The trouble is that such a 2◇ opening cannot do justice to the huge hands. Wishing to retain 2♣ for the huge hands, players have turned to opening 2◇ for strong, balanced hands, not quite good enough for a 2NT opening. This is one such scheme:

The 2◇ opening covers the hands of around 18-19 points that would bid 1X : 1Y, 2NT in standard methods. It can include a 5-card major, just like a 2NT opening can.

2◇ : Pass. With a very weak hand and 5+ diamonds, responder may pass.

2◇ : 2♡ = offer to play, 4+ hearts and weak. Opener can pass with 3-4 hearts, bid 2♠ with 4-5 spades, bid 2NT with no major or raise to 3♡ with a really good maximum. Partner accepts with (4)/5-6 points.

2◇ : 2♠ = Puppet to 2NT. Then continue as after a 2NT opening.

2◇ : 2NT = transfer to clubs. It could be to sign off in 3♣ or to bid a second suit with a 6-4 pattern and slam potential or to continue with 4♣ to ask for key cards or to rebid 3NT to start cues.

2◇ : 3♣ / 3◇ = transfer to diamonds / hearts. It shows slam interest with a 6+ suit. After opener accepts the transfer, 3NT asks for cues, repeat suit = RKCB, new suit = 6-4 pattern (see later).

2◇ : 3♡ = 5+ spades. Opener bids 3♠ with 3+ spades and 3NT with only two spades. After 3♠, 3NT starts cue-bidding, 4♠ is to play, 4NT asks for key cards, based on spades, and a new suit = a 6-4 pattern. If opener rebid 3NT (only two spades), new suit = a 6-4 pattern and 4NT asks for key cards, based on spades.

2◇ : 3♠ = slam values and at least 5-5 in the minor suits. Opener must support one minor or the other.

2◇ : 4♣ / 4◇ = transfers to 4♡ / 4♠ (like South African Texas, p. 36)

2◇ : 4♡ = 5-5 in the majors, no slam interest, pass or correct

2◇ : 4♠ = 5-5 in the majors, slam potential, forcing. Opener can bid 4NT, key-card ask, setting hearts or 5♣, key-card ask, setting spades.

After 2◇ : 2NT / 3♣ / 3◇ (all transfers)

After opener accepts the transfer, responder's 3NT rebid is forcing and starts cues, regardless of the suit. If responder raises opener, this asks for key cards, even in the 2◇ : 3◇, 3♡ : 4♡ auction.

2◇ : 2♠, 2NT : 3♡, 3♠ : 3NT = choice of contracts. Responder is happy to be declarer in 4♠, but would prefer to have partner declarer in 3NT if opener is 4-3-3-3. If not, opener should bid 4♠ with three or four spades.

2◇ : 3NT sets spades, starts cue-bidding. Warning: Memory danger.

2◇ : 3NT, 4♠ = every suit controlled and wants to be declarer

2◇ : 3NT, 4♡ = every suit controlled and does not need to be declarer

If opener bids a new suit after any of the 2◇ : 2NT / 3♣ / 3◇ / 3♡ transfers, a new suit from responder shows slam interest with a 6-4 pattern. A cue-bid now by opener sets the 4-card suit as trumps. Otherwise opener will revert to the 6-suit to set that as trumps and start cue-bidding or let responder ask for key cards.

2◇ : 3♡, 3♠ : 4♡ or 2◇ : 3♡, 3NT : 4♡ = six spades, four hearts and is forcing. Then 4♠ sets spades, while 4NT = key card ask, hearts set.

DEFENCE AGAINST 2◇ 18-19 balanced

Double to show strong diamonds. Overcall with a strong suit.

COUNTERMEASURES BY THE OPENING SIDE

After 2◇ : (Double), responder may pass with a weak hand, but decent diamonds, at least a 5-card suit OR redouble to ask opener to bid 2♡ and then pass responder's next bid (except for a rebid of 2NT, which is weak with both minors). All other bids = system on.

After 2◇ : (2♡ or 2♠), responder can double (for takeout and forcing to game), Pass (inviting opener to re-open with a double with a suitable hand). 2◇ : (2♡) : 2♠ = puppet to 2NT and higher bids = system on, but 3♡ by responder = game-force and a 4-1-4-4 pattern.

After 2◇ : (2NT), Double = penalties. If they run to a new suit, next double is takeout, third double is penalties.

After 2◇, if they bid at the 3-level or higher, double for takeout or a suit bid (5+ suit) is forcing to game. Opener may always pass a double here.

NEW IDEAS IN THE SLAM ZONE

Key-card asks after a 3-level pre-empt by partner

Method 1: After a 3 ◇ / 3 ♡ / 3 ♠ opening, 4 ♣ asks for key cards. Opener gives the usual replies. After a 3 ♣ opening, a jump to 4 ◇ asks for key cards. Opener gives the usual replies.

Method 2: After a 3 ◇ / 3 ♡ / 3 ♠ opening, 4 ♣ asks for key cards. Opener bids 4 ◇ with a poor pre-empt, otherwise gives the usual replies. After the 4 ◇ bid, if responder still wants to know about key cards, responder bids 4 ♡ to ask, but if the suit is hearts, responder bids 4 ♠ to ask.

After a 3 ♣ opening, a jump to 4 ◇ asks for key cards. Opener bids 4 ♡ with a poor pre-empt, otherwise gives the usual replies. It is true that after 3 ♣ : 4 ◇, opener will bid 5 ◇ with two key cards and the trump queen. If that is not enough for a slam, responder should not have asked with 4 ◇. After the 4 ♡ (poor pre-empt) reply to 4 ◇, responder can still ask for key cards with 4 ♠. A 5 ◇ reply, two key cards, no trump queen, must be enough for responder to bid the slam.

Key-card asks and cue-bidding after agreeing a minor suit

Using 4NT to ask for key cards with a minor suit set as trumps can take you too high. Most pairs want a cheaper method to ask for key cards in a minor suit contract. This is simple and effective. Regardless of which minor suit has been agreed as trumps by the 3-level, 4 ♣ says, 'Please start cue-bidding' and 4 ◇ says, 'Please show your key cards'. Also, 4 ♣ and 4 ◇ have the same meanings if they cannot sensibly be natural. For example, after 1 ♣ : 1 ♠, 3 ♣, 4 ♣ = start cues and 4 ◇ = key-card ask. You do lose the opportunity for a 4 ◇ splinter in these kind of auctions, but the compensation is more than worthwhile.

4 ♠ as the key card ask when hearts are trumps

If hearts are trumps and 4NT asks for key cards, if the reply is 5 ◇, there is no convenient ask for the trump queen without committing to a small slam. This is so, whether 5 ◇ = 0 or 3 key cards or 1 or 4 key cards. It is worthwhile to give up 4 ♠ as a splinter or as a cue-bid and use it as asking for key cards if hearts have clearly been agreed as trumps already or if it cannot be sensible as a natural bid. Thus, 1 ♣ : 1 ♡, 2 ♡, 4 ♠ = key-card and 1 ♡ : 2 ◇, 2 ♡ : 3 ♣, 3 ♡ : 4 ♠ = asking for key cards.

After the 4 ♠ key-card ask and a 4NT or 5 ♣ reply, (0 or 3 / 1 or 4, either way), there is always room to ask for the queen of trumps.

THE KABEL 3NT OPENING: A NEW VERSION

The Kabel 3NT opening, asking for specific aces, was described on page 121. In that version, 3NT : 4♣ showed no aces. Although the opening would still be rare, one can increase the opportunitie for 3NT specific-ace ask by making the 4♣ response shows 0 or 1 ace. You still need about a 10-trick hand or better and a powerful suit, but this is how it works:

3NT : 4♣ = 0 or 1 ace. After that, 4♡ / 4♠ / 5♣ / 5♢ = to play.

3NT : 4♣ , 4♢ asks. In reply 4♡ = no ace. Opener can pass with hearts or bid 4♠ / 5♣ / 5♢ = to play.

3NT : 4♣ , 4♢ asking : 4♠ / 5♣ / 5♢ = ace in that suit and 4NT = ♡A. Any suit bid by partner now is to play.

3NT : 4♢ = two aces, ♢A + ♡A

3NT : 4♡ = two aces, ♡A and ♠A

3NT : 4♠ = two aces, ♠A and ♣A

3NT : 4NT = two aces, ♣A and ♡A *OR* ♢A + ♠A (non-touching)

3NT : 5♣ = two aces, ♣A and ♢A

Memory aid: 3NT : 4♢ / 4♡ / 4♠ / 5♣ = that ace and the next along, while 3NT : 4NT = non-touching aces (N-T = Non-Touching). If the opener cannot tell which two aces responder holds from the 4NT reply, it was probably wrong to have opened 3NT with no aces.

After two aces have been shown, any suit bid by opener is to play.

3NT : 5♢ / 5♡ / 5♠ / 5NT = three aces, excluding the ace in the bid suit. 5NT = no ♣A.

After any number of aces have been shown, a suit bid by opener is to play. A no-trump bid asks for specific kings. See page 121 for details.

WEST	EAST	WEST	EAST
♠ AKQJ8764	♠ 5	3NT	4NT
♡ KQJ9	♡ A 8 2	6♠	Pass
♢ 6	♢ J 8 5 3		
♣ ---	♣ A 9 6 3 2		

If East had bid 4♢ (♢A + ♡A), West would bid 7♠. Had East bid 4♣, West would ask with 4♢. After 4♡ (no ace), West bids 4♠. After 5♢ or 4NT (♡A), West bids 6♠. After 5♣ (♣A), West signs off in 5♠.

ANOTHER DEFENCE TO A 1NT OPENING

(1NT) : Double = penalties, whether the 1NT is weak or strong. If either opponent runs to a suit, next double is takeout, third double is penalties.

(1NT) : 2♣ = majors *OR* minors *OR* 6+ diamonds. A suit bid by partner is 'pass or correct'. Do not bid 2-Major unless prepared to hear 3◇. 2NT by partner asks for clarification: 3♣ = minors, 3◇ = diamonds, 3♡ / 3♠ = 5-card suit, with four in the other major, and 3NT = 5-5 in the majors.

(1NT) : 2◇ = a 6+ one-suiter, but not in diamonds. A suit bid by partner is 'pass or correct'. 2NT by partner asks for the suit: 3♣ = clubs, 3◇ = a major, but weak for the 2◇ bid (then 3♡ / 3♠ is 'pass or correct') and 3♡ / 3♠ = good 1-suiter in the bid suit.

(1NT) : 2♡ / 2♠ = major-minor two-suiter, normally 5 major, 4+ minor. Partner can use 2NT to ask for the minor: 3♣ / 3◇ = that minor, 3♡ / 3♠ = clubs / diamonds, a 5-5 pattern and a good hand.

ANOTHER VERSION OF SPECIFIC TWO-SUITERS

In (1♡) : 2♡ or (1♠) : 2♠, a drawback to the Michaels Cue-bid is that the minor suit is not identified. That can cost if third hand raises opener's major and partner has shortage in one minor and length in the other. Roman Jump Overcalls (p. 130) showed specific two-suiters, but you could not afford these with a very strong hand, as you are bidding one of the suits. The following method allows you to show specific two-suiters with any strength, since you never bid a suit that you actually have.

1. Bidding the opposition suit shows the next two suits. (1♣) : 2♣ = diamonds and hearts, (1◇) : 2◇ = hearts and spades, (1♡) : 2♡ = spades and clubs and (1♠) : 2♠ = clubs and diamonds.

2. The cheapest jump-overcall in a suit shows the next two suits. You lose that weak jump, but that is not much of a loss. (1♣) : 2◇ = hearts and spades, (1◇) : 2♡ = spades and clubs, (1♡) : 2♠ = clubs and diamonds and (1♠) : 3♣ = diamonds and hearts.

3. 2NT = two non-touching (N-T) suits. (1♣) : 2NT = diamonds and spades, (1◇) : 2NT = clubs and hearts, (1♡) : 2NT = diamonds and spades and (1♠) : 2NT = clubs and hearts.

Once partner picks a suit, you bid again if strong. 2NT, if available, asks for strength: cheaper suit = seven losers, other suit = six losers, unbid suit = five losers and opener's suit = four losers or fewer.

INDEX